S. B. Herrick

Essays and Reviews of George Eliot not hitherto Reprinted

Together with an Introductory Essay on the Genius of George Eliot

S. B. Herrick

Essays and Reviews of George Eliot not hitherto Reprinted
Together with an Introductory Essay on the Genius of George Eliot

ISBN/EAN: 9783337250669

Printed in Europe, USA, Canada, Australia, Japan

Cover: Foto ©Thomas Meinert / pixelio.de

More available books at **www.hansebooks.com**

ESSAYS AND REVIEWS

OF

GEORGE ELIOT

NOT HITHERTO REPRINTED

𝔗𝔬𝔤𝔢𝔱𝔥𝔢𝔯 𝔴𝔦𝔱𝔥 𝔞𝔫 𝔍𝔫𝔱𝔯𝔬𝔡𝔲𝔠𝔱𝔬𝔯𝔶 𝔈𝔰𝔰𝔞𝔶

ON

THE GENIUS OF GEORGE ELIOT

BY

MRS. S. B. HERRICK

BOSTON
ALDINE BOOK PUBLISHING COMPANY
1887

𝔘𝔫𝔦𝔟𝔢𝔯𝔰𝔦𝔱𝔶 𝔓𝔯𝔢𝔰𝔰:
JOHN WILSON AND SON, CAMBRIDGE.

CONTENTS.

GENIUS OF GEORGE ELIOT.

By Mrs. S. B. HERRICK.

———•o;•;o•———

IT is said that George Eliot spent years of her literary life in translating, and in writing review articles, before she ventured upon a creation of her own. Her first appearance as an author was made in "Blackwood's Magazine." She there published three stories of English rural life, called "Scenes in Clerical Life." Their literary merit was at once acknowledged; but they did not attract the attention which they merited until she had made herself famous in her second work, "Adam Bede."

Perhaps no book of fiction, since the days of the Great Unknown, has attracted so much attention, and been the subject of such universal discussion, as this first novel by George Eliot. Before the *nom de plume* had vanished in the light of eager inquiry, she was claimed as a man by men, and as a woman by women. She seems to us to be the only woman, in all the wide range of fictitious literature, who has drawn a genuine, manly man — one who is manly in his faults as well as in his virtues.

It seems given to the noblest and most gifted of each sex to possess so large and inclusive a humanity, as to be a representative of both man and woman. Where do we find a more exquisite tenderness, tact, and refinement, than in the highest type of man; and where a more noble courage, a deeper sense of truth and honor, than in the noblest of women? George Eliot truly possesses an intellect which is so far above ordinary womanhood as to include the strength and grasp, the critical acumen and large outlook of a man, with the tenderness and purity of a woman.

We are told that God said, " Let us make man in our image, after our likeness . . . . So God created man in his own image, in the image of God created he him ; male and female created he them." The divine nature, then, must include within itself both the masculine and feminine attributes. The higher nature is, and the more fully it is developed, if the moral growth be co-ordinate with the intellectual, the more godlike will it be, and the more certainly will it escape from the limitations of ignorance, of conventionality and finally of sex itself.

Naturalists tell us that every organ and every member which is fully developed in the higher animal is possessed in a rudimentary condition by the lower. The organism of man shows the same members, in a high state of development, which we find in the lower vertebrates. The hand of man, with its wonderful capabilities and exquisite adaptability to an infinite variety of labor and uses, is but a full expression of the idea suggested in the fin of the fish, the hoof of the horse, the wing of the bat, and the paddle of the mole. Every bone which gives the power of grasp and flexibility, so necessary in supplying the needs of his higher existence, is found in the lower in a modified form. The whole natural world is pointing, by successive and increasingly perfect organisms, to man, the crowning glory of the animal kingdom. He possesses powers which, in their just proportion and harmonious co-ordination, are far beyond the physical powers of the brute. Though he is less strong than the lion, less agile than the monkey ; though his hearing is less acute, and his vision less sensitive than those of the insect and the bird, yet he is far beyond them all in his powers of self-protection, self-development, and progress. This is because his powers are so adjusted to each other, and so co-ordinated with that higher spiritual being which constitutes him man, as to produce the most perfect result. The soul and mind of man are made in the image of God. In the more wretched and degraded members of the human family, we see the germs folded, the power and faculties latent; but who will say, in the light of missionary enterprise, that the soul is wanting in any race of men? It only lies dormant, waiting the awakening touch of divine truth. As we go from the lower to the higher forms of human life, we see, as we do in the analogous forms of animal existence, a life which approaches nearer and nearer to the divine type. The spiritual world points no' less unerringly to the perfect and divine prototype.

In the true artist, whether his creations be by the aid of pen or pencil, by the chisel of the sculptor, or the fingers of the musician, the work is creative, the attitude is godlike. The divine power of imagination is at work; and the world is receiving beauty, wrought from the very life of the artist. There are a few, a very few, who deserve the title of artist in this high sense. The man who may rightfully lay claim to such a title must possess the gift, not only of seeing the truth and rendering it, but he must also have that all-comprehensive glance, and that vitalizing power, which is rather a spiritual than an intellectual faculty. He must lay under contribution all the physical beauty of earth and sea and sky, besides all the subtler moral beauty of tenderness and heroism and devotion. When such men do bless the earth, they are cosmopolitan, and can be claimed exclusively by no age and no country. They are heaven-born souls, who have only made some unworthy spot of earth their abiding-place for a little time. The birthplace of a genius like this may well be proud that it was chosen for such a manifestation; but it cannot claim him as its own. The world is his home, and mankind his compatriots.

Into this noble army, how many women have ever been admitted, or how few! It is strange that the world has seen almost no creative mind among women. The apology which is always offered for the inferiority of women, in every branch of severe intellectual labor, cannot be offered here. The cultivation of art has always been considered eminently proper for her sex. The most stringent conservative does not imagine that a woman must overstep her allotted sphere in order to excel in art. The facilities for artistic training, which have been open to women during the last two centuries, are certainly greater than those possessed by the men of earlier times. We confess to a deeply rooted scepticism in regard to "mute inglorious Miltons" of either sex. There is something in the essence of genius which compels it to express itself, even if it perish in the expression. But when we do see this high order of creative talent among women, we hail it with delight. George Eliot has vindicated the divine right of her sex, if it needed vindication. In the estimation of the best critics of England and America, she has no superior, — we had almost said no peer, — in her own province, among living artists.

It would be worth our while to examine carefully the character of her mind and the method of her working. She is, perhaps, the truest and highest exponent of the age in which we live. She is essentially modern in her mode of thought; and yet, in spite of this quality, she has given us one of the most vivid pictures of past days which can be found in literature. She is intensely modern; but, more than that, deep down in the recesses of her nature, she is still more intensely human. The loves and joys, the disappointment and anguish, of antique Florentine life, are made to glow with vitality and beauty by the magic of her pen. The human heart, which throbs in all the ages, and under the garbs of those old times, appeals to, and finds a response in, the common humanity of the present. There is a charm about old times, old customs, old habits of thought and mode of life, which appeals to the æsthetic in all of us. The great trouble with most writers is that they make all which is old partake of the nature of a fossil, and that is not interesting. Fossils are very excellent things in their way, but they must be genuine bits of ancient existence, not the result of a modern fossil manufactory. Pictures of a life which has passed away with the rolling centuries can never be painted from nature; and it is only the

most vivid and powerful imagination which should attempt
to cope with the difficulties in the way of their reproduction.
When such an imagination does give us a picture of the olden
time, it possesses an indescribable charm. We look back
upon the strange, fantastic garbs, the curious inexplicable customs of past times, with a sense of being alien and
astray, until we are made to feel that the same joys and
sorrows stir the hearts, beating under those odd vestments,
which move our own ; and that the same human eyes, shining
with joy or shaded with sorrow, are looking at us from under
the quaint head-dresses, which we see in the faces of our
friends and of our children. We give our recognition with
something of the heart-leap with which we greet an old acquaintance in a foreign land, and which proclaims, in silent
but eloquent language, that we are all of one kin.

Look at Kingsley's "Hypatia" and "Amyas Leigh." One
is never tired of returning again and again to them, and is
rewarded each time by discovering new beauties. Beauty —
true, noble beauty — never palls, but rather becomes more
lovely in our eyes, as it is softened and hallowed by the clustering of tender associations around it. Shall we look but
once at a beautiful picture, and never feel the desire to see it
again ? Shall we hear only once exquisite music, and be forever satisfied because, forsooth, we know what is coming ?
Shall we look once on a glorious landscape, and the eye never
again be thirsty to drink in delight from the same source ?
Can our souls vibrate but once to any beauty, which reaches
it through any channel, and then be forever afterward
mute ?

It must be that the motive which impels the public to the
enjoyment of any work of art, is generally a restless desire
to be amused; not any deep love of truth or beauty, or it
would not go away so soon filled. It is the highest order
of creations alone which can bear the test of time, of different nationalities, and different creeds. There is only a giant
here and there, who has infused into his work the exhaustless
vitality which keeps it alive, — though, in the mean time, em-

pires have risen, flourished, and sunk into decay; though generation after generation has been born, lived out its little day of joy and anguish, and then passed away forgotten, — while it goes forward rejoicing in its eternal youth, and finding a home wherever beats a human heart. Into such works a man must have cast his very soul. There is nothing but life, freed from its shackles and its human limitations, which causes a work of art to live such a life as this, adapting itself to the requirements and needs of every new phase of existence, and amid all changes reappears

"Forever lovely and forever young."

George Eliot possesses this creative power of imagination. Her characters are never imaginative beings to our minds, — they are people. We are no more afraid of confounding them, one with another, than we are of forgetting which is which in the circle of our friends. Each character preserves its individuality in our memories. She does not find it necessary to resort to the cheap expedient of putting an invariable form of words or mode of expression into the mouths of her *dramatis personæ*, as a sort of mechanical make-shift, which shall do duty for a higher kind of individuality. This expedient, which is not entirely unknown among good writers, is painfully suggestive to us of our juvenile attempts at sketching, with the essential addition of a label below to prevent mistakes, and does not indicate high art.

Her earlier works were almost too dazzling to be effective. It is not the best and truest art which forever stimulates the imagination, and keeps the wits constantly on the *qui vive*. There is sometimes a sense of pain at the profusion of good things she spreads before us. We feel that such prodigality is the prophet of coming want. It is not possible to enjoy everything at once; the mind requires quiet intervals, in which it may assimilate what has been given it. Without these intervals of rest, neither body nor mind, nor our æsthetic faculties, can attain their most perfect development. The grossest form of the error into which an exuberant imagination, and a memory teeming with rich material are hurried, is the sensational novel. George Eliot has a mind too full of high thoughts and a heart too full of noble purposes to prostitute her art. These qualities have expressed themselves in her maiden efforts by a tracery which occasionally is too rich to allow the design to show itself to full advantage, by an ornamentation which a little obscures the general design. There is never anything turgid in language, or highflown in illustration, or exaggerated in sentiment, only many touches of color here and there, which, though admirable in themselves, mar the purity of the design. We are bewildered at the brilliancy of the display. It is a fault — if it may be called a fault at all — of a too exuberant fancy, of an imagination which cannot contain itself, but must overflow and enrich everything around it.

Have we not all felt, in the presence of some great beauty, a sense of pain at the limitations in ourselves? Have we not all sighed to see the great ocean of delight stretching out before us, at the consciousness that we had only one little pint-cup of capacity to fill? Not that we want more from any greedy desire of appropriation, but that it is a pain to think of the dreary stretches of life, barren of all the loveliness which is so lavishly spread before us. Each one of us has, at times, as the journey of life lay over the desert, felt the very soul parching with thirst; and then the consciousness that one drop of all this wasted delight would cool the tongue, has become a pang amid the pleasures of memory. The essence of every bygone pain is, indeed, not so much memory, as it is the prophecy which it holds within itself of a possible future like it. What is the minor tone, which softens and sobers the most exquisite delight of earth, but this memory of past sorrow, which casts its vague but lengthening shadow across the future?

Our author is learning a truer economy as she is gaining a riper and fuller development. It is a noble thrift, after all, where all go away filled, and yet care is taken that nothing be wasted. A comparison of " Scenes in Clerical Life," or

"Adam Bede," with "Middlemarch," will show what we are aiming to illustrate. In "Adam Bede," for instance, there is more incident, more description of external life, more characters, more pointed sayings, detachable from the main current of the story, than there is in "Middlemarch;" and yet there is just half as much writing. "Adam Bede" is sparkling and scintillating from beginning to end with bits of pathos and humor, with occasions for laughter and tears. But in "Middlemarch" there is a more perfect development of character, a closer analysis of feeling, and a more noble repose than we find in her earlier works. It is hard to say which is the finer book. Each has its own peculiar merits and its own individual blemishes.

We lay down this great work from the pen of George Eliot in anything but a critical mood. It invites criticism more decidedly as we read it in detached portions, and disarms it more completely when we consider it as a finished whole, than do any of her previous productions. Without repeating herself in plot or character, we feel that her mind is becoming every year more deeply set in its original mould. She has lived a real, earnest, intense life, such a life as leaves deep traces behind it. The sufferings of the very least and meanest of God's creatures find a response in the great human heart, that beats under the keen analytic power of the mental philosopher and the quick-sighted discrimination of the critic.

"Adam Bede" is in no sense crude; it is from the pen of a trained writer, — from one who was skilled in analysis, and trained in style, by her earlier literary efforts. It has, in this way, missed the faults of "first novels;" but it is a younger book than "Middlemarch;" it shows a fuller appreciation of outward life, a keener enjoyment of its external conditions, but not the same chastened and purified soul. We see the same clear-sighted vision and even-handed justice, but not the large-hearted sympathy, that comes from a bitter struggle with self which has ended in victory. She possessed the same object, first as last; but she had not estimated the public, with which she had to deal, quite correctly. The same deep, significant lesson is taught in "Adam Bede," which rang out in such unmistakable tones in "Romola." It is the lesson which is generally taught, not by books, but by the noble and lovely lives which are lived around us, — the lesson that there is just one thing on earth which is worth the seeking, and that is, the Right.

The lesson taught in the character of Arthur Donnithorne is, that there is one, and only one, safeguard against baseness and dishonor, and that this safeguard is a supreme love of virtue, a high moral principle, which cannot be tampered with. No magnanimity, no natural generosity, no sweetness of temper or desire to please, is of a texture strong enough to bear the stress of temptation. The whole fabric of the story is so inwoven with the moral purpose that it is entirely inseparable; and so the moral purpose is, to some extent, missed by some readers. It is not the first time that the moral of a fable has been missed by the public, because the judicious precaution was omitted of stating it in succinct form as an addendum. But her purpose lay too deep in her heart to admit of any uncertainty as to its results; her message must be given to the world, and it was delivered with an accent that no one could miss, in the delineation of the beautiful Greek in "Romola." We consider that her power culminated in "Romola;" the exuberance of life is present, but the slower measure is reached.

Her novels are not the favorites of young, ardent souls, untouched by the troubles of life and unchastened by its discipline. It is only suffering, and suffering which has been a discipline, that can attune a soul to respond to the vibrations of her music. The story in her books is like the narration of a real life, the incidents are always subordinate to the results. The progress which we follow, with ever-increasing interest, is the progress of a soul toward perfection, not the progress of a plot toward completion. The issues are moral issues; the crises, spiritual crises; and the culmination of interest consists, not in some well-laid scheme crowned with success, or some happy marriage consummated, but in the victory of a noble soul over the powers of darkness. The happiness which is reached is of that deep, sure nature which can be ruffled only on the surface by any of earth's disappointments, trials, or sufferings.

There is manifested all through her works a passionate sympathy with joy and sorrow, with struggle, and even with failure. There is never a touch of the Pharisee in her. She has felt that there are moments in every battle when the result hangs trembling in the balance, even though it may turn on the side of victory. Though she recognizes, with the utmost clearness, the truth that victory is not the result of chance, yet those moments have taught her to look upon defeat with a large indulgence. She looks at things as they are in their own just proportions, not as they seem in relation to her own thoughts and prejudices. There is a curiously impersonal character in her writings, because she stands only as the interpreter of her own creations; and yet there is the deep personality pervading them which must characterize the fruit of every living soul. They are her children, bone of her bone, and flesh of her flesh ; and yet they maintain, each and every one, an individuality, intact and impregnable.

There is no peculiarity which more truly characterizes our great novelists than the presence or absence of this conscious personality in their writings. For instance, Dickens threw himself into his work with a self-forgetful ardor, which has made the least prominent of his *dramatis personæ* men and women to us. It is said that when he wrote he shut himself in alone, and yielded himself up utterly to the spell of enchantment which he was weaving for the world. He forgot to eat and to sleep. He laughed and wept over the humorous and pathetic scenes he was delineating. The life he depicts passes before him like a panoramic view. He is conscious of himself only as a passive spectator, and feels that his work is to translate for the world what already exists in his own imagination. How often we feel inclined to say, when we meet an odd, or grotesque, or genial-looking figure, "That man has just stepped out of Dickens." As if Dickens had created a little world of his own, whose inhabitants interchanged occasional civilities with ourselves. His writings are sparkling and rippling over with an exuberance of life; and yet, where is Charles Dickens?

Then we turn to Charles Reade, a writer who stands deservedly high in fictitious literature, and who has never been surpassed in a certain dramatic power. He shows us a wonderful picture: but he is always there himself, pointing out a beauty here and a deformity there; joining in the derisive scorn, which he bespeaks from his audience, for every ignoble and vicious quality; not forgetting to add his applause at every touch of tenderness or nobleness. He is always sure to be there, standing with his discriminating pointer between us and his own creations.

Again, Anthony Trollope, who is undoubtedly a man of great talent, close in his analysis of motives, true in his insight, discriminating in his praise or blame, is only a photographer of a very high order. He possesses the artistic sense which makes him choose his subjects well; which directs him in his arrangement of color and selection of pose; but, after all, it wants the divine spark of imagination to make it true art. He seems to recognize this, for he keeps himself modestly in the background, as a photographer should.

George Eliot is utterly unlike Dickens, and yet they are nearly enough on the same plane to admit of comparison. She possesses the same wonderfully acute observation, which enables her to enrich her writings with touches of nature, bits of description, and hints of exquisite sentiment, which we find in Dickens. She is far more analytic and introverted, and less genial and laughter-loving than Dickens. Under the pathos of Dickens is the ripple of laughter. Under her wit or humor, or that which partakes of the nature of both, and yet is neither, is the recognition of all the misery and sin in the world. She is the exponent, in the world of fiction, of that spirit of the nineteenth century which has been so well described by another. " Christianity ended," says the writer referred to, "by producing that peculiar passion for self-analysis, that rage for the anatomy of emotion, and that reverence for the individual soul, which was almost entirely unknown to the ancient world. . . . If we were now asked roughly to define what we mean by the Spirit of the Age, we should say the genius of the nineteenth century is analytic. There is hardly anything on earth which Goethe — the very incarnation of modern culture — has not done something toward analyzing. Scientific research has taken complete possession of the unexplored regions of the physical world. Kant and Hegel have endeavored to define the limits of pure reason. Swedenborg strove to give law and system to the most abnormal states of human consciousness. There is not an aspect of nature, or complication of character, or contrast of thought and feeling, which has not been delineated by modern novelists and painted by modern artists ; while the national poets of Europe, whether we think of Goethe, Heine, Lamartine, De Musset, or our own living poets, Tennyson and Browning, have all shown the strongest disposition to probe and explore the hidden mysteries of thought and feeling : to arrange and rearrange the insoluble problems of life, which never seemed so insoluble as now ; to present facts with all their by-play ; and to trace emotion through all its intricate windings."

It is rather strange that, with her great powers of imagination and command over the language of emotion, her poems have not been more successful. We heartily agree with the words of the best criticism which, in our opinion, has been written upon George Eliot. "The poems," says this critic, "are conspicuously inferior to the novels ; and a striking indication that poetry is not George Eliot's element as an artist is this, that in her poems the idea and the matter do not really interpenetrate ; the idea stands above the matter as a master above the slave, and subdues the matter to its will.

The ideal motives of 'The Spanish Gypsy,' of 'Jubal,' and of 'Armgart' can be stated in a concise form of words. For the mystery of life there is substituted the complexity of a problem of moral dynamics, a calculable composition of forces. And with this the details of the poem are necessarily in agreement. A large rhythm sustains the verse, similar in nature to the movement of a calmly musical period of prose; but at best the music of the lines is a measurable music; under the verse there lies no living heart of music with curious pulsation and rhythm, which is a miracle of the blood. The carefully executed lyrics of Juan and Fedalma are written with an accurate knowledge of what song is, and how it differs from speech. The author was acquainted with the precise position of the vocal organs in singing; the pity is, she could not sing. The little, modelled verses are masks taken from the dead faces of infantile lyrics that once lived and breathed." What Lowell says so happily of Dryden is conspicuously true of her: "In his prose you come upon passages that persuade you he is a poet, in spite of his verses so often turning state's evidence against him, as to convince you he is none. He is a prose writer, with a sort of Æolian attachment."

The reason why she lends herself so much more readily to prose than to poetry, lies probably in the predominating characteristic of her nature, her deep moral earnestness. Art must not have for its primary object the presentation of high moral truth. It must be a delineation of life as it is, glorified and idealized by the medium through which it has passed. If what it delineates be not true, — true, either historically or ideally, — the art is false. We must have what is true, either in strict adherence to facts, or else in that wider sense of being in harmonious accord with the great underlying principles of human life. If the truth be not spiritualized by the imagination through which it has passed, it cannot be properly called art at all. Art lends itself readily to the high, spiritual truths of religion; it finds itself at home among the purer and softer emotions; but it rejects, as unfit for its purposes, the sterner and more uncompromising element of religion which we call morality. And it is with morality that George Eliot chiefly has to do. It is with man's relations with man, and not man's relations with God, that she deals. We so commonly associate the fruits of human tenderness and charity and truth with the hidden life of divine communion, that we involuntarily assume this life when we see the fruits depicted.

The human element, which is so strong in her, manifests itself very clearly here. The morality in her books is so pure and high that we recognize it as being the morality of the Bible. It is not a cold, clear-cut philosophy which she inculcates, but a faith rich in all the tender charities which characterize the religion of Jesus. And yet there is not an allusion to a power higher than a lofty purpose taking root in a noble nature. She provides the seed and the soil, but the heaven-born influences of vitalizing dew and sunshine and air are all ignored. It is hardly possible to believe that the practical truths of Christianity should have been so perfectly apprehended by one who was at the same time ignorant of the divine life. It is difficult to conceive that one who had never felt the workings of God's Spirit should have been able to describe so perfectly its fruits; for, if she rests upon the great central truth of the doctrine of Christ, she has left it to inference. There is no word to indicate it in her works.

We find in her novels, on almost every page, beautiful bits of descriptive writing, exquisite touches of sentiment, and pointed illustration, glimmering all over with the fitful play of humor and pathos. Yet under all the music, whether it be bright and sparkling, fresh and pure, measured and solemn, or soul-stirring and heroic, there is a low monotone of pain. It is often so low that it may be overwhelmed by the lighter strain that is carried on above it, except to the ear which has been attuned by personal suffering to catch the wail. All the higher notes of her wonderful music give, besides the melodies and chords which are their natural and direct consequence, a low, resultant tone that imparts a sorrowful cadence to the whole, but which can be distinguished only by a trained and attentive ear.

Though she is wandering in a world full of beautiful possibilities, they are not what she wants; she sees afar off the gates of heavenly truth, but she has let go the guiding hand, and the clew she trusted in is gone. Does not the secret of this undertone of sorrowful longing lie here? She appreciates the high moral beauty of the Christian standard, but at the same time recognizes how far the lives of Christians fall short of their profession. She sees the end to be attained and approves it; she recognizes the *apparent* inadequacy of the means and rejects them. She is striving in her own way to work out the solution of the problem. She has taken into consideration all the elements concerned; her view is wide and inclusive; and if her solution is not the true one, it is because her method is false, and not because the problem, with which she is endeavoring to grapple, is inadequately stated. She seems to make Christ the great teacher, the divine exemplar, all but the Saviour, of poor, storm-tossed, sin-stained humanity. She has never drunk in, with the divine teachings, the divine power of fulfilment which accompanies them. Her recognition of truth is very clear, even of the highest type of divine truth; there is none of the morbid sentimentality which tolerates sin, and which is such an ominous characteristic of modern infidelity. She scorns the specious charity which is really a cloak for sin, while it pretends to be the divine love " which thinketh no evil; which rejoiceth not in iniquity, but rejoiceth in the truth." Her nature is too true to permit her to make any compromise with evil, no matter how alluring its guise may be. It is the instinct of her strong and truthful soul to tear off the flimsy coverings of modern sentimentalism, and to call things by their plain unvarnished names. She looks steadily at the truth, however painful; she recognizes every symptom of the disease, but she does not see the only remedy. If her solution of the difficulty is untrue, it is because it still is incomplete, not because it is one-sided.

She makes of suffering and disappointment a savior. Life, with its varied discipline of joy and sorrow, is the great purifier of souls. Her philosophy is an accurate copy of the divine system of Christianity, and wants only the divine life.

Like the artist king of old, her whole soul revolts against the impurity of the lives she sees around her; and she strives to create for herself an ideal which shall be worthy of her best worship. Out of her imagination is wrought the beautiful but lifeless semblance of the truth; the body of truth waiting for its soul. She looks upon her own creation with the agonized longing of the artist, and feels in it the lack of that which alone can satisfy her cravings. She gives her passionate but despairing love to the cold perfection of her own creation. Will the divine touch come, as it did to the fabled image of Pygmalion? Will this longing, hungry soul ever be filled with the bread of life, so that she may be numbered with those of whom it is said: "They shall hunger no more, neither thirst any more; neither shall the sun light on them, nor any heat: for the Lamb that is in the midst of the throne shall feed them, and shall lead them into living fountains of waters; and God shall wipe away all tears from their eyes"?

With an author's historical self, we, as critics, have nothing to do, but we are drawn within the circle of his real individuality. We do not know, as matters of fact, through what storms and sunshine this soul has ripened to such fulness. But we do know, from internal evidence, that it is a nature rich in all capabilities of happiness, and possessing commensurate capabilities for suffering. We see everywhere the tokens of strife and of victory. The whole moral poise is upright; there is no single instance where tenderness, for suffering or temptation or failure, degenerates into a compromise with evil. One thing has always been to us an inexplicable mystery: she deals with just those incidents which are so peculiarly hard to touch firmly and yet delicately. There is no thought of impurity in her rendering of the most

difficult subjects. We feel the innate refinement and purity
of the woman in the main current of the story ; and yet, scattered through her earlier works, are passages, here and there,
which are coarse. They do not seem to belong to the texture
of the narration, and are so utterly unnecessary. We do not
hold that there is any indelicacy in dealing with truth plainly.
Where there are high ends to be subserved, vice is a perfectly
legitimate subject for fiction ; but it is the plane on which the
writer stands, the standpoint from which he looks at the sin
and folly in the world, which makes his work moral or immoral in its tone. In the words of an eloquent writer we
would say : " The best art is like Shakspeare's art and Ti-
tian's art, always true to the great, glad, aboriginal instincts of
our nature, severely faithful to its foibles, never representing
disease in the guise of health, never rejoicing in the exercise
of morbid fancy, many-sided without being unbalanced, tender without weakness, and forcible without ever losing the
fine sense of proportion. Nothing can be falser than to suppose that morality is served by representing facts other than
they are. No emasculated picture of life can be moral ; it may
be meaningless, and it is sure to be false. No ; we must
stand upon the holy hill with hands uplifted, like those of
Moses, and see the battle of Good against Evil, with a deep
and inexhaustible sympathy for righteousness, and a sense of
victory in our hearts."

As her powers find a fuller development, we note a more
direct and absorbing moral purpose, and less lingering by the
wayside. We have less of the picturesque as accessories to
her delineations, but more of close analysis. The inner life
is more full, and the outer life more meagre. Though we
have lost something, yet we have gained more. We may console ourselves for the loss of the rosy beauty of the orchard
while we are enjoying the mellower fruitage of a later day ;
and yet the eye misses the beauty of the blossoms, and is
not quite satisfied with the fruit.

In " Middlemarch " the story is so entirely subordinated to
the development of character, and to the purpose of the book,

that it requires a little effort to remember that there is a story or plot. The incidents flow on in a calm and steady current, which is worthy of notice only because it bears upon its bosom the rich treasure of immortal interests. In the light of eternity, it is a matter of comparative insignificance whether life be joyful or sorrowful. The great concern is, shall it purify and ennoble the soul? She has an intense yearning for happiness, and feels that delight of every innocent kind is good and to be desired; but she does not call this little strip of time which borders eternity, *existence;* she does not make this ante-chamber to the Temple of God the only theatre of life.

She recognizes the indissoluble connection between sin and suffering, and between virtue and happiness. She does not reward goodness with success, or punish evil with failure, or play with puppets in which the wires are pulled in accordance with the requirements of poetic justice. She recognizes the great truth, that the very essence of sin lies in the revolt of the soul against its Maker, in the severing of the relation between God and man, and that suffering, ignorance, and death are but the fruits of this severance. God no more punishes a planet with sterility and death, which has broken away from its allegiance to the central sun, and is wandering aimlessly in space, than he punishes the human race by sorrow and death, because it has severed the relation between itself and him. The divine justice plants its foundations far down beneath the shifting sands of circumstance. The Almighty does not merely issue decrees, and carry them into execution. Disobedience to the moral law carries, within itself, its own punishment. Our author seems to recognize this truth fully; she sees it as a part of that system of administration which makes an indissoluble connection between the violation of physical laws and physical suffering and death. In the natural world these laws, which regulate the relations of things, are permitted to work out their results unchecked by divine interposition. Christ refused to cast himself down from the pinnacle of the Temple, not because the divine aid which could hinder the consequences was wanting, but because he conformed himself to the laws of nature. We have no proof, indeed, that any miracle he ever performed was a violation of any natural law; all that his miracles were intended to manifest was that his power was supernatural. If he modified the effects of the laws of nature, which are beyond all human control, so as to produce supernatural results, the object of miracles was attained. That is to say, his divine power, by coworking with the unchanged laws and forces of nature, achieved those resultant effects which reveal his divinity, or godhead.

In the divine government God has placed himself between the violation of the moral law and the consequences; and this, it seems to us, our author fails to see. She does not recognize the cords of divine love, which are to draw alienated man back into his true relations with God. It is strange that such clear-sighted vision should just come short of the glory of God!

The intense and full delight which she takes in beauty produces a responsive delight in her readers. In no other prose writer do the descriptions of purely physical and natural beauty produce the same impression upon us as do hers, the impression from her description is so like the impression from the reality; it is the same beauty, reaching us through different channels. She has sunned herself in the light, and we catch the reflected rays. The allurements of luxury and beauty are full of power for her; and it is because she feels the force of such temptation, and the necessity for a counterbalancing and correcting moral force, that she deals so sternly with self-indulgence. The warning comes with a personal accent, that tells of a personal struggle and a personal victory. She reiterates with passionate fervor the refrain of all her stories. Again and again she tells us, that it is not only wickedness, but folly, to make happiness the supreme object of our lives; that no direct and unscrupulous search after pleasure will ever be crowned with success; that abiding happiness lies nowhere but in the path of honor and duty.

It is only her human way of repeating the divine teachings :
"Seek ye first the kingdom of God and his righteousness,
and all these things shall be added unto you." She has stood
upon the edge of the abyss, and looked with horror down
into the frightful depths which have swallowed up so many
precious souls ; and necessity is laid upon her to speak ·and
give warning.

She has never drawn any characters which more fully justify her reputation as a creative artist, than three in "Middlemarch," — Dorothea, Lydgate, and Rosamond. There is
in Dorothea some suggestion of one of her previous creations.
She possesses the same pure and simple lines of character
with Romola; she is the same grand type of woman, full of
unconscious heroism, and a large-hearted generosity. Yet
despite these resemblances, the one is not a repetition of the
other, much less a copy. Each is, on the contrary, a distinct,
separate, and original creation ; and if they bear a sort of
family likeness to one another, this is only because they have
a common parentage.

We do not propose giving any synopsis of the story, or
analysis of the characters. We shall, however, endeavor to
illustrate the justice of some of our criticisms by extracts.
There are thickly scattered through "Middlemarch" illustrations drawn from a wide range of reading upon subjects
not considered exactly feminine "specialties." For instance :
"Miss Brooke argued from words and dispositions not less
unhesitatingly than other young ladies of her age. Signs are
small, measurable things, but interpretations are illimitable ;
and in girls of sweet, ardent natures, every sign is apt to con-
jure up wonder, hope, belief, vast as a sky, and colored by a
diffused thimbleful of matter in the shape of knowledge."
Again : "For in truth, as the day fixed for his marriage came
nearer, Mr. Casaubon did not find his spirits rising ; nor did
the contemplation of that garden-scene, where, as all experience showed, the path was to be bordered with flowers, prove
persistently more enchanting to him than the accustomed
vaults where he walked, taper in hand. He did not confess

to himself, still less would he have breathed to another, his surprise that, though he had won a lovely and noble-hearted girl for his wife, he had not won delight, which he had also regarded as an object to be found by search.   It is true that he knew all the classical passages implying the contrary ; but knowing classical passages, we find, is a mode of motion which explains why they leave so little extra force for their personal application."   Again : " But Mr. Casaubon's theory of the elements which made the seed of all tradition was not likely to bruise itself unawares against discoveries.   It floated among flexible conjectures, no more solid than those etymologies which seemed strong because of the likeness of sound, until it was shown that likeness of sound made them impossible."   Without the knowledge of the latest theory upon the color of the sky, or the modern doctrine of the correlation and conservation of force, or of the principles of comparative grammar, or recent researches in philology, she could not have illustrated her point in each case so perfectly. Superficial knowledge will often enable one to draw analogies from the facts of science, but not from the great fundamental principles.   With all her wealth of illustration, she has, we believe, never been betrayed into an error in history or science.

In the delineation of character we note a peculiarly impartial judgment, which would lead to the belief that each one is a study from the life.   There is, perhaps, no character in all her writings who is less calculated to arouse any strong feeling of admiration or reprehension than Mr. Casaubon ; an elderly scholar, with no high belief in himself or his work, entirely self-centred, though not utterly selfish, is the last type of man to stir her sympathies ; and yet she pleads his cause against herself, with that intensely human sympathy which is her strongest characteristic.   She says, in her calm, judicial way : " If, to Dorothea, Mr. Casaubon had been the mere occasion which set alight the inflammable material of her youthful illusions, does it follow that he was fairly represented in the minds of those less impassioned personages who have hitherto delivered their judgments concerning him? I protest against any absolute conclusion, any prejudice derived from Mrs. Cadwallader's contempt for a neighboring clergyman's alleged greatness of soul, or Sir James Chettam's poor opinion of his rival's legs — from Mr. Brooke's failure to elicit a companion's ideas, or from Celia's criticism of a middle-aged scholar's personal appearance. I am not sure that the greatest man of his age, if ever that solitary superlative existed, could escape these unfavorable reflections of himself in various small mirrors; and even Milton, looking for his portrait in a spoon, must submit to have the facial angle of a bumpkin."

The habit of questioning facts, and giving a careful interpretation of them to the world, is a characteristic of modern art. It is the accurate truth of the delineation, rather than the ideal and religious sentiment, which recommends the work as genuine art. The impression which "Middlemarch" leaves, in contradistinction to that made by her earlier writings, is, that each character has been carefully studied from nature; and, in consequence, the delineation is more close, accurate, and analytic, though not more true than in her earlier works. She wrote "Scenes in Clerical Life" when her mind was teeming with the accumulated experience of years; the exuberance of fancy, the multitude of characters, sometimes indicated in a few masterly lines, show her confidence in an inexhaustible reserve of material. We do not feel this prodigality in "Middlemarch;" every conception is worked up carefully, and made to do full duty.

The artist is manifested more clearly in the admirable manner in which she sustains relations, than even in the perfection of each bit of the painting. The moral perspective is never forgotten. The minor characters are well sustained, but they keep their appointed places modestly. We find the neutral tints and masses of distinct color necessary to throw out into most effective relief the main features and characters of the story. The whole meaning and interest of "Middlemarch" is spiritual. It is the growth of a soul, out of the crudities and illusions of youth, into a beautiful, rounded womanhood. Dorothea goes through an experience which could more easily find its counterpart in real life than in fiction. Her discipline is not one of treachery and cruelty and persecution, but the daily, wearing discipline, to an eager soul, of missing the work she is longing to do, as well as the help and sympathy she needs in her effort to live a high and noble life. With the ardent enthusiasm, which looks upon life as something to be done, goes the usual accompaniment, in a young and earnest soul, of a tendency to asceticism. Her greatest delight was in riding. "She loved the fresh air and the various aspects of the country; and, when her eyes and cheeks glowed with mingled pleasure, she looked very little like a devotee. Riding was an indulgence which she allowed herself in spite of conscientious qualms; she felt that she enjoyed it in a pagan sensuous way, and always looked forward to renouncing it." Her notions of life were very childlike and unpractical. "She felt sure she would have accepted the judicious Hooker, if she had been born in time to save him from that wretched mistake he made in matrimony; or John Milton when his blindness had come on; or any of the other great men whose odd habits it would have been glorious piety to endure; but an amiable, handsome baronet, who said 'Exactly' to her remark, even when she expressed uncertainty — how could he affect her as a lover?"

The tragedy which awaits such a nature, in a world full of sordid cares and considerations, came in due time to her. Under the stress of her peculiar needs and longings she married; but the higher and fuller life never came. It was not long before the veil of youthful illusion and glorifying fancy fell from her eyes, and she saw and felt how barren her life promised to be. "The clear heights where she expected to walk in full communion had become difficult even in imagination; the delicious repose of the soul on a complete superior had been shaken into uneasy effort, and alarmed with dim presentiment. When would the day begin of that active, wifely devotion, which was to strengthen her husband's life and exalt her own? Never, perhaps, as she had preconceived them; but somehow — still somehow. In this solemnly pledged union of life, duty would present itself in some new form of inspiration, and give a new meaning to wifely love."

"Meanwhile there was the snow and the low arch of dun vapor; there was the stifling oppression of that gentle-woman's world, where everything was done for her and none asked her aid; where the sense of connection with a manifold, pregnant existence had to be kept up painfully as an inward vision, instead of coming from without, in claims that would have shaped her energies. 'What shall I do?' 'What ever you please, my dear:' that had been her brief history since she had left off learning morning lesson, and practis-ing silly rhythms on the hated piano. Marriage, which was to bring guidance into worthy and imperative occu-pation, had not yet freed her from the gentlewoman's oppressive liberty; it had not even filled her leisure with ruminant tenderness. Her blooming, full-pulsed youth stood there in a moral imprisonment, which made itself one with the chill, colorless, narrowed landscape." But this nature was too full of vigorous spiritual vitality to be crushed by her narrow, hopeless life. When love and a noble ambi-tion were forced to be silent, a tender, womanly compassion took up the strain. At first she felt only the blight upon her own hopes. "She was as blind to his inward troubles as he to hers; she had not yet learned those hidden conflicts in her husband which claim our pity. She had not yet listened patiently to his heart-beats, but only felt that her own was beating violently." The sweet, womanly nature soon righted itself; the world should never know her disappointment, how-ever bitter it might be, and her husband should have all the tender care which the most admiring love could bestow.

Mr. Casaubon's disappointment is touched no less tenderly than is Dorothea's. The infinite pathos of a failure, where life and health have been cast into the decisive throw, encir-cles him with a halo to the eyes of our author; and yet she does not spare him. "When he had seen Dorothea" (this was before their marriage) "he believed that he had found even more than he demanded; she might really be such a helpmate as would enable him to dispense with a hired secretary — an aid which Mr. Casaubon had never yet employed, and had a suspicious dread of. (Mr. Casaubon was nervously conscious that he was expected to manifest a powerful mind.) Providence, in its kindness, had supplied him with the wife he needed; for a modest young lady, with the purely appreciative, unambitious abilities of her sex, is sure to think her husband's mind powerful. Whether Providence had taken equal care of Miss Brooke, in presenting her with Mr. Casaubon, was an idea which could hardly occur to him. Society never made the preposterous demand that a man should think as much about his own qualification for making a charming girl happy, as he thinks of hers for making him happy. As if a man should choose not only his wife, but his wife's husband. . . . It is an uneasy lot, at best, to be what we call highly taught, and yet not to enjoy; to be present at this great spectacle of life, and never be liberated from a small, hungry, shivering self; never to be fully possessed by the glory we behold ; never to have our consciousness rapturously transformed into the vividness of a thought, the ardor of a passion, the energy of an action, but always to be scholarly and uninspired, ambitious and timid, scrupulous and dim-sighted. . . . He had not much foretaste of happiness in his previous life. To know intense joy, without a strong bodily frame, one must have an enthusiastic soul. Mr. Casaubon had never had a strong bodily frame, and his soul was sensitive without being enthusiastic; it was too languid to thrill out of self-consciousness into passionate delight; it went on fluttering in the swampy ground where it was hatched, thinking of its wings, and never flying. His experience was of that pitiable kind which shrinks from pity, and fears most of all that it should be known ; it was that proud, narrow sensitiveness, which has not mass enough to spare for transformation into sympathy, and quivers thread-like in small currents of self-preoccupation, or at best of an egotistic scrupulosity. . . . To this mental estate, mapped out a quarter of a century before, to sensibilities thus fenced in, Mr. Casaubon had thought of annexing happiness with a lovely young bride; but even before marriage, as we have seen, he found himself under a new depression in the consciousness that the new bliss was not blissful to him. Inclination yearned back to its old, easier custom; and the deeper he went into domesticity, the more did the sense of acquitting himself and acting with propriety predominate over any other satisfaction." He was sensitively alive to the indifference and criticism of the literary world; because he possessed no self-confidence which could sustain him under adverse criticism. "These were heavy impressions to struggle against, and brought that melancholy embitterment which is the consequence of all excessive claim. . . . There was no denying that Dorothea was as virtuous and amiable a young lady as he could have obtained for a wife; but a young lady turned out to be a something more troublesome than he had conceived. She nursed him, she read to him, she anticipated his wants, and was solicitous about his feelings; but there had entered into her husband's mind the certainty that she judged him, and that her wifely devotedness was like a penitential expiation for unbelieving thoughts — was accompanied by a power of comparison by which himself and his doings were seen too luminously as a part of things in general. His discontent passed vapor-like through all her gentle, loving manifestations, and clung to that inappreciative world which she had only brought nearer to him. Poor Mr. Casaubon! This suffering was the harder to him, because it seemed like a betrayal; the young creature who had worshipped him with perfect trust had quickly turned into the critical wife; and early instances of criticism and resentment had made an impression which no tenderness and submission afterward could remove. . . . In Mr. Casaubon's ear Dorothea's voice gave loud, emphatic iteration to those muffled suggestions of consciousness, which it was possible to explain as mere fancy, the illusion of exaggerated

sensitiveness : always when such suggestions are unmistaka-
bly repeated from without, they are resisted as cruel and
unjust. . . . We are angered even by the full acceptance of our
humiliating confessions; how much more by hearing in hard,
distinct syllables, from the lips of a mere observer, those con-
fused murmurs which we try to call morbid, and strive against
as if they were the oncoming of numbness! And this cruel,
outward accuser was there in the shape of a wife — nay, of a
young bride — who, instead of observing his abundance of pen-
scratches and amplitude of paper, with the uncritical awe of an
elegant-minded canary-bird, seemed to present herself as a
spy, watching everything with a malign power of inference.
Here, toward this particular point of the compass, Mr. Casaubon had a sensitiveness to match Dorothea's, and an equal
quickness to imagine more than the fact. He had formerly
observed with approbation her capacity for worshipping the
right object; he now foresaw with sudden terror that this
capacity might be replaced by presumption, this worship by
the most exasperating of all criticism — that which sees
vaguely a great many fine ends, and has not the least notion
what it costs to reach them."

We have purposely made long quotations from these reflections by the author, because they illustrate so pointedly her
distinguishing characteristics. They show a subtle analysis
of character, and of that hidden current of motive which
forever ebbs and flows underneath the surface, as well as
underneath the ostensible motives and feelings which are
acknowledged to the world and to one's self. She seems to
see as clearly "all the little, mean work of our natures,"
which "is generally done in a small, dark closet, just a little
back of the subject we are talking about," as she does the
hidden springs of nobleness and of unconscious heroism.
The close analysis of such a character as Mr. Casaubon's
shows wonderful clearness in one whose nature is so full of
intense vitality as George Eliot's.

" Middlemarch " does not offer to the reader so many pithy
sentences, detachable from the current of the story, as we

have in "Adam Bede." Still it does not lack brightness and
point. The sharp-tongued Mrs. Cadwallader does not say so
many good things as Mrs. Poyser; yet there are remarks
here, there, and everywhere, which are sparkling with wit
and satire. . . .

It is impossible to speak too strongly of the masterly power
of the pen which has drawn Lydgate and Rosamond. There
is a tragedy in Lydgate's fate, before which the tragedy of
death itself sinks into insignificance; and which comes home
to us with peculiar force, because it lies so close to the
experience of our daily lives and struggles. The chief artistic merit of the book is its unity. It is a growth which may
not be fairly represented by any fragment. If we cut a bit
of the stalk, or carry away with us a leaf as a memento, it
can only recall, it can never represent, the existence of which
it was a part. Toward the end, when the whole outcome of
Dorothea's life is shown in her passionate sufferings at what
she believed was her broken trust; in her woman's scorn of
the treachery shown her, and strong self-contempt at her own
delusion; and finally in the noble reassertion of her better
nature, we see the glorious bloom which crowns the plant and
which gives meaning to the hidden processes of growth. In
the light of this beautiful culmination we see the reason of
the bursting of the seed-sheath, and the casting off of the en-
cumbering yet life-sustaining earth. The dark creations of
nature or of art are then understood and self-vindicated, when,
out of the elements by which they are surrounded and which
threaten to stifle their existence, they burst into the open air
and sunshine of a higher life. Thus do we look upon the
growth of character, whether real or fictitious, as upon that of
a plant whose culmination in the flower sheds meaning and
beauty on all the slow and doubtful stages of its development.
The real question of life is, in story as in history, what we
are, and not what we possess. This question lies beneath all
the hard conditions of uneventful lives, pressed down by sordid cares and conventional trammels, and preaches a sermon
which sinks into the heart like dew from heaven. It helps

us to see that, although a life may be full of repression and misery, yet, under all this, there is a divine alchemy which turns all the baser metal of existence into pure gold, seven times refined.

We gratefully acknowledge that we owe much to the genius of George Eliot, not less, perhaps, to its short-comings and defects than to its achievements and perfections. It has made life seem a better and nobler thing to us, and has shown us that truth, when illuminated by genius, finds its way where the same truth would, in other guise, fail to penetrate. But if it has shown us what life *ought* to be, it has, at the same time, shown us what life *must* be if it comes short of the hopes and the joys of the Christian's faith. Give us these, and others may, if they please, or if they *can*, find rest in the riches, the honors, or the pleasures of a perishable world.

Her faith in the God-given possibilities of human nature has, it is true, " gathered round itself a fair shape " of words; and other souls, stirred by the same faith, may worship with her at the same shrine. But the surer faith, "which is founded upon a rock," begets a higher and more certain hope, converting the *possibilities* of our nature into the *realities* of the eternal, unchanging, and unfading glory of the divine life within us. These are the sublime heights, the " delectable mountains," on which the Christian worships, and in no temple made with hands; and from which he looks down upon all the shrines erected by human genius, however exalted, as upon the lower plains in the gilded valley of death.

c

ESSAYS AND REVIEWS

OF

GEORGE ELIOT.

————◦◦°•◦°◦◦————

THE LADY NOVELISTS.

THE appearance of Woman in the field of literature is a
significant fact. It is the correlate of her position in
society. To some men the fact is doubtless as distasteful as
the social freedom of women in Europe must be to an Eastern
mind; it must seem so unfeminine, so contrary to the real
destination of woman; and it must seem so in both cases
from the same cause. But although it is easy to be supercilious and sarcastic on Blue Stockings and Literary Ladies; —
and although one may admit that such sarcasms have frequently their extenuation in the offensive pretensions of
what are called "strong-minded women," — it is certain that
the philosophic eye sees in this fact, of literature cultivated
by women, a significance not lightly to be passed over. It
touches both society and literature. The man who would
deny to woman the cultivation of her intellect, ought, for
consistency, to shut her up in a harem. If he recognize in
the sex any quality which transcends the qualities demanded in a plaything or a handmaid, if he recognize in her
the existence of an intellectual life not essentially dissimilar
to his own, he must, by the plainest logic, admit that life to
express itself in all its spontaneous forms of activity. It is
very true that ink on the thumb is no ornament, but we have
yet to learn that stains upon the blouse or the dissecting-

sleeves are ornamental; few incidents of work are. What then? Moreover we confess it is very awkward and uncomfortable to hear a woman venture on Greek, when you don't know Greek, or to quote from a philosophical treatise which would give you a headache; and something of this feeling doubtless lies at the core of much of the opposition to "learned women;" the men are "put out" by it. The enormity seems equivalent to the domestic partner of your joys assuming the privilege of a latch-key! "Where is our supremacy to find a throne if we admit women to share our imperious dominion — Intelligence?" So reasons the intellectual Jones. But one might quietly ask him whether he professed any immense delight in the society of the *man* who threw Greek and philosophy at his head? Pedantry is the ostentation of learning, the scholar's coxcombry; no one likes it, any more than he likes other forms of obtrusive self-assertion. Therefore we may say with Mademoiselle de Scudéry: "Je veux donc bien qu'on puisse dire d'une personne de mon sexe qu'elle sait cent choses dont elle ne se vante pas, qu'elle a l'esprit fort éclairé, qu'elle connait finement les beaux ouvrages, qu'elle parle bien, qu'elle écrit juste et qu'elle sait le monde; mais je ne veux pas qu'on puisse dire d'elle, *c'est une femme savante:* car ces deux caractères sont si différents qu'ils ne se ressemblent même point." [1]

One may admit that much folly is spoken and written on the subject of "woman's mission" and "emancipation," folly *pro* and folly *con;* one may admit that literary women are not *always* the most charming of their sex (are literary men of theirs?) — but let us leave all such side questions, and definitely ask ourselves, What does the literature of women really mean? To aid us in arriving at something like distinctness, it will be well to settle a definition of literature itself.

Literature must be separated from philosophy and science, at least for our present purpose. Science is the expression of the forms and order of Nature; literature is the expression of the forms and order of Human Life.

[1] "Le Grand Cyrus."

All poetry, all fiction, all comedy, all *belles lettres*, even to the playful caprices of fancy, are but the expression of experiences and emotions; and these expressions are the avenues through which we reach the sacred adytum of Humanity, and learn better to understand our fellows and ourselves. In proportion as these expressions are the forms of universal truths, of facts common to all nations or appreciable by all intellects, the literature which sets them forth is permanently good and true. Hence the universality and immortality of Homer, Shakspeare, Cervantes, Molière. But in proportion as these expressions are the forms of individual, peculiar truths, such as fleeting fashions or idiosyncrasies, the literature is ephemeral. Hence tragedy never grows old, for it arises from elemental experience ; but comedy soon ages, for it arises from peculiarities. Nevertheless, even idiosyncrasies are valuable as side glances ; they are aberrations that bring the natural orbit into more prominent distinctness.

It follows from what has been said that literature, being essentially the expression of experience and emotion, — of what we have seen, felt, and thought, — that only *that* literature is effective, and to be prized accordingly, which has *reality for its basis* (needless to say that emotion is as real as the three-per-cents), *and effective in proportion to the depth and breadth of that basis.*

It was M. de Bonald, we believe, who gave currency to the famous definition, so constantly accepted as accurate, " Literature is the expression of society." To make it acceptable, however, we must depart very widely from its direct meaning. The most cursory glance at literature on the one hand, and at society on the other, will detect the glaring discrepancy. So far from literature being a mirror or expression of society, it is under most aspects palpably at variance with society. Idyls flourish on the eve of violent social outbreaks, as we see in Florian, Gesner, and George Sand; chivalry finds a voice as chivalry is passing from the world; wild, adventurous novels, agitated with hair-breadth 'scapes, solace a money-making society "so eminently respectable ; " love in a cottage makes the heart flutter that is about to sell itself for a splendid match. The remark is as old as Horace:—

> "Luctantem Icariis fluctibus Africum
> Mercator metuens otium et oppidi
> Laudat rura sui ; mox reficit rates
> Quassas, indocilis pauperiem pati."

Not only so, but our novels and plays, even when pretending to represent real life, represent it as no human being ever saw it.

If, however, instead of regarding literature as the expression of society, we regard it as the expression of the emotions, the whims, the caprices, the enthusiasms, the fluctuating idealisms which move each epoch, we shall not be far wrong ; and inasmuch as women necessarily take part in these things, they ought to give them *their* expression. And this leads us to the heart of the question, What does the literature of women mean ? It means this : while it is impossible for men to express life otherwise than as they know it, and they can only know it profoundly according to their own experience, the advent of female literature promises woman's view of life, woman's experience,—in other words, a new element. Make what distinctions you please in the social world, it still remains true that men and women have different organizations, consequently different experiences. To know life you must have both sides depicted.

> "Der Mann muss hinaus
> Ins feindliche Leben,
> Muss wirken und streben ! "

Let him paint what he knows. And if you limit woman's sphere to the domestic circle, you must still recognize the concurrent necessity of domestic life finding its homeliest and truest expression in the woman who lives it.

Keeping to the abstract heights we have chosen, too abstract and general to be affected by exceptions, we may further say that the Masculine mind is characterized by the predominance of the intellect, and the Feminine by the predominance of the emotions. According to this rough division the regions of philosophy would be assigned to men, those of literature to women. We need scarcely warn the reader against too rigorous an interpretation of this statement, which is purposely exaggerated, the better to serve as a signpost. It is quite true that no such absolute distinction exists in mankind, and therefore no such correlative distinction will be found in authorship. There is no man whose mind is shrivelled up into pure intellect; there is no woman whose intellect is completely absorbed by her emotions. But in most men the intellect does not move in such inseparable alliance with the emotions as in most women; and hence, although often not so great as in women, yet the intellect is more commonly dominant. In poets, artists, and men of letters, *par excellence,* we observe this feminine trait, that their intellect habitually moves in alliance with their emotions; and one of the best descriptions of poetry was that given by Professor Wilson, as the "intellect colored by the feelings."

Woman, by her greater affectionateness, her greater range and depth of emotional experience, is well fitted to give expression to the emotional facts of life, and demands a place in literature corresponding with that she occupies in society; and that literature must be greatly benefited thereby, follows from the definition we have given of literature.

But hitherto, in spite of splendid illustrations, the literature of women has fallen short of its function, owing to a very natural and very explicable weakness; it has been too much a literature of imitation. To write as men write is the aim and besetting sin of women; to write as women is the real office they have to perform. Our definition of literature includes this necessity. If writers are bound to express what they have really known, felt, and suffered, that very obligation imperiously declares they shall not quit their own point of view for the point of view of others. To imitate is to abdicate. We are in no need of more male writers; we are in need of genuine female experience. The prejudices, notions, passions, and conventionalisms of men are amply illustrated; let us have the same fulness with respect to women. Unhappily the literature of women may be compared with that of Rome; no amount of graceful talent can disguise the internal defect. Virgil, Ovid, and Catullus were assuredly gifted with delicate and poetic sensibility; but their light is, after all, the light of moons reflected from the Grecian suns, and such as brings little life with its rays. To speak in Greek, to think in Greek, was the ambition of all cultivated Romans, who could not see that it would be a grander thing to utter their pure Roman natures in sincere originality. So of women. The throne of intellect has so long been occupied by men, that women naturally deem themselves bound to attend the Court. Greece domineered over Rome; its intellectual supremacy was recognized; and the only way of rivalling it seemed to be imitation. Yet not *so* did Rome vanquish Pyrrhus and his elephants, — not by employing elephants to match his, but by Roman valor.

Of all departments of literature, Fiction is the one to which, by nature and by circumstance, women are best adapted. Exceptional women will of course be found competent to the highest success in other departments; but, speaking generally, novels are their forte. The domestic experiences, which form the bulk of woman's knowledge, find an appropriate form in novels; while the very nature of fiction calls for that predominance of sentiment which we have already attributed to the feminine mind. Love is the staple of fiction, for it "forms the story of a woman's life." The joys and sorrows of affection, the incidents of domestic life, the aspirations and fluctuations of emotional life, assume typical forms in the novel. Hence we may be prepared to find women succeeding better in *finesse* of detail, in pathos and sentiment, while men generally succeed better in the construction of plots and the delineation of character. Such a novel as "Tom Jones" or "Vanity Fair" we shall not get from a woman, nor such an effort of imaginative history as "Ivanhoe" or "Old Mortal-

ity ; " but Fielding, Thackeray, and Scott are equally excluded
from such perfection in its kind as " Pride and Prejudice,"
" Indiana," or " Jane Eyre." As an artist, Miss Austen surpasses all the male novelists that ever lived ; and, for eloquence and depth of feeling, no man approaches George
Sand.

We are here led to another curious point in our subject,
viz., the influence of Sorrow upon female literature. It may
be said without exaggeration that almost all literature has
some remote connection with suffering. " Speculation," said
Novalis, " is disease." It certainly springs from a vague
disquiet. Poetry is analogous to the pearl which the oyster
secretes in its malady.

> " Most wretched men
> Are cradled into poetry by wrong;
> They learn in suffering what they teach in song."

What Shelley says of poets, applies with greater force to
women. If they turn their thoughts to literature, it is —
when not purely an imitative act — always to solace by some
intellectual activity the sorrow that in silence wastes their
lives ; and by a withdrawal of the intellect from the contemplation of their pain, or by a transmutation of their secret
anxieties into types, they escape from the pressure of that
burden. If the accidents of her position make her solitary
and inactive, or if her thwarted affections shut her somewhat
from that sweet domestic and maternal sphere to which her
whole being spontaneously moves, she turns to literature as
to another sphere. We do not here simply refer to those notorious cases where literature has been taken up with the
avowed and conscious purpose of withdrawing thoughts from
painful subjects, but to the unconscious unavowed influence
of domestic disquiet and unfulfilled expectations, in determining the sufferer to intellectual activity. The happy wife
and busy mother are only forced into literature by some hereditary organic tendency, stronger even than the domestic ;
and hence it is that the cleverest women are not always
those who have written books.

Having said thus much on the general subject of female novel writing, let us glance rapidly, and without pretence of exhaustive criticism, at some of the novelists; doing in careless prose what Leigh Hunt has done in genial verse in his "Blue Stocking Revels." We have been great readers and great admirers of female novels; and although it is difficult to give authors a *satisfactory* reason for not including their names among the most celebrated, we beg our fair novelists to put the most generous construction upon all our "omissions," and to believe that when we are ungallant and omissive, there is "a design under it" as profound as that under Swift's dulness. To include *all* would obviously be impossible in these limits; and we shall purposely exclude some names of undoubted worth and renown, in order not even to seem invidious.

First and foremost let Jane Austen be named, the greatest artist that has ever written, using the term to signify the most perfect mastery over the means to her end. There are heights and depths in human nature Miss Austen has never scaled nor fathomed, there are worlds of passionate existence into which she has never set foot; but although this is obvious to every reader, it is equally obvious that she has risked no failures by attempting to delineate that which she had not seen. Her circle may be restricted, but it is complete. Her world is a perfect orb, and vital. Life, as it presents itself to an English gentlewoman peacefully yet actively engaged in her quiet village, is mirrored in her works with a purity and fidelity that must endow them with interest for all time. To read one of her books is like an actual experience of life; you know the people as if you had lived with them, and you feel something of personal affection towards them. The marvellous reality and subtle distinctive traits noticeable in her portraits has led Macaulay to call her a prose Shakspeare. If the whole force of the distinction which lies in that epithet *prose* be fairly appreciated, no one, we think, will dispute the compliment; for out of Shakspeare it would be difficult to find characters so typical yet so nicely demarcated within the

limits of their kind. We do not find such profound psychological insight as may be found in George Sand (not to
mention male writers), but taking the type to which the
characters belong, we see the most intimate and accurate
knowledge in all Miss Austen's creations.

Only cultivated minds fairly appreciate the exquisite art of
Miss Austen. Those who demand the stimulus of "effects,"
those who can only see by strong lights and shadows, will
find her tame and uninteresting. We may illustrate this by
one detail. Lucy Steele's bad English, so delicately and
truthfully indicated, would in the hands of another have
been more obvious, more "effective" in its exaggeration; but
the loss of this comic effect is more than replaced to the cultivated reader by his relish of the nice discrimination visible
in its truthfulness. And so of the rest. *Strong* lights are
unnecessary, *true* lights being at command. The incidents,
the characters, the dialogue — all are of every-day life; and
so truthfully presented, that to appreciate the art we must
try to imitate it, or carefully compare it with that of others.

We are but echoing an universal note of praise in speaking
thus highly of her works; and it is from no desire of simply
swelling that chorus of praise that we name her here, but to
call attention to the peculiar excellence, at once womanly and
literary, which has earned this reputation. Of all imaginative writers, she is the most *real*. Never does she transcend
her own actual experience, never does her pen trace a line .
that does not touch the experience of others. Herein we
recognize the first quality of literature. We recognize the
second and more special quality of womanliness in the tone
and point of view ; they are novels written by a woman, an
Englishwoman, a gentlewoman; no signature could disguise
that fact; and because she has so faithfully (although unconsciously) kept to her own womanly point of view, her works
are durable. There is nothing of the *doctrinaire* in Jane
Austen, not a trace of woman's "mission;" but as the most
truthful, charming, humorous, pure-minded, quick-witted, and
unexaggerated of writers, female literature has reason to be
proud of her.

Of greater genius, and incomparably deeper experience, George Sand represents woman's literature more illustriously and more obviously. In her, quite apart from the magnificent gifts of Nature, we see the influence of Sorrow, as a determining impulse to write, and the abiding consciousness of the womanly point of view as the subject-matter of her writings. In vain has she chosen the mask of a man; the features of a woman are everywhere visible. Since Goethe, no one has been able to say with so much truth, " My writings are my confessions." Her biography lies there, presented, indeed, in a fragmentary shape, and under wayward disguises, but nevertheless giving to the motley groups the strange and unmistakable charm of reality. Her grandmother, by whom she was brought up, disgusted at her not being a boy, resolved to remedy the misfortune as far as possible by educating her like a boy. We may say of this, as of all the other irregularities of her strange and exceptional life, that whatever unhappiness and error may be traceable thereto, its influence on her writings has been beneficial, by giving a greater range to her experience. It may be selfish to rejoice over the malady which secretes a pearl, but the possessor of the pearl may at least congratulate himself that at any rate the pearl has been produced; and so of the unhappiness of genius. Certainly few women have had such profound and varied experience as George Sand; none have turned it to more account. Her writings contain many passages that her warmest admirers would wish unwritten; but although severe criticism may detect the weak places, the severest criticism must conclude with the admission of her standing among the highest minds of literature. In the matter of eloquence, she surpasses everything France has yet produced. There has been no style at once so large, so harmonious, so expressive, and so unaffected; like a light shining through an alabaster vase, the ideas shine through her diction; while as regards rhythmic melody of phrase, it is a style such as Beethoven might have written, had he uttered in words the melodious passion that was in him.

But deeper than all eloquence, grander than all grandeur of phrase, is that forlorn splendor of a life of passionate experience painted in her works. There is no man so wise but he may learn from them, for they are the utterances of a soul in pain, a soul that has been tried. No man could have written her books, for no man could have had her experience, even with a genius equal to her own. The philosopher may smile sometimes at her philosophy, for *that* is only a reflex of some man whose ideas she has adopted; the critic may smile some-times at her failure in delineating men; but both philosopher and critic must perceive that those writings of hers are *original*, are genuine, are transcripts of experience, and as such fulfil the primary condition of all literature. It is not our present purpose to enter upon details, but we may add in passing that although *all* her works will be found to partake of the character of confessions, there is one wherein the biographical element takes a more definite and literal shape, viz., in "Lucrezia Floriani." Wide as the incidents of this story are from the truth, the characters of Lucrezia, Karol, and Vandoni are more like portraits than is usual with her.

By a whimsical transition our thoughts wander to Lady Morgan, the "Wild Irish Girl," who delighted our fathers, and gave the "Quarterly" an opportunity of displaying its accustomed amenity and nice feeling for the sex. Lady Morgan has been a stanch upholder of the rights of woman, and in her own person vindicated the claims of the sex to be heard as authors. But Leigh Hunt shall touch her portrait for us : —

"And dear Lady Morgan! look, look how she comes,
With her pulses all beating for freedom, like drums —
So Irish, so modish, so *mixtish*, so wild;
So committing herself, as she talks, like a child,
So trim yet so easy, polite yet high-hearted,
That truth and she, try all she can, won't be parted.
She'll put on your fashions, your latest new air,
And then talk so frankly, she'll make you all stare."

2

From the same hand you shall have a sketch of Miss Edgeworth — a strange contrast to her countrywoman just
named : —

> " At the sight of Miss Edgeworth, he [1] said, ' Here comes one
> As sincere and as kind as lives under the sun ;
> Not poetical, eh ? — nor much given to insist
> On utilities not in utility's list.
> (Things, nevertheless, without which the large heart
> Of my world would but play a poor husk of a part.)
> But most truly within her own sphere sympathetic —
> And that 's no mean help towards the practice poetic.'
> Then smiling he said a most singular thing —
> He thanked her for making him ' saving of string '!!
> But, for fear she should fancy he did n't approve her in
> Matters more weighty, praised much her ' Manœuvring ; '
> A book, which, if aught could pierce craniums so dense,
> Might supply cunning folks with a little good sense.
> And her Irish (he added), poor souls! so impressed him,
> He knew not if most they amused, or distressed him ! "

Miss Edgeworth possesses in a remarkable degree the peculiarly feminine quality of Observation ; though but little of
that other quality, Sentiment, which distinguishes female
writers, and which, combined with observation, constitutes
the staple of novels.   Indeed one might class novelists thus :
1st, those remarkable for Observation ; 2d, those remarkable for Sentiment ; 3d, those remarkable for the combination
of the two.   Observation without sentiment usually leads to
humor or satire ; sentiment without observation to rhetoric
and long-drawn lachrymosity.   The extreme fault of the one
is flippant superficiality ; that of the other is what is called
" sickly sentimentality."

Miss Burney, for example, had a quick observation, notably of ridiculous details, and with a certain broad vulgar
gauge of human nature, contrived to write one or two novels
that admirably reflected the passing manners of her age ; but
when — as in the " Wanderer " — she attempted to interest by
sentiment, her failure was hopeless.   L. E. L., on the other

------

[1] Apollo.

hand, was essentially deficient in that which made the reputation of Fanny Burney; but her quick emotive nature, trembling with sensibility, enabled her to write passages of
exquisite beauty, which were not, however, more durable
than mere emotion is. Mrs. Gore, again, — who might, perhaps, with more care bestowed upon her works, have been
the Fanny Burney of our age, — exhibits in every chapter the
marvellous finesse and quickness of observation, winged with
a certain airy gayety of style which, if it be not wit, has half
the charm of wit; and this faculty of observation has allowed her to write heaps of fashionable novels, as fugitive as
the fashions they reflect, yet as gay and pleasant. But who
does not miss in them that element of serious sentiment
which gives to other novels their pathos, their poetry, their
psychology ?

We might run through the list of female writers, thus con-
trasting them, noting the strong sarcastic observation of Mrs.
Trollope and the wearisome sentimentality of Mrs. Marsh
(who has, nevertheless, written one most powerful tale,
" The Admiral's Daughter," and whose most popular work,
" Emilia Wyndham," we are willing to take upon trust, not
having read it); but the excursion would carry us beyond our
limits. Enough, if we have indicated the point of view.

Two celebrated women whose works have produced an extraordinary " sensation " — the authoress of " Jane Eyre,"
and the authoress of " Mary Barton " — owe their success, we
believe, to the union of rare yet indispensable qualities.
They have both given imaginative expression to actual experience; they have not invented, but reproduced; they have
preferred the truth, such as their own experience testified, to
the vague, false, conventional notions current in circulating
libraries. Whatever of weakness may be pointed out in their
works will, we are positive, be mostly in those parts where
experience is deserted, and the supposed requirements of fiction have been listened to; whatever has really affected the
public mind is, we are equally certain, the transcript of some
actual incident, character, or emotion. Note, moreover, that

beyond this basis of actuality these writers have the further advantage of deep feeling united to keen observation. The presence of observation is more apparent in "Mary Barton" than in "Jane Eyre," as it is possibly more predominant in the mind of the authoress; and this is why there never was even a momentary doubt as to the writer's sex, a woman's delicate hand being visible in the strongest pages; whereas "Jane Eyre" was not only attributed to a man, but one of the most keen-witted and observing of female writers dogmatically pronounced, upon internal evidence, that none but a man could have written it. The force and even fierceness of the style certainly suggested doubts, but what man could have drawn Jane herself; above all, what man could *so* have drawn Rochester! The lyrical tendency — the psychological and emotional tendency — which prevails in "Jane Eyre" may have blinded some to the rare powers of observation also exhibited in the book; a critical examination, however, will at once set this right, — the more so when we know that the authoress has led a solitary life in a secluded part of Yorkshire, and has had but little opportunities of seeing the world. She has made the most of her material.

The deep impression produced on Europe by George Sand has naturally caused many imitations, notably in Germany and France. As to the Germans, *palmam qui meruit ferat!* "let the most gifted bear away the palm;" and the palm of bad novel-writing certainly belongs to them. However, as the names of these Indianas and Lelias have scarcely crossed the German Ocean, we will leave them in untroubled emancipation —

> "non ragioniam di lor
> Ma guarda e passa."

The name of Daniel Stern (pseudonyme for the Comtesse d'Agoult) has had more attention. Her first appearance was in "Nélida," a novel in which she idealized herself, and branded her truant lover, Franz Liszt. It had a certain "succès de scandale." The assumption of a man's name, and the abiding imitation of Madame Sand, lessened, perhaps, the admiration the novel would otherwise have excited, because it claimed a standard to which, in no sense, could it be compared. Since that, Daniel Stern has earned a more serious reputation as a political and historical writer. Her "History of the Revolution of 1848" is the best that has been written on that subject.

Apropos of "Nélida," and of Lady Bulwer Lytton's novels, it may be pertinent to distinguish between writing out your actual experience in fiction, and using fiction as a medium for obtruding your private history on the sympathies of the public. We hold that the author is bound to use actual experience as his material, or else to keep silent; but he is equally bound by all moral and social considerations not to use that experience in such forms that the public will recognize it, and become, as it were, initiated into the private affairs of his characters. If he avow himself as the Juvenal or Aristophanes of his age, and satirize his friends and foes, he has, at any rate, the excuse that every one is on guard against avowed satire. But if he have been mixed up in some deplorable history which has become notorious, and if he take advantage of that notoriety to tell *his* version of it under the transparent disguise of fiction, then we say he violates all principle of truth and of literature ; because in fiction he has an immunity from falsehood. He does not profess to tell you the story, yet he gives you to understand what he wishes. He paints himself as an injured innocent ; and if you object to his portrait of you, as that of an incarnate demon, his answer is ready : " *That* is a character in my novel ; who said it was a portrait of you ? "

It was notorious, for example, that Madame Sand had lived for some years with Chopin, and that Madame d'Agoult had children by Liszt, and that both women had finally separated from their lovers. Now, although we hold that if Madame Sand or Madame d'Agoult wished to write, they were bound to go back for material to their own personal experience, it is quite clear that, in so doing, they were bound, by the very notoriety of their histories, to work up that material into shapes so unlike the outward form of these histories, that no one should detect the origin. Instead of doing so, they both take the public into confidence, and manage to paint themselves as victims, and their lovers as insupportable. We are touching upon a delicate distinction, but the moral sense of every impartial·reader easily distinguishes between the legitimate and illegitimate employment of experience.

As examples of the legitimate employment, let us name the works of Geraldine Jewsbury and Eliza Lynn, two writers in whom the influence of George Sand is traceable, and in whom, although we know that actual experience is taken as the material used, no one ever pretends to recognize private life. Recurring to our rough classification, we should cite Miss Jewsbury as one in whom observation and sentiment were about equal; but although she possesses, in an eminent degree, both qualities, she does not work them harmoniously together. Her keen womanly observation of life gives to her novels the piquancy of sarcasm, and her deep womanly feeling of life gives to them the warmth and interest of sentiment; but — there *is* a but! — the works seem rather the offspring of two minds than of one mind; there is a want of unity in them, arising, perhaps, from want of art. Curious it is to trace the development of her mind in the three novels she has published at wide intervals : "Zoe," in which the impetuous passionate style clearly betrays the influence of George Sand; "The Half-Sisters," in which the style is toned down to a more truthful pitch; and "Marian Withers," in which there is scarcely any trace of the turbulence and fervor of "Zoe." If we look closely we shall find that age and experience have had their customary influence, and, while subduing the exuberance of sentiment, have brought into greater prominence the strong characteristics of observation. Miss Jewsbury excels in subtle and sometimes deep observation of morals as of manners ; and we look to her for still finer works than any she has yet written.

Miss Lynn occupies a strange and defiant position. In her first work, "Azeth," she astonished by the recondite reading exhibited in her Egyptian coloring, and by the daring voluptuousness of her eloquence. In her second romance, "Amymone," she quitted Egypt for Greece, showed an equal amount of laborious study and of exuberant rhetoric, but assumed a still more hostile position against received notions by a paradoxical defence of Aspasia. In "Realities," a novel of our day, the antagonism was avowed, incessant, impetuous ; it was a passionate and exaggerated protest against conventions, which failed of its intended effect, because it was too exaggerated, too manifestly unjust. Splendor of diction, and a sort of rhythmic passion, rising oftentimes into accents of startling power, have never been denied her ; but one abiding defect of her novels we must allude to, and that is, the want of that observation which we have insisted on as a requisite in fiction. In "Realities" this want was singularly apparent, and gave it the air of unreality so detrimental to such a work. The realm of imagination is better suited to her powers than that of fact ; she feels deeply, paints vividly what she feels, but she sees dimly.

Miss Muloch has also a great gift of eloquence, and considerable power in the dramatic presentation of character. "The Ogilvies," "Olive," and the "Head of the Family " may be compared with Miss Jewsbury's three novels, as indicating the rapid progress in observation, and a more subdued employment of sentiment ; although sentiment, after all, remains her forte. Not so the authoress of " Rose Douglas " and the " Two Families," in whom we recognize a wonderful truthfulness of touch in the portraiture of quiet village life and quiet village character. The authoress of " Margaret Maitland " excels in delineation of character of greater range and depth, and her pictures of Scottish life are among the most memorable and agreeable we know. They place her beside the charming Madame Charles Reybaud, — whose novels, we may parenthetically add, are among the few French fictions admissible into the libraries of young ladies.

But we must cease this rapid flight over the large field of female literature. We have done enough if in this bird's-eye view we have indicated the most characteristic details; and we have proved our case if we have proved the right of Woman to citizenship in the Republic of Letters.

WEIMAR AND ITS CELEBRITIES.

THERE is no country which presents so many difficulties to the national historian as Germany, — none in which the principle of centralization was so long and so completely excluded, and in which it still exists in so imperfect a degree. The Roman Germanic Empire was in its very essence opposed to that principle. It was the secular representation of the universality of the Church. Divided into above two hundred little states, which are completely independent of the other, being connected by no link save one common tongue, Germany, despite her poets' continual invocation of the "Fatherland," has never had any real existence as a nation. Indeed, until the present century, the patriotic attachments and sympathies of her sons had always been confined to the particular spot which gave them birth. Whether in the Middle Ages, after the Reformation, or during the Thirty Years' War, we find the same civil feuds and divisions. The Germans were Guelphs and Ghibellines, Saxons or Thuringians, Bavarians or Swabians. The triumphs of Frederick the Great, the most popular of German heroes, were the triumphs of one German over the other, the humiliation of the House of Hapsburg by that of Brandenburg. It was not till the galling yoke of Napoleon, by pressing with equal weight upon the whole empire, roused one universal thrill of shame and indignation, that for the first time, and for a brief space only, the Germans became indeed one nation. The peril over, the victory achieved, they relapsed once more into their former condition, and in this they still remain. This was strikingly exemplified in the Revolution of 1848, when the mutual jealousies between the various states, large and small, prevented the realization of their long-cherished project of forming a "united Germany."

Under these circumstances, a national history must be admitted to be a most difficult undertaking. It is only within the last fifty years that it has been attempted, and even now, despite the high merits and popularity of Wenzel, Haüser, and some others, with but partial success. On the other hand, the number of provincial and dynastic historians is particularly large. Justes, Moeser, Spittler, Schlosser, &c., have treated successively with more or less talent the origin and history of the little principalities to which they severally belong. Dr. Vehse has followed in their footsteps. His "History of the Prussian Court and People," which appeared in 1851, though very verbose and somewhat wearisome, still attracted sufficient attention to induce the author to follow it up by others of the Courts of Austria, Bavaria, Saxony, &c. It is the last of these which has just reached a second edition, to which we now invite the reader's attention, deriving as it does a peculiar attraction from the individuals of whom it treats, — the eccentric John Frederic Carl Auguste, the friend and patron of Goethe, his mother Amelia, the noble and high-minded Duchess Louise, who forced even the conqueror and oppressor of her native land to respect and admiration, and, above all, Goethe himself, and his contemporaries, Wieland, Herder, and Schiller. The other volumes prefixed to this article also throw some new light on the habits, manners, and history of the Court of Weimar. We shall therefore freely avail ourselves of them while sketching, as we now propose to do, some of the more salient features and incidents of that Court.

Weimar, indeed, is but a little spot on the map of Europe; but in the history of the empire to which it belongs, and, above all, in the history of the human mind, it occupies a far more conspicuous place than the proud capitals of Austria and Prussia. Its most brilliant days were at the close of the eighteenth and beginning of the nineteenth century. This was the golden age of German philosophy and literature, and almost all the celebrated men of the epoch seem to have met in the capital of Carl Auguste's dominions. The German rulers had never evinced much inclination to favor the development of literary genius in their own land. They either despised it as unworthy their attention, or dreaded it as inimical to their authority. It was to a foreign monarch that Klopstock was indebted for his pension, and all his worldly advantages. Schubert languished for ten long years in the prisons of Hohen-Asberg, without one neighboring sovereign interesting himself in his behalf, and was at length indebted for his freedom to the intercession of an English prince. Burger, poor and neglected, applied in vain to the greatest of German kings in his distress. Lessing owed nothing to any earthly potentate. Thus unaided and unprotected, German poetry had slowly but successfully emerged from obscurity, and worked out its way to the light. As yet, indeed, it had achieved no signal triumph ; no mighty master of song — no Homer, no Dante, Milton, or Shakspeare — had shone forth with dazzling splendor, to form the wonder of succeeding ages. Even the "Messiah" of Klopstock, hailed as it had been with rapturous applause, could not claim a place beside the glorious monuments of human genius of which Greece, Italy, and England may be so justly proud. But enough had been achieved to give hope and promise of brighter days. It was at this moment that a woman-regent of a little principality — numbering scarcely thirty thousand inhabitants, and hitherto almost unknown and unnoticed — stepped forward as the good genius of her country's muse, and forever associated her name with that of its most gifted sons. While Goethe, Schiller, Wieland, and Herder are remembered, Amelia of Weimar will not be forgotten in the literary annals of the land those great names adorn.

The founder of the present reigning House of Weimar (the younger branch of the Saxon line, the "Ernestonians," called after the first of their race) was the Duke William, born in 1598. He was one of eleven brothers, among whom was that Bernard, so famous in the Thirty Years' War, and the unfor-

tunate John Frederic, whose strange and tragic story st.ll
lives in the recollection of his countrymen. Like his brother,
John Frederic offered his sword to the Protestant cause ; but
the singularity of his character, and the dark reports already
attached to his name, made him rather shunned than sought
by his companions-in-arms. It was rumored that he had
devoted himself to forbidden studies, and the faith in witch-
craft and demonology was at that time so universally diffused that the tale found easy credence. Far from seeking
to destroy this impression, John Frederic did his best to confirm it. Shutting himself up in his hereditary castle, he
devoted his days and nights to the study of Paracelsus, Cor-
nelius Agrippa, and other necromantic writers, in the hope
of discovering the awful secrets of magic ; his name became
a byword, and nothing but his rank and position saved him
from the fate of a sorcerer. In the year 1625 he entered the
service of King Christian of Denmark, then at the head of
the Protestant cause, in whose ranks his younger brother,
the famous Bernard, had already enlisted. But a dispute
with a Danish officer, in which his violent and unjustifiable
conduct excited general indignation, soon brought about his
dismissal. Burning with rage, he abandoned the Protestant
cause and faith, and joined the Imperial army, where he was
well received. Ere long, however, he was compelled to fly,
in consequence of a duel in which he ran his adversary
through the body, and falling into the hands of the enraged
Protestants, was thrown into a dungeon and loaded with
fetters, as at once a renegade, a traitor, a maniac, and magician — attributes, one alone of which would have sufficed to
render him an object of universal horror and detestation.
The Court of Weimar claiming him, he was given up to it
on condition of his being kept in close custody — a condition rigorously fulfilled. Caged like a wild beast, conscious
that he was the object of general hatred and terror, the mind
of the wretched captive, already deeply shaken, completely
gave way, till, in a fit of despair or insanity, he declared he
had entered into a pact with the devil, had signed it with his

blood, and hourly expected his deliverance by the Prince of Darkness. What passed on a certain awful night in the captive's chamber has never been revealed to human ear; but the next morning the wretched man was found dead on the floor, bathed in blood. The report was industriously spread that the foul fiend, enraged by his disclosure of their secret intercourse, had destroyed the wretched prisoner, as he had destroyed Faust, and so many others who had pledged their eternal weal; and that in the dead of night unearthly howlings had rent the air, and that the very walls had trembled as though shaken by an earthquake. But the immediate reception of the guards, who had watched the captive, into the Duke's service, the lavish bestowal of presents on the captains and officers, and the absence of all investigation, seem to point to a more probable, though scarcely less horrid, solution of the gloomy tale. However this may be, the popular belief, as usual in Germany, inclined to the supernatural version of the story. The building which had been the scene of the tragedy was shut up; and such was the terror with which it was regarded, that an inhabitant of Weimar would have gone miles out of his way, rather than pass it after sunset. At length, in 1817, it was pulled down, and its place supplied by modern houses, to which is attached no such fearful mystery. This crime of fratricide, if indeed it was committed by the Duke of Weimar, is strangely in contrast with his general character — that of an honest, openhearted man. He reigned peacefully for twenty years; his successor was so deeply engrossed by theological pursuits that he found little time for the duties of government, — holding religious conferences, and examining his hearers on the state of their consciences, instead of attending to public affairs. His grandson, Ernest Augustus, was one of the most singular characters of the day, and occupies some amusing pages in the memoirs of the Margravine of Baireuth, who met him at her father-in-law's court in 1732. He was carried off by a fever when his son, the father of Carl Auguste, had attained his eleventh year; and that prince likewise dying, at the age of one-and-twenty, his widow, Amelia, became Dowager Duchess of Weimar.

Amelia of Brunswick was born the 14th of October, 1742. The Court of Brunswick was at that period the most highly cultivated in Germany, and the princess enjoyed the advantages of a careful and solid education. Her youth, however, was far from happy. Her father, stern, cold, and haughty, regarded his children, especially his daughters, as mere household appendages, to be disposed of as best suited his personal convenience and his political interests. The strict etiquette on which he insisted, not only deprived the young girl of all the delights of intimate friendship with those of her own age, but exercised a chilling influence even over the heart of her royal mother, and introduced itself like a dark spectre between parent and child. In 1756 she was given in marriage to the Duke of Weimar. It was a union in which the heart had little share. "I was married as princesses generally are," she said; nevertheless, she could not but rejoice at her deliverance from the harsh treatment to which she had been subjected under the parental roof, and which, it appears, went even to the length of blows. Her gentle sweetness gained the confidence and affection of her not very congenial spouse, so as to render her married life at least supportable, if not happy. In 1757 she became the mother of Carl Auguste. A year later her husband died, leaving her *enciente* with her second son, Constantine. By the Duke's will, Amelia's father was appointed Regent, and guardian of mother and children; but at the expiration of a twelvemonth, the fair widow was declared of age by the Emperor, and invested with the sole regency of her little realm.

Her position was a difficult one for a young, lovely, and inexperienced woman; but the zeal and earnestness with which she applied herself to her new duties went far to supply the place of the knowledge of affairs and practical wisdom in which she was necessarily deficient. The following document, found among her papers after her decease, will give some idea of her thoughts at this momentous epoch of her existence, and proves that it was not only in the family of Frederic William of Prussia that princesses were subject to corporeal chastisement : —

My Thoughts.

From childhood my lot has been nothing but self-sacrifice. Never was education so little fitted as mine to form one destined to rule others. Those who directed it themselves needed direction ; she to whose guidance I was entrusted was the sport of every passion, subject to innumerable wayward caprices, of which I became the unresisting victim. Unloved by my parents, ever kept in the background, I was regarded as the outcast of the family. The sensitive feelings I had received from nature made me keenly alive to this cruel treatment ; it often drove me to despair. I became silent, reserved, concentrated, and thus gained a certain firmness, which gradually degenerated into obstinacy. I suffered myself to be reproached, insulted, *beaten*, without uttering a word, and still, as far as possible, persisted in my own course. At length, in my sixteenth year, I was married. In my seventeenth I became a mother. It was the first unmingled joy I had ever known. It seemed to me as though a host of new and varied feelings had sprung into life with my child. My heart became lighter, my ideas clearer ; I gained more confidence in myself. In my eighteenth year arrived the greatest epoch in my life. I became a mother for the second time, a widow, and Regent of the Duchy. The sudden changes, which one after another had taken place in my existence, created such a tumult in my mind, that for some time I could scarcely realize what had occurred. A rush of ideas and feelings, all undeveloped, and no friend to whom I could open my heart! I felt my own incapacity, and yet I was compelled to find everything in my own resources. Never have I prayed with truer or deeper devotion than at that moment. I believe I might have become the greatest of saints. When the first storm was over, and I could look within and around with more calmness, my feelings were, I confess, those of awakened vanity. To be Regent, so young ! to rule and command ! It could not be otherwise. But a secret voice whispered, Beware ! I heard it, and my better reason triumphed. Truth and self-love struggled for the mastery ; truth prevailed. Then came war. My brothers and nearest relations were crowned with laurels. Nothing was heard but the name of Brunswick. It was sung alike by friend and foe. This roused my ambition. I, too, longed for praise. Day and night I studied to render myself mistress of my new duties. Then I felt how absolutely I needed a friend in whom I could place my entire confidence. There were many who courted my favors, — some by flattery, others by a show of disinterestedness. I seemed to accept all, in the hope that among them I should find the pearl of great price. At length I did find it, and it filled me with the same joy which others experience at the discovery of a treasure. If a prince, and the individual he selects as a confidant, are both noble-minded, the sincerest affection may exist between them; and thus the question is decided, whether or no princes can have friends.

These extracts prove how deeply the young Duchess felt the responsibility of her new position. She soon displayed talents for government which, in a wider sphere of action, might have given her a name in history. The state of the little Duchy was lamentable; the treasury was empty, agriculture was neglected, and the people were discontented. With the aid of her faithful ministers she succeeded in restoring something like order to the exhausted finances, established schools and charitable asylums, and left untried no means of promoting the general prosperity. Disgusted by the wearisome etiquette of which her youth had been a victim, she banished all that was not absolutely indispensable to the due maintenance of her dignity; while in her love of literature she succeeded in drawing round her a galaxy of genius which recalled the Court of Ferrara in the days of Alfonso. The first who answered her call was Herder. After spending some years at Bückeburg, one of the innumerable little principalities into which Germany was then divided, he accepted her proposal to settle at Weimar, as chaplain, and superintendent of the schools she had established there.

Few men have possessed greater virtues, or faculties more lofty and varied than Herder. Like Lessing, he may be regarded as one of the pioneers of the German intellect. But his temper was too uncertain, his sensibility too morbidly keen, to permit him to live on very good terms with those around him. He was perpetually imagining some offence where none was intended, and lending every word and action

an import of which their authors probably had never even
dreamt. He reminds us of an instrument of exquisite tone,
in which, by some fault of mechanism, a slight but oft-recur-
ring jar mars the delicious harmony. Perhaps his frequent
attacks of ill health, his position, which never exactly suited
his taste or his temperament, may in some degree account
for the fits of irritability and hypochondria which at times
darkened his noble nature. These defects, however, did not
prevent him from being generally loved and admired, both
as a writer and a man. A poet, in the highest sense of the
word, perhaps he was not, for in the creative faculty he was
deficient; but no man had a deeper sense of the beautiful, or
keener powers of analysis and criticism. Indeed, whatever
the defects of his works, they are forgotten amid their many
beauties. In every line we trace a pure, noble, lofty spirit,
the love of God and man; a mind equally removed from
incredulity and bigotry. "He was inspired," says Edgar
Quinet, one of his warmest admirers, "by something nobler
than love of fame, — by a sincere and constant desire to pro-
mote the best and highest interests of humanity."

Wieland played a more conspicuous part than Herder at
the little Court of Weimar. When he first made his appearance, he was at the very zenith of his popularity, the pride
and darling of his countrymen. His "Oberon," indeed, on
which his celebrity principally if not entirely rests, the only
one of his numerous productions which still maintains its
place among the classic works of Germany, was not yet composed; but his poem of "Musarion," in which Goethe delighted, and the classic romance, the "Agathon," now almost
forgotten, sufficed to raise him to the very pinnacle of literary fame. The latter, indeed, had called forth the unmingled
praises of the severe Lessing, who, in his "Dramaturgie,"
declared it, without contradiction, "the most remarkable
work of its era." Carl Auguste was then in his sixteenth
year. The high and varied endowments, and the private
virtues of Wieland, decided the Duchess on selecting him as
the preceptor of the young prince. The appointment, indeed,

3

was not unopposed, for spotless as was Wieland's life, his
works were by no means equally immaculate; and it was but
too easy to point out passages, both in the "Agathon" and
"Musarion," strangely at variance with that sound and lofty
morality which ought to form the basis of every education,
more especially that of one born to rule the destinies of his
fellow-men.   But the Duchess, who, despite her unsullied
purity, was somewhat tainted by the philosophy of the day,
and who held the delusive though plausible theory that no
license of tone, or warmth of coloring, could injure any really
healthful and high-toned mind, cast these objections to the
wind.   We have Wieland's well-known honor as guarantee
that he never betrayed the sacred trust reposed in him.   But
there were not wanting many who attributed that tendency
to licentious habits — which was the only stain upon Carl
Auguste's many virtues — if not to the instructions of his
tutor, at least to the perusal of his works, the evil effects of
which even his example could not suffice to neutralize.   The
emolument offered to Wieland was so small as to appear
almost ludicrous in our eyes.   He was to receive 1000 gulden,
or £90 per annum, for three years, to be followed by the
magnificent pension of 300 gulden, or £23 per annum for
life.   But in this world everything is comparative.   The
£90 went further in Germany in the eighteenth century
than £300 would in England at the present day.

The tastes of the inhabitants were simple.   The price of
all the necessaries of life was comparatively small.[1] Schiller,
some years later, declared that he could live charmingly at
Jena for 300 florins, or £60 per annum, with wife and children ; that he had a servant who, when necessary, could perform the part of a secretary, for 18s. per quarter, and a
carriage and horses for £60. per annum.   Thus Wieland's
salary, with what he gained by his literary labors, was sufficient for his wants and those of an increasing family.   The
close intimacy between the Duchess Amelia and her son's

---

[1] Beef was 4 kreutzers (a penny farthing) per pound; wood, 6 gulden, or
11s. a load (it is now 28 gulden) ; and everything in proportion.

tutor was broken only by death. Nor could even the more brilliant glory of a Goethe or a Schiller eclipse his in the estimation of this devoted friend.

In 1776 the Duchess resigned the reins of government to Carl Auguste, then eighteen years of age, and set out for Italy, that land which had ever been the darling dream of her existence.

" My son," were her last words on quitting her little capital, " I confide to your hands the happiness of your subjects; be it your care as it has been mine." In many respects Carl Auguste was no ordinary man. Frederick the Great, who saw him at the Court of Brunswick in 1771, when he was but fourteen, declared he had never beheld a youth who at an early age justified such lofty hopes; and in 1775, the prince-primate Dalberg, writing to Görres, observes : " He unites an excellent understanding to all the frankness and true heart-iness of his age ; he has a princely soul such as I have never yet seen. Taught both by precept and example to place little value upon empty pomp and splendor, he carries his dislike to all courtly forms and ceremonials to an even exaggerated degree." How early and how well Carl Auguste had learnt to value genius, is evident from the discourse he addressed to his Council in his nineteenth year, in which he expressed his intention of inviting Goethe to his Court. " The judgment of the world," observes the young prince, " may perhaps censure me for placing Dr. Goethe in my most important university, without his having passed the grades of professor, chancellor, &c. The world judges according to its own prejudices ; but I do not act like others, for the sake of fame or the approbation of the world, but to justify myself before God and my own conscience."

Occasionally the thoughtlessness and reckless love of pleasure, which in his earlier years contrasted so strangely with the Duke's loftier qualities of head and heart, may have led him astray ; but his nature was essentially gener-ous and noble, — his ear ever open to the cry of the suffering and distressed, his hand ever ready, so far as his means al-

lowed, to aid them. In 1774 the Duke left Weimar to cele-
brate his union with the Princess Louise. On his way
through Frankfort, Goethe, already celebrated as the author
of "Götz von Berlichingen" and "Werter," was introduced
to him. Fascinated by the charm of his genius, by the grace
and gayety of his manner, the Duke invited him to visit his
Court; and Goethe, only too happy to escape from Frankfort,
and from the vicinity of the fair Lili, — that bright being he
had, at least as he imagined, once so passionately loved, but
whom he had, as usual, discovered was not a meet partner for
his glorious destinies, — at once accepted the proposition.

It was arranged that the Duke's chamberlain, Herr von
Kalb, who having lingered behind at Strasburg to execute
some commissions for his master, was to arrive at Frankfort
on a certain day, should call for the new guest. But days
and weeks passed on, and no Von Kalb made his appearance.
Goethe's father was a burgher of the old school, and, thoroughly disliking kings and princes, had always been exceed-
ingly averse to the project. He now insisted that the whole
affair was a hoax, and urged his son to wait no longer, but to
set off at once on his long-proposed journey to Italy, and
Goethe at length consented. In the journal he now commenced, which, however, was carried on only for a very brief
period, we find certain expressions which induce the belief
that his resolutions to break off his marriage with Lili were
aided by a dawning inclination for another, Augusta Stolberg,
sister to the two counts of that name. "How shall I call
thee," he writes, "thou whom I cherish as a spring blossom
in my heart? Thou shalt bear the name of fairest flower.
How shall I take leave of thee? Comfort — for it is time —
the full time. A few days, and already — oh, farewell!
Am I, then, only in the world to involve myself eternally in
involuntary guilt?"

The meaning of these last words is not very apparent, unless it be that Goethe's feelings toward Augusta were of a
warmer nature than has generally been supposed. The correspondence is altogether of the most romantic cast; and

many of the letters, written long before Goethe's engagement with Lili was broken off, sound not a little strange from a man passionately attached and already affianced to another. "My dearest," he writes, in one of the earliest of these epistles, "I will give you no name, for what are the names of friend, sister, beloved, bride, or even a word which would comprehend all these, in comparison with my feelings? I can write no more." To this he added his silhouette, entreating she would send him hers in return. The receipt of it seems to have filled him with delight. "How completely is my belief in physiognomy confirmed," he writes; "that pure thoughtful eye, that sweet firm nose, those dear lips. Thanks, my love, thanks. Oh! that I could repose in your heart, rest in your eyes." It is true that Goethe had never seen Augusta, and that her rank as Countess rendered a union with her in those days almost impossible; so strict was the line of demarcation between the nobles and burghers, that even Goethe's already brilliant fame would not have enabled him to surmount the barrier. Nor, perhaps, did the idea ever take a tangible form; but it seems pretty certain that this half-ideal, half-romantic passion for one whom imagination invested with every conceivable perfection, tended somewhat to cool his affection for the gay open-hearted young creature, who, while loving him with truth and tenderness, was too much accustomed to homage to hang upon his every word and look as Fredricka had done, and Augusta seemed inclined to do.[1]

Goethe proceeded to Heidelberg, and from thence was about to depart to Italy when the long-expected messenger from Weimar arrived, and he set off post-haste for the little capital of which he was henceforth to be the brightest ornament. His appearance was the signal for fêtes and rejoicings, and he himself seems to have given free vent to the spirit of youthful gayety and love of pleasure which at this time possessed him.

[1] Mr. Lewes does not appear to attach any importance to this correspondence, and scarcely notices it; but it will be found published in extenso.

The author of the "Musen Hof," who is nevertheless one of
his warmest admirers, declares that his *immediate* influence
over the young Duke was not peculiarly beneficial, as he led
him into dissipations prejudicial alike to his health and domestic happiness; and certainly the letters of his contemporaries — of Bottiger, Berteuch, Knebel, nay of Madame von
Stein herself — seem to have corroborated this assertion.
"Goethe," says the latter, "causes a terrible commotion
here; all our happiness has disappeared. A ruler dissatisfied
with himself and every one about him, risking his life constantly in mad follies, with little health to sustain him, a
mother annoyed and vexed, a wife discontented, &c." It is
evident that the strange mode of existence in which the Duke
and Goethe indulged, and the infelicity of the royal pair
which seems to have been the result, must have attracted
general attention, since it reached the ears of Klopstock, and
induced the aged poet to address a letter to Goethe on the
subject, which, like most advice of a similar nature, served
only to displease all parties.

We will not enter further into this much-vexed question.
At all events, Goethe soon grew weary of a mode of life so
little in accordance with the higher aspirations of the poet's
soul. He gradually retired more and more from the noisy
pleasures of the Court, spending a considerable portion of his
time in the quiet retirement of his garden pavilion. A new
and all-engrossing passion had likewise its share in withdrawing him from pursuits unworthy of his nobler nature.
He loved, not indeed for the first, second, or third time, as
his annals attest, but with a warmth, a tenderness, and,
above all, a constancy, which neither the fair, innocent, and
trusting Fredricka, nor the bright and graceful Lili, had
been able to inspire. And yet the woman to whom was reserved the triumph of fettering for ten long years the heart
of one of the most gifted and most inconstant of mortals, was
no longer in the early bloom of womanhood; she had attained
her thirty-third year, and Goethe was but twenty-eight.
Beautiful in the strict sense of the word she had never been,

but there was a mingled grace, sweetness, and dignity in her glance and demeanor which exercised a singular fascination on all around her. Goethe, the young, the gallant, the admired of all admirers, was at once enthralled by her spell. "I can only explain," he writes to Wieland, "the power she exercises over me, by the theory of the transmigration of souls. Yes! we were formerly man and wife. Now, I can find no name for us, for the past, the future." Unluckily, Charlotte von Stein was already the wife of another, the mother of six children. That she returned the passion of her adorer cannot be doubted; but — if we are to believe the assurance of her son, in his preface to Goethe's letters to his mother, and the testimony of many of her contemporaries, among others that of Schiller — she never transgressed the strictest bounds of virtue. She had been indoctrinated with the questionable morality of the eighteenth century, and was married, while yet a girl, to a man infinitely her inferior in all mental endowments, and for whom she had little sympathy or affection. She was thrown, by her position as lady-of-honor to the Dowager Duchess, into the constant society of the young and brilliant genius, already the day-star of his age and country. Proud in conscious virtue, it is perhaps not to be wondered at that she could not prevail on herself to break an intercourse so replete with every charm of intellect and fancy, to refuse an homage so flattering alike to her heart and her vanity, if she permitted herself to be the Laura of this new Petrarch.

"Indeed," observes Frederick von Stein, "if this correspondence proves that emotions even dangerous in their warmth were not far distant from this intercourse, it also serves to place in a still stronger light the virtue and prudence of the woman who, while keeping her young, gifted, and ardent lover within the limits of the strictest reserve, still contrived to reconcile him to her severity, by sincere sympathy in all his trials, both mental and material, by fully comprehending his glorious vocation, and by soothing him with the most sincere and lasting friendship."

More than one German author, especially Adolphe Stahr, in his well-known work, "Weimar and Jena," has actually censured Madame von Stein in no measured terms for refusing to accede to Goethe's entreaties that she would obtain a divorce from her husband, the father of her children, against whom she had no just cause of complaint, and become his wife, — that is, when he found it impossible to induce her to listen to a suit of any other description. Upon this refusal is thrown the whole responsibility of the poet's subsequent *liaison* with Christina Vulpius. These authors seem never even to imagine that there may be some slight fault on Goethe's side; that if Madame von Stein was blamable in admitting him to an intimacy endangering her peace of mind, if not her conjugal fidelity, he was not perfectly justifiable in seeking, with all the eloquence of genius, to win the heart of a woman already bound by the most sacred ties to another. But Nemesis was not forgetful. The connection which in a moment of ennui and weariness Goethe formed with Christina Vulpius — a connection which he had not the courage or cruelty to break, and which he ultimately confirmed by marriage — embittered his latter years, and could not but exercise an unfavorable influence on his whole nature. Would not Fredricka or Lili have been a more genial companion than Christina Vulpius for that great poet of whom his native land is so justly proud? Who could have dreamt of such a bride for the beautiful gifted Apollo, as Adolphe Stahr calls him, when he first set foot in the dominions of Carl Auguste!

Weimar, consecrated to all lovers of poetry, scarcely deserved the name of a town when Goethe first lived there. Schiller, in a letter to Körner, calls it "something between a town and a hamlet." Goethe laughingly observed one day to his friend Zetter, when the latter spoke of building a theatre for the people, "How is it possible to talk of the people of Weimar in this little residence, where there are ten thousand poets and five hundred inhabitants?"

The park did not then exist. A few trees alone waved on the spot now so beautifully diversified with verdant wood

and grassy lawn. On the Curplatz, now covered with stately
houses, stood nothing save the straw-thatched huts of the
Weimar peasants. One thing only have we to regret in the
changes which have gradually transformed an insignificant
village into a stately city. On the esplanade, which as late
as 1770 was the favorite promenade of the good inhabitants,
stands a dwelling so humble as scarcely to attract attention
among the more conspicuous buildings around. It is the
house of Schiller. Here, in this modest retreat, did the
author of " Wallenstein " spend the latter years of his existence. He purchased it at the high price, as he called it, of
4,000 gulden, £ 360. He entered it on the 29th of April, full
of delight at possessing one spot on earth he could call his
own. A heavy domestic calamity soon came to damp this
joy. Within a few days he received a letter informing him
of the death of his mother, that mother to whom he was so
devotedly attached. The blow was a heavy one. Amid
every change of place and scene, domestic joys and sorrows,
amid fame, homage, toil and suffering, his heart had ever
clung with inexpressible fondness to the home of his childhood, and above all to the parent who had watched over his
infant years.

" Would," he writes to his sister, " that I had been able to aid you
in tending our beloved mother during her last illness. Oh, dear sister,
now our parents are sunk to rest, the most holy bond which united us
is torn asunder. It makes me unspeakably sad, and I feel desolate,
though surrounded by the loved and loving. Yet I have *you* too, my
sister, to whom I can fly in joy and sorrow. Oh! let us, now there
are but three of us remaining in the paternal house, cling close to each
other. Never forget you have a loving brother. I remember vividly
the days of our youth, when we were all in all to each other. Life
has divided our destiny ; but confidence and affection may at least remain unalterable."

It is scarcely possible to enter, without a feeling of deep
emotion, that humble dwelling, where so many glorious works
of genius were brought forth, where one of the purest and
noblest spirits that ever breathed on earth passed away.

Three years only was Schiller permitted to inhabit this lowly but pleasant abode, so modest that even Goethe's house, though not particularly splendid, looks like a palace in comparison. The middle story, in which the family resided, is let; only the room which Schiller himself inhabited is shown to the visitor, the town having at length purchased the house. In the centre stands the table on which he was in the habit of writing, that very table which, as he informs his friend Körner, "cost two carolines," a heavy sum for his narrow finances at that period. It is of the very commonest wood, and so low as perfectly to explain his unfortunate habit of bending over it when composing. One drawer was always filled with half-rotten apples, the smell of which was peculiarly agreeable to the poet. The walls are covered with green paper; the furniture is of light mahogany, covered with leather. A little guitar, a few bad-colored prints of Palermo, the bed in which Schiller breathed his last, a portrait taken from his bust, and a second painted after death — these complete the picture. When Schiller resided at this cottage it had nothing but green trees around and upland shades before it.

Improvements, however, so far as the Duke's finances allowed, went on rapidly under the supervision of the almost ubiquitous Goethe. The park owes its origin to a tragic incident which occurred about the beginning of 1780 — the suicide of a young and blooming girl, Christel von Lasberg, who, in despair at the infidelity of her lover, destroyed herself on a spot Goethe was compelled to pass on his way to and from the ducal castle. This affected him painfully, the more so as his "Werther" was found in her pocket, though it appeared that this was but an accidental coincidence. At first he resolved on erecting a monument to her memory, but abandoned this project, "because," as he said, "one could neither pray nor love there." But the gloom of the spot, overhung by dark pine-trees, and peopled by such terrible recollections, became intolerable to Goethe, and he determined to try and lend it a more cheerful aspect. To this end he had some of the trees cut down, the rocks planted with shrubs and flowers.

This suggested the idea of further changes, which at length resulted in that beautiful park which is now the principal ornament of Weimar.

"The Duke and Goethe," says Wieland to Merck, June 3, 1778, "came back yesterday afternoon from their trip to Leipsig, Dessau, and Berlin. In the evening I went with my wife and both my eldest girls to see the exercise-grounds opposite Goethe's garden, and arranged according to his own plans; thence I proceeded to the so-named Star, to show my wife the new *Poemata*, which has been made by the Duke, after Goethe's designs, and is laid out with wonderful skill, to represent a wild, solitary, yet not completely sequestered assemblage of rocks, where Goethe and the Duke often dine together, with some goddess or half-goddess. We met both with the fair Corinna Schröder, who with her exquisite Attic elegance, her lovely form, her simple yet inexpressively graceful attire, looks like the very nymph of this sequestered spot."

The words "in the society of some goddess," let us into something of the secret origin of the Weimar scandal. There were other pleasures, however, of a less objectionable character.

"Last Saturday," writes Wieland to Merck, August 21, 1779, "we drove to Goethe's, who had invited the Duchess Amelia to spend the evening with him in his garden, to regale her with all the poems he had composed during her absence. We dined in a charming solitary spot. When we rose from table, and the doors were thrown open, we beheld before us a scene which resembled a realization of a poet's dream. The whole banks of the Ilm were illuminated quite in the taste of Rembrandt, a wondrous enchanting mixture of light and shadow, which produced an effect beyond all description. The Duchess was delighted; so were we all. As we descended the little steps of the hermitage, and wandered along the banks of the Ilm, amid the rocks and bushes which unite this spot with the Star, the whole vision changed into a number of small pictures *au* Rembrandt, which one could have looked on forever. The carnival time," he continues, "has brought with it its usual gayeties, and we have done our best to make the ordinary Court malady, *ennui*, as brilliant as possible."

The limited finances of the little Court somewhat interfered with these courtly amusements. Carl Auguste often found himself in difficulties, which neither his own skill nor that of his counsellors could suffice to remove. When tormented by some of these petty annoyances, or fatigued with the cares of state, he would retire to a little country-house, where, dismissing all his train, he would remain alone.

"It is just ten o'clock," he writes to Knebel. "I am sitting at the window, and writing to you. The day has been exquisitely beautiful, and this, my first evening of liberty, I have enjoyed to the utmost. I feel so far removed from the affairs of earth, so completely in a better, a higher sphere. Man is not destined to be the miserable *phlister* of this every-day life. Never do we feel so noble, so elevated, as when we behold the sun sink to rest, and the stars rise, and know that all this is created for its *own* sake alone, not for that of man; and yet we enjoy it as though it were all made for us. I will bathe with the evening star, and draw in new life. Till then, farewell. . . . I come from my bath. The water was cold; night already lay upon its bosom. It seems as though I had plunged into the cold night itself when I took the first dip, all was so calm, so holy. Over the distant hills rose the full moon. All was silent, and the intense stillness made me hear, or fancy I heard purer sounds, than those which really reached the ear."

The individual to whom this letter is addressed enjoyed, next to Goethe, the confidence and affection of the Duke. Knebel, better known as the friend and companion of poets and princes than by any celebrity of his own, was one of those peculiarly constituted natures which seem destined to act rather in calling forth the powers of others, than in displaying their own. These perhaps are, on the whole, the happiest. Free from those feverish impulses, that burning thirst for fame, which so often torment more highly gifted spirits, they can enjoy to the full the productions of genius without envy or regret. They, too, are poets; but they are content to find poetry in life and nature, in the summer flowers, in the murmur of the fountain, in the whispering of the breeze, instead of attempting to give it form and shape in verse. They compose, but only for the amusement of a leisure hour; yet no men have had more influence on the great minds of their age. Most rare and valuable are such spirits, sufficiently gifted to appreciate the lofty endowments of genius, to sympathize in all its varied moods and sublime aspirations, and yet content to play the humble part of confidant and admirer. Such a man was Knebel. His literary works, though not absolutely devoid of merit, have been long since forgotten; but the ascendancy he exerted over the intellect of the great men of his country and his time has associated his name lastingly with theirs.

Descended from a Flemish family, he was born at Wallenstein, in Ottingen, 1744. One of his ancestors having paid the penalty of his religious opinions by a cruel death under Philip II., the family had fled from the land of their birth, and taken refuge in Germany. Stern, harsh, and unbending, Knebel's father was feared rather than loved by his son, and the youth always attributed his timidity in after life to the severity exercised towards him in childhood. His delicate and somewhat fastidious tastes seemed continually in the way. At the university they rendered the rude habits of his companions insupportable. When he entered the service of Frederick the Great, he found the want of education and literary taste among his brother officers still more intolerable. He felt like an automaton, deprived of all individuality of action; and despite the royal notice, with which he was occasionally honored, he grew sad and dispirited.

Knebel spent ten years in the Prussian service — ten long and weary years, as he calls them. In 1772 he obtained his discharge, with a small pension, and a letter of introduction to the young Duchess of Weimar from the Crown Prince, in whose regiment he had served. By her he was graciously received; while by Wieland, who had already resided at Weimar, as tutor to the young duke, he was warmly welcomed. In 1773 he was himself appointed professor of mathematics to Carl Auguste and his brother. Shortly afterwards he accompanied the princes on a visit to some of the courts of Germany, and afterwards to Paris. Knebel was delighted with the novelty of all he beheld, and especially with the grace of French manners. "They may say what they like," he wrote to Wieland, "the French are an agreeable and amiable people; nowhere else does one find so much urbanity." "I saw a good deal of Diderot," he adds in a subsequent letter. He expressed his amazement that Mendelssohn was not admitted to the Royal Academy of Berlin. Though royalty still seemed to reign supreme, the Revolutionary spirit was already abroad. "Many young men of distinguished talent," says Knebel in his letters, "repeated to me continually that henceforward all must be equal — nobles, peers, burghers, and peasants, and *such like trash.*" He was not keen-sighted enough to discern, through the bright and glowing atmosphere that surrounded him, the dark clouds, big with the mighty changes, already slowly looming on the verge of the horizon, so soon to cover all with its gloomy folds, and to burst in thunder over Europe.

Next to Goethe and Knebel, the most intimate friend of Carl Auguste was his chamberlain, Frederick von Einsedel. Born 1750, he commenced his Court career as page; he was then promoted to the rank of chamberlain to the Dowager Duchess Amelia; in 1770 he was named privy-councillor. Himself gay, joyous, and light-hearted, he had, while page, played prank upon prank, which had already become proverbial in the court chronicles of Weimar. In after life his gladsome temperament, his frank and open manners, and generous nature secured him the lasting favor of his royal master. His very failings served as subjects of amusement rather than anger. His constitutional laziness, varied by fits of feverish activity, and his strange absence of mind, during which he might be *robbed* of hat, gloves, or watch, without his ever perceiving it, diverted the ennui to which, despite the presence of a Goethe, or a Herder and a Wieland, this little Court seems to have been peculiarly subject. Einsedel, however, must have had merits of a higher order than mere harmlessness and good-humor, or he would scarcely have been admitted to the intimate friendship of Herder and Schiller.

"He is an excellent, unaffected man," writes the latter to Körner, in 1803, "and far from devoid of talent." Einsedel's private life, however, was anything but immaculate, and some of his adventures might serve as a curious illustration of the times and the atmosphere in which he lived. He had become desperately enamored of a Madame von Werthein, who, yielding to her passion, abandoned home, husband, friends, and country, to follow her seducer. Not completely dead, however, to the shame of thus publicly violating all her holiest duties, she had recourse to one of the most extraordinary stratagems ever devised by a romantic female head. She took advantage of the fainting fits to which she was occasionally subject, to feign death. With the connivance of her attendants, she contrived to steal out of the house unperceived, while a doll was buried in her stead. She then proceeded with her lover to Africa, where he proposed exploring certain gold-mines, by which he expected to make his fortune. The affair turned out a complete failure, and Einsedel returned poorer than he went, with his fair and frail companion. Great was the amazement and indignation of husband and friends on beholding the resuscitation of her they believed long since buried in the vaults of her ancestors. But in German courts in the eighteenth century such affairs were not regarded as involving any very great amount of moral turpitude. The Court of Weimar indeed was virtue itself, compared with those of Dresden, of Wurtemberg, and Hanover; but even *here* "excess of love" was held as sufficient excuse for every sin. There was a strange mixture of the maudlin and the licentious, French immorality grafted on German sentimentality. A separation was obtained, and Madame W. became the wife of her lover. Einsedel lived to the age of seventy-eight, and died in 1828.

In 1796 Weimar received a new visitor in the author of "Hesperus." The mingled naïveté and singularity of his demeanor, his animated and poetic language, full of thoughts and images at once tender and ironical, — for he spoke as he wrote, — his enthusiastic belief in the progress of humanity,

charmed Herder to such a degree, that he wrote to Jacobi:
" Heaven has given me in Jean Paul a treasure which I dare
not hope I merit. He is all intellect, all soul, a melodious
sound from the mighty golden harp of humanity, that harp
of which so many chords are snapped or broken." By Goethe he was more coldly received.

'It was with apprehension, almost with terror," he writes to his
friend Otto, " that I entered the abode of Goethe. Every one depicted
him as cold and indifferent to all earthly things. Madame von Kalb
had told me that he no longer admired anything, not even his own
works. Every word, she said, is an icicle, especially to strangers,
whom he is with difficulty persuaded to admit to his presence. His
house struck me. It was the only one in Weimar built in the Italian
style ; from the very staircase it is a museum of statues and pictures.
The god at length appeared. He was cold ; he expressed himself in
monosyllables only, and without the slightest emphasis. ' Tell him,'
said Knebel, ' that the French have just entered Rome.' ' Hein,' replied the god. His person is bony, his physiognomy full of fire, his
look a sun. At length our conversation on the arts and on the opinions of the public, perhaps also the champagne, animated him, and
then at length I felt I was with Goethe ! His language is not flowery
and brilliant, like that of Herder ; it is incisive, calm, and resolute.
He concluded by reading, or rather performing, one of his unpublished
poems, a composition truly sublime. Thanks to this, the flames of
his heart pierced their crust of ice, and he pressed the hand of the enthusiast Jean Paul. How shall I describe his mode of reading ? It
was like the distant roar of thunder, mingled with the soft dripping of
a summer shower. No ! there is no one in the world like Goethe !
We must be friends."

This desire was not destined to be fulfilled. The author
of " Quintus Filein " was too diametrically opposed, not only
as a writer but as an individual, to the poet of " Faust " or
" Tasso," to allow of any real or lasting intimacy.

One of the most eccentric and most troublesome personages
of the little Court of Weimar was Constantine, the Duke's
brother. He possessed neither the intellectual endowments
nor the generous nature of Carl Auguste. Knebel, who was appointed his tutor in 1782, had in vain endeavored to inspire

him with loftier tastes. An unfortunate *liaison* with a beautiful girl, Carolina von S——, produced so much scandal, that the Duke sent him from Weimar, on his travels to Italy, accompanied by the Councillor Albrecht von ——, a talented and excellent man, but apparently not a very amusing companion. Constantine soon grew weary of so grave a Mentor. Arrived at Paris, he plunged, despite his companion's admonitions, into all the dissipations of that brilliant capital, and ere long fell into the snare of a clever actress, Mademoiselle Darsaincourt, whose wit, intrigue, and beauty completely enthralled him. Yielding to her counsel, he got rid of the perpetual presence of his guardian, by assigning him, under some pretext, a place in another carriage, while his mistress took hers beside him. He then set off, not for Italy, but to London.

Poor Albrecht, from a sense of duty, followed him, but finding his admonitions utterly useless, returned in despair to Weimar. In vain did Carl Auguste recall his brother; he disregarded his commands. Of his life in London little is recorded, but it is probable that it was not of a very reputable nature. At length, in 1803, his resources failing, he set out for Germany. Somewhat embarrassed how to dispose of his companion, he despatched her beforehand. Carl Auguste, however, would not permit her to set foot on his dominions, and she was forced to return to France, despite the entreaties and remonstrances of her despairing lover.

" This last catastrophe," writes Carl Auguste to Knebel, January 5, 1784, " has been of service to Constantine, — apparently at least. The society here endeavored to prove its adherence to me by openly blaming his conduct, and shunning his company, so that he was left to almost complete solitude. This decided condemnation was very painful to him, and made him feel how essential is a certain degree of exterior decency at least, to procure a reception in good society, and that even his rank could not protect him from contempt and neglect. He has now adopted an appearance of respectability, fulfils more exactly the ordinary duties of life, and performs his part well enough to be regarded as an educated member of society. I am seeking to obtain his admission into the Saxon service."

4

Constantine died in 1803.

Amid this circle of genius, wit, fancy, and gallantry, sometimes verging on libertinism, stood the Duchess Louise, like
one of those pure, calm, beautiful, though somewhat stiff and
stately figures of Holbein or Vandyke, among the loose and
lovely groups of a Rubens or a Lily. Endowed with every
grace of mind and person, seemingly formed to enjoy and
bestow felicity, united to one of the most charming and
noble-minded princes of the age, Louise was still unhappy
and alone. The circumstances which led to this sense of
isolation were trifling in themselves ; yet in such a position
as that of the young Duchess, they sufficed to darken all
her prospects of domestic bliss. Educated with the utmost
severity, accustomed to the observance of the most rigid etiquette and the strictest reserve, Louise found herself suddenly
transplanted into an atmosphere diametrically opposite to that
in which her whole existence had hitherto been passed. We
have seen how completely, both in private and public life,
the Duchess Amelia and her son had thrown aside those
wearisome observances which in other German Courts were
still held as necessary appendages to royalty, and which the
young Louise had learned to regard with almost superstitious
reverence. At Weimar, on the contrary, all was simplicity,
gayety, equality, and fraternity. In their desire to do away
with the useless encumbrances imposed by their rank, the
Duke and Duchess had in fact unconsciously gone a little too
far, and infringed something of that strict decorum which is
one of the best safeguards of royalty.

Louise was surprised, pained, even shocked. Her high
and perhaps exaggerated sense of what was due alike to the
bride and the princess was perpetually wounded. The
charms of intellectual intercourse with such men as Goethe,
Herder, Wieland, and Schiller, the gay good-humor of her
thoughtless but really noble-minded consort, the grace and
sweetness of her mother-in-law, would have reconciled most
women to the sacrifice of some of their early prejudices.
But Louise, with all her lofty qualities, was wanting in that

flexibility of character which could alone have secured her felicity under existing circumstances; and though she never by word or deed expressed her feelings, her pallid cheek, her saddened mien, her cold, reserved manner, too plainly showed what passed within. If Carl Auguste had passionately loved his young wife, all might have been well. But Louise's was a nature so utterly antagonistic to his own that he never fully understood her, or at least not till too late. Her timidity and reserve prevented her expressing her sentiments, while her daily increasing silence and coldness chilled her husband, and led him to believe he was utterly indifferent to her. Nay, he conceived an equally erroneous opinion of her intellect as of her heart. "She is incomprehensible," he wrote to his friend Knebel; "before her marriage she lived quite alone in the world, without ever finding a being who answered her expectations of what friends ought to be, without exercising a single talent which would have softened her nature. She runs the risk of becoming completely isolated, and losing all that grace and amiability which form the principal charm of her sex." These words speak volumes. They explain the clouds which from day to day grew darker over the domestic horizon of the royal pair. Louise felt that her husband neither understood nor appreciated her, as she was conscious she deserved to be appreciated. Wounded alike in her affections and her pride, too timid to remonstrate, too haughty to complain, she withdrew more and more from his society, till at length, though living together, the two consorts became almost strangers to each other. " The young Duchess," observes Knebel, "shone like a darkened star in a hazy atmosphere. The first meeting did not produce very favorable impressions on either side, and she certainly had in part reason to complain of the want of *convenances* in her court. She endured much with infinite patience, and maintained her dignity with unvarying consistency. The characters of the two princesses, which did not quite agree, gave rise to much disunion. That this exercised a painful influence on those who surrounded them may easily be supposed. Nevertheless the prudence of their *entourage*, the moderation of the Duchess, and the desire of her mother-in-law to love and be loved, prevented any violent outbreak." Even the powerful bonds of parental love did not suffice to draw the royal pair closer together. For many years, indeed, the Duke had cherished another passion; he loved a beautiful and gifted actress, Caroline Jägernau. With a virtue and self-denial rare in her class and time, she had long repelled his entreaties, though her heart pleaded his cause. Louise was no stranger to this attachment; it scarcely sought concealment. It had often rent her heart and embittered her existence; but she knew the passionate temperament of her husband; she felt that Caroline, with whose gentle and generous character she was well acquainted, might save him from worse seduction.

Affection, womanly pride, religious principle, all opposed such a compromise of her own paramount claims and duty. But, as with Burger's Dora,[1] Louise's devoted tenderness overcame every other consideration. She not only did nothing to prevent or oppose the *liaison*; she wrote the fair actress to entreat her to listen to the Duke's suit. However we may wonder at such a course, we are bound to render justice to the unselfish motives which inspired it. Louise did not, like Caroline of England, give her lord a mistress in order to rule him more easily, or less ostensibly, through her influence. It was to save him from worse courses, to confer on him a happiness she felt she had not been able to bestow. Caroline yielded, yet not without a struggle. She was elevated to the dignity of Madame von Hagendorf, and presented with a superb estate in Saxony. Her influence over Carl Auguste was boundless, and ended only with his life. It is to her credit that she never abused her position, and that she always preserved a most perfect fidelity to her royal lover. She was a blonde, with light hair, and features

[1] See "Poets and Poetry of Germany," by Madame de Pontés; vol. ii. p. 337.

and complexion of surpassing beauty. The Duchess treated her happier rival with the delicacy and kindness natural to her own pure and noble soul, both before and after the death of the Duke. How Carl Auguste's mother regarded this *liaison*, we are not informed. Between herself and her daughter-in-law there was too little congeniality of taste or character to admit of intimacy or confidence; yet that Amelia fully appreciated the lofty virtues of her son's wife can scarcely be denied. On her return from Italy the Dowager Duchess resided at the Belvidere, or her jointure house some little distance from Weimar, where, in the society of the gifted men she had drawn to her son's Court, and the enjoyment of innocent and intellectual pleasures, she passed the remainder of her days. Her health, which had latterly shown many symptoms of decay, sank completely beneath the terrible incidents of 1806 — the death of her brother, the Duke of Brunswick, the ruin of her ancestral house, and the danger which impended over the land of her adoption. She died in 1807.

But the events which overwhelmed the sensitive nature of the Dowager Duchess only called into action the noble qualities of her daughter-in-law. When Weimar was threatened by the victorious army of the conqueror, when all deserted a town which seemed doomed to destruction, the Duchess Louise remained firm and unshaken at the post which she believed Providence assigned her.

Her lord, on whom Napoleon had vowed vengeance, had been forced by prudence to fly. Her children, in her maternal tenderness, she had sent to a place of safety, her troops were scattered, her friends trembling and defenceless, but still Louise, Duchess of Weimar, remained firm and unshrinking, in that town which every instant might become a prey to the flames, in that palace which was so soon to receive the presence of the imperious victor, among the people of whom she had always been the friend and protector, and of whom she was now the guardian angel. "When," says Falk, in his personal reminiscences of Goethe, "the people learnt that the Grand Duchess was still in the Castle, their joy knew no bounds. When they met they threw themselves in each others' arms exclaiming, 'The Grand Duchess is here.'"

Nor were they mistaken in the sense of safety with which her presence inspired them. The Duchess received the conqueror (who had previously announced his intention of passing the night of the 15th of October at the Castle) at the head of the grand staircase. Pale, but calm and dignified, she awaited the approach of the terrible Emperor, on whom the fate of her people depended. Napoleon turned towards her with an angry mien. "Qui êtes-vous, madame?" "The Duchess of Weimar, sire," was the answer. "Je vous plains," replied Napoleon, abruptly; "I must crush your husband." Then turning rudely away, "Qu'on me fasse diner dans mes apartements," he exclaimed, and left the Duchess without addressing her another word. But Louise would not suffer herself to be discouraged. The following morning she requested another interview; it was granted.

Night had brought counsel. The conqueror, though still haughty and imperious, condescended at least to lend an ear to her remonstrance and appeal. Unmoved by his darkening brow and impatient gestures, she defended, with all the eloquence of a noble nature, the conduct of the Duke in adhering to the Prussian cause, as commanded alike by honor and necessity. She painted in vivid colors the personal friendship which bound him to Frederic William, the marks of affectionate interest he had received from that monarch, and inquired with generous indignation whether "it was in the hour of peril and misfortune that he could desert his friend and ally." She pictured the fearful condition of the land, — the stain that would forever rest upon the fame of the victor if the city were, as he threatened, abandoned to pillage. Struck and impressed despite himself, Napoleon relented so far as not only to give strict orders that the town should be respected, but to rescind his repeated declaration that the Duke should never again set foot on his native soil. True, the conditions appended to this concession were rigorous enough.

Carl Auguste was to quit the Prussian camp within twenty-four hours. In vain the anxious wife endeavored to obtain some delay. Here Napoleon was inflexible; and Louise, finding her efforts useless, retired to take instant measures to inform her lord of what had occurred. She despatched messengers in all directions, for the exact spot where he was to be found was not known.

Next morning Napoleon returned the visit, accompanied by all his principal officers. Desirous, it would seem, of effacing all recollection of his former harshness, he expressed the deepest regret for the excesses committed by his soldiery, lamenting the cruel necessity of war, and declaring *that it had been forced upon him.* "Croyez-moi, madame, il y a une Providence qui dirige tout, et dont je ne suis que l'instrument," he repeated. On descending to his apartment he exclaimed, "Voilà une femme à qui nos deux cents canons n'ont pas pu faire peur."

Perhaps political considerations induced Napoleon to prolong the term originally fixed for the Duke's return to Weimar, and to admit some modification of the severe conditions he had imposed. No entreaties or remonstrances, however, could obtain any reduction of the contribution of two hundred million francs, a fearful burden on a country already so terribly impoverished. All that the Duchess could do to alleviate the sufferings of the people, she did. Her private purse was drained to aid their necessities, and it is even said that she disposed of many of her jewels for the same purpose. This noble conduct found its reward in the adoration of her people, in the increasing regard of her lord, in the admiration of Europe. "She is the true model of a woman," writes Madame de Staël, "formed by nature for the very highest position. Equally devoid of pretension or weakness, she awakens at the same time, and in an equal degree, both confidence and veneration. The heroic soul of the olden days of chivalry still animates her, without in the slightest degree diminishing the gentleness of her sex."

Though in the latter years of their union a sincere if not

ardent friendship had succeeded the coldness of early life,
Louise was not destined to be beside her husband at the hour
of his death.   He had undertaken a journey to Berlin to visit
his granddaughter, the Princess Marie, who had lately married the Prince of Prussia.   On his return he was suddenly
seized with illness, and died at Graditz, near Torgau, 14th
June, 1828, at the age of seventy.   Alexander Humboldt had
been his constant companion during the latter days of his
life, and with him he conversed hours together, on all those
subjects in which he had even felt so lively an interest.

"In Potsdam," says this gifted man, in a letter to Chancellor Müller, "I spent many hours alone with the Grand Duke on the sofa.
He drank and slept alternately, drank again, rose to write to his consort, then again sank to sleep.   He was cheerful, but very much exhausted.   During the interval he pressed me with the most difficult
questions on physics, astronomy, meteorology, and geology, on the
transparency of a comet, the atmosphere of the moon, the influence of
the spots on the sun, on the temperature, &c.   In the midst of our
conversation he would fall asleep, and was often uneasy.   When he
awoke, he would quickly and kindly entreat forgiveness for his want
of attention.   'You see, Humboldt, it is all over with me.'   All at
once he would commence a desultory conversation on religion.   He
complained of the increase of fanaticism, the close connection of this
religious tendency with political absolutism, and the oppression of all
the free movements of the intellect.   'Besides, they are false and
treacherous,' he exclaimed; 'all they try for is to render themselves
agreeable to princes, to receive stars and ribbons.   They sneaked in
with their poetical love of the Middle Ages.'   Soon, however, his indignation appeased itself; he began to speak of all the consolation he
had found in the Christian faith.   'That is a truly philanthropic
doctrine,' he observed, 'but from the very commencement it has
been deformed.'"

It was on occasion of this letter of Humboldt that Goethe
pronounced his well-known eulogium on Carl Auguste : —

"The Duke was a born nobleman; he had taste and interest for
everything good and great.   He was but eighteen when I came to Weimar; but even then the bud and blossom showed what the tree would
become.   He soon chose me for his friend, and evinced the sincerest

sympathy in everything I did. My being nearly ten years older than himself was favorable to our intimacy. He would sit whole evenings beside me in deep conversation on nature, art, or anything else that was worth his attention. Often did we converse thus till nearly midnight, and it not unfrequently happened that we fell asleep beside each other on the sofa. Fifty years did we continue this intercourse. There are many princes capable of speaking admirably on subjects of interest ; but they have not the real love of them in their hearts, it is only superficial. And it is no wonder, when we remember all the distractions and dissipations attending a Court life to which a young prince is peculiarly exposed. He must notice everything, and know a bit of this and a bit of the other ; but in this way nothing can take deep root in the mind, and it requires a really powerful nature not to turn to mere empty smoke in such an atmosphere. The Grand Duke was a man, in the full sense of the term. He was animated by the noblest benevolence, the purest philanthropy ; and from his whole soul desired to do the best he could. His first thought was always his people's happiness ; his own was the very last.

"His hand was ever open, and ready to aid noble individuals and noble aims. There was much that was divine in his nature. He would fain have showered happiness on all mankind.

"He was by nature taciturn ; but the action followed close upon the words. He loved simplicity, and was an enemy to all coddling and effeminacy. He never drove out except in a drosky, which really hardly kept together, wrapt in an old gray mantle and a military cap. He loved travelling ; but not so much to amuse himself as everywhere to keep his eyes and ears open, and observe everything good and useful, that he might introduce it into his own country. Agriculture and manufactures owe him no common debt of gratitude. He did not seek to win the favor of his people by fine words ; but the people loved him, because they knew his heart beat for them."

Carl Auguste was buried, by his own desire, in the same vault in which Schiller already reposed, and where Goethe himself was one day to sleep beside him.

WOMAN IN FRANCE: MADAME DE SABLÉ.

IN 1847 a certain Count Leopold Ferri died at Padua, leaving a library entirely composed of works written by women, in various languages, and this library amounted to nearly thirty-two thousand volumes. We will not hazard any conjecture as to the proportion of these volumes which a severe judge, like the priest in Don Quixote, would deliver to the flames; but for our own part, most of those we should care to rescue would be the works of French women. With a few remarkable exceptions, our own feminine literature is made up of books which could have been better written by men, — books which have the same relation to literature in general, as academic prize poems have to poetry; when not a feeble imitation, they are usually an absurd exaggeration of the masculine style, like the swaggering gait of a bad actress in male attire. Few English women have written so much like a woman as Richardson's Lady G. Now we think it an immense mistake to maintain that there is no sex in literature. Science has no sex; the mere knowing and reasoning faculties, if they act correctly, must go through the same process, and arrive at the same result. But in art and literature, which imply the action of the entire being, in which every fibre of the nature is engaged, in which every peculiar modification of the individual makes itself felt, woman has something specific to contribute. Under every imaginable social condition, she will necessarily have a class of sensations and emotions, the maternal ones, which must remain unknown to man; and the fact of her comparative physical weakness, which, however it may have been exaggerated by a vicious civilization, can never be cancelled, introduces a distinctively femi-

nine condition into the wondrous chemistry of the affections
and sentiments, which inevitably gives rise to distinctive
forms and combinations. A certain amount of psychological
difference between man and woman necessarily arises out of
the difference of sex, and instead of being destined to vanish
before a complete development of woman's intellectual and
moral nature, will be a permanent source of variety and
beauty, as long as the tender light and dewy freshness of
morning affect us differently from the strength and brilliancy
of the midday sun. And those delightful women of France
who, from the beginning of the seventeenth to the close of
the eighteenth century, formed some of the brightest threads
in the web of political and literary history, wrote under circumstances which left the feminine character of their minds
uncramped by timidity and unstrained by mistaken effort.
They were not trying to make a career for themselves; they
thought little, in many cases not at all, of the public; they
wrote letters to their lovers and friends, memoirs of their
every-day lives, romances in which they gave portraits of
their familiar acquaintances, and described the tragedy or
comedy which was going on before their eyes. Always refined and graceful, often witty, sometimes judicious, they
wrote what they saw, thought, and felt, in their habitual language, without proposing any model to themselves, without
any intention to prove that women could write as well as
men, without affecting manly views or suppressing womanly
ones. One may say, at least with regard to the women of
the seventeenth century, that their writings were but a
charming accident of their more charming lives, like the pet-
als which the wind shakes from the rose in its bloom. And
it is but a twin fact with this, that in France alone woman
has had a vital influence on the development of literature;
in France alone the mind of woman has passed like an electric current through the language, making crisp and definite
what is elsewhere heavy and blurred; in France alone, if the
writings of women were swept away, a serious gap would be
made in the national history.

Patriotic gallantry may perhaps contend that English women could, if they had liked, have written as well as their neighbors; but we will leave the consideration of that question to the reviewers of the literature that might have been. In the literature that actually is, we must turn to France for the highest examples of womanly achievement in almost every department. We confess ourselves unacquainted with the productions of those awful women of Italy who held professorial chairs, and were great in civil and canon law; we have made no researches into the catacombs of female literature, but we think we may safely conclude that they would yield no rivals to that which is still unburied; and here, we suppose, the question of pre-eminence can only lie between England and France. And to this day Madame de Sévigné remains the single instance of a woman who is supreme in a class of literature which has engaged the ambition of men; Madame Dacier still reigns the queen of blue-stockings, though women have long studied Greek without shame;[1] Madame de Staël's name still rises first to the lips when we are asked to mention a woman of great intellectual power; Madame Roland is still the unrivalled type of the sagacious and sternly heroic, yet lovable woman; George Sand is the unapproached artist, who, to Jean Jacques' eloquence and deep sense of external nature, unites the clear delineation of character and the tragic depth of passion. These great names, which mark different epochs, soar like tall pines amidst a forest of less conspicuous, but not less fascinating, female writers; and beneath these, again, are spread, like the thicket of hawthorns, eglantines, and honey-suckles, the women who are known rather by what they stimulated men to write, than by what they wrote themselves — the women whose tact, wit, and personal radiance created the atmosphere of the *Salon*, where literature, philosophy,

---

[1] Queen Christina, when Madame Dacier (then Mademoiselle Le Fèvre) sent her a copy of her edition of "Callimachus," wrote in reply: "Mais vous, de qui on m'assure que vous êtes une belle et agréable fille, n'avez-vous pas honte d'être si savante?"

and science, emancipated from the trammels of pedantry and technicality, entered on a brighter stage of existence.

What were the causes of this earlier development and more abundant manifestation of womanly intellect in France? The primary one, perhaps, lies in the physiological characteristics of the Gallic race — the small brain and vivacious temperament which permit the fragile system of woman to sustain the superlative activity requisite for intellectual creativeness; while on the other hand, the larger brain and slower temperament of the English and Germans are, in the womanly organization, generally dreamy and passive. The type of humanity in the latter may be grander, but it requires a larger sum of conditions to produce a perfect specimen. Throughout the animal world, the higher the organization, the more frequent is the departure from the normal form; we do not often see imperfectly developed or ill-made insects, but we rarely see a perfectly developed, well-made man. And thus the physique of a woman may suffice as the substratum for a superior Gallic mind, but is too thin a soil for a superior Teutonic one. Our theory is borne out by the fact that, among our own countrywomen, those who distinguish themselves by literary production more frequently approach the Gallic than the Teutonic type; they are intense and rapid rather than comprehensive. The woman of large capacity can seldom rise beyond the absorption of ideas; her physical conditions refuse to support the energy required for spontaneous activity; the voltaic-pile is not strong enough to produce crystallizations; phantasms of great ideas float through her mind, but she has not the spell which will arrest them, and give them fixity. This, more than unfavorable external circumstances, is, we think, the reason why woman has not yet contributed any new form to art, any discovery in science, any deep-searching inquiry in philosophy. The necessary physiological conditions are not present in her. That under more favorable circumstances in the future, these conditions may prove compatible with the feminine organization, it would be rash to deny. For the present, we are only concerned with our theory so far as it presents a physiological basis for the intellectual effectiveness of French women.

A secondary cause was probably the laxity of opinion and practice with regard to the marriage tie. Heaven forbid that we should enter on a defence of French morals, most of all in relation to marriage! But it is undeniable that unions formed in the maturity of thought and feeling, and grounded only on inherent fitness and mutual attraction, tended to bring women into more intelligent sympathy with men, and to heighten and complicate their share in the political drama. The quiescence and security of the conjugal relation are doubtless favorable to the manifestation of the highest qualities by persons who have already attained a high standard of culture, but rarely foster a passion sufficient to rouse all the faculties to aid in winning or retaining its beloved object — to convert indolence into activity, indifference into ardent partisanship, dulness into perspicuity. Gallantry and intrigue are sorry enough things in themselves; but they certainly serve better to arouse the dormant faculties of woman than embroidery and domestic drudgery, especially when, as in the high society of France in the seventeenth century, they are refined by the influence of Spanish chivalry, and controlled by the spirit of Italian causticity. The dreamy and fantastic girl was awakened to reality by the experience of wifehood and maternity, and became capable of loving, not a mere phantom of her own imagination, but a living man, struggling with the hatreds and rivalries of the political arena; she espoused his quarrels, she made herself, her fortune, and her influence the stepping-stones of his ambition; and the languid beauty, who had formerly seemed ready to "die of a rose," was seen to become the heroine of an insurrection. The vivid interest in affairs which was thus excited in woman must obviously have tended to quicken her intellect, and give it a practical application; and the very sorrows, the heart-pangs and regrets which are inseparable from a life of passion, deepened her nature by the questioning of self and destiny which they occasioned, and by the energy demanded to surmount them and live on. No wise person, we imagine, wishes to restore the social condition of France in the seventeenth century, or considers the ideal programme of woman's life to be a *mariage de convenance* at fifteen, a career of gallantry from twenty to eight-and-thirty, and penitence and piety for the rest of her days. Nevertheless, that social condition has its good results, as much as the madly superstitious Crusades had theirs.

But the most indisputable source of feminine culture and development in France was the influence of the *salons* ; which, as all the world knows, were *réunions* of both sexes, where conversation ran along the whole gamut of subjects, from the frothiest *vers de société* to the philosophy of Descartes. Richelieu had set the fashion of uniting a taste for letters with the habits of polite society and the pursuits of ambition ; and in the first quarter of the seventeenth century, there were already several hôtels in Paris, varying in social position from the closest proximity of the Court to the debatable ground of the aristocracy and the bourgeoisie, which served as a rendezvous for different circles of people, bent on entertaining themselves, either by showing talent or admiring it. The most celebrated of these rendezvous was the Hôtel de Rambouillet, which was at the culmination of its glory in 1630, and did not become quite extinct until 1648, when the troubles of the Fronde commencing, its *habitués* were dispersed or absorbed by political interests. The presiding genius of this *salon*, the Marquise de Rambouillet, was the very model of the woman who can act as an amalgam to the most incongruous elements : beautiful, but not preoccupied by coquetry or passion ; an enthusiastic admirer of talent, but with no pretension to talent on her own part ; exquisitely refined in language and manners, but warm and generous withal ; not given to entertain her guests with her own compositions, or to paralyze them by her universal knowledge. She had once meant to learn Latin, but had been prevented by an illness ; perhaps she was all the better acquainted with Italian and Spanish productions, which, in default of a

national literature, were then the intellectual pabulum of all
cultivated persons in France who were unable to read the classics. In her mild, agreeable presence was accomplished that
blending of the high-toned chivalry of Spain with the caustic
wit and refined irony of Italy, which issued in the creation of
a new standard of taste — the combination of the utmost exaltation in sentiment with the utmost simplicity of language.
Women are peculiarly fitted to further such a combination,—
first, from their greater tendency to mingle affection and imagination with passion, and thus subtilize it into sentiment;
and next, from that dread of what overtaxes their intellectual energies, either by difficulty or monotony, which gives
them an instinctive fondness for lightness of treatment and
airiness of expression, thus making them cut short all pro-
lixity and reject all heaviness. When these womanly characteristics were brought into conversational contact with the
materials furnished by such minds as those of Richelieu, Cor-
neille, the Great Condé, Balzac, and Bossuet, it is no wonder
that the result was something piquant and charming. Those
famous *habitués* of the Hôtel de Rambouillet did not apparently first lay themselves out to entertain the ladies
with grimacing "small-talk" and then take each other by the
sword-knot to discuss matters of real interest in a corner;
they rather sought to present their best ideas in the guise
most acceptable to intelligent and accomplished women.
And the conversation was not of literature only; war, politics, religion, the lightest details of daily news — everything
was admissible, if only it were treated with refinement and
` intelligence. The Hôtel de Rambouillet was no mere literary
réunion ; it included *hommes d'affaires* and soldiers as well
as authors; and in such a circle women would not become *bas
bleus* or dreamy moralizers, ignorant of the world and of human nature, but intelligent observers of character and events.
It is easy to understand, however, that with the herd of imi-
tators who, in Paris and the provinces, aped the style of this
famous *salon,* simplicity degenerated into affectation, and nobility of sentiment was replaced by an inflated effort to out-

strip nature, so that the *genre précieux* drew down the satire which reached its climax in the "Précieuses Ridicules" and "Les Femmes Savantes," the former of which appeared in 1660, and the latter in 1673. But Madelon and Caltros are the lineal descendants of Mademoiselle Scudéry and her satellites, quite as much as of the Hôtel de Rambouillet. The society which assembled every Saturday in her *salon* was exclusively literary, and, although occasionally visited by a few persons of high birth, bourgeois in its tone, and enamoured of madrigals, sonnets, stanzas, and *bouts rimés*. The affectation that decks trivial things in fine language belongs essentially to a class which sees another above it, and is uneasy in the sense of its inferiority; and this affectation is precisely the opposite of the original *genre précieux*.

Another centre, from which feminine influence radiated into the national literature, was the Palais du Luxembourg, where Mademoiselle d'Orleans, in disgrace at Court on account of her share in the Fronde, held a little court of her own, and for want of anything else to employ her active spirit, busied herself with literature. One fine morning, it occurred to this princess to ask all the persons who frequented her court, among whom were Madame de Sévigné, Madame de la Fayette, and La Rochefoucauld, to write their own portraits, and she at once set the example. It was understood that defects and virtues were to be spoken of with like candor. The idea was carried out, those who were not clever or bold enough to write for themselves employing the pen of a friend.

" Such," says M. Cousin, " was the pastime of Mademoiselle and her friends during the years 1657 and 1658 ; from this pastime proceeded a complete literature. In 1659 Ségrais revised these portraits, added a considerable number in prose and even in verse, and published the whole in a handsome quarto volume, admirably printed, and now become very rare, under the title, ' Divers Portraits.' Only thirty copies were printed, not for sale, but to be given as presents by Mademoiselle. The work had a prodigious success. That which had made the fortune of Mademoiselle de Scudéry's romances — the pleasure of seeing

5

one's portrait a little flattered; curiosity to see that of others; the passion which the middle class always have had and will have, for knowing
what goes on in the aristocratic world (at that time not very easy of
access); the names of the illustrious persons who were here for the
first time described physically and morally with the utmost detail;
great ladies transformed all at once into writers, and unconsciously in-
venting a new manner of writing, of which no book gave the slightest
idea, and which was the ordinary manner of speaking of the aristocracy; this undefinable mixture of the natural, the easy, and at the
same time of the agreeable and supremely distinguished — all this
charmed the Court and the town, and very early in the year 1659
permission was asked of Mademoiselle to give a new edition of the
privileged book for the use of the public in general."

The fashion thus set, portraits multiplied throughout
France, until in 1688, La Bruyère adopted the form in his
"Characters," and ennobled it by divesting it of person-
ality. We shall presently see that a still greater work than
La Bruyère's also owed its suggestion to a woman, whose
salon was hardly a less fascinating resort than the Hôtel de
Rambouillet itself.

In proportion as the literature of a country is enriched and
culture becomes more generally diffused, personal influence
is less effective in the formation of taste and in the further-
ance of social advancement. It is no longer the coterie which
acts on literature, but literature which acts on the coterie;
the circle represented by the word "public" is ever widening,
and ambition, poising itself in order to hit a more distant
mark, neglects the successes of the *salon*. What was once lav-
ished prodigally in conversation is reserved for the volume
or the "article;" and the effort is not to betray originality,
rather than to communicate it. As the old coach-roads have
sunk into disuse through the creation of railways, so journalism tends more and more to divert information from the channel of conversation into the channel of the Press; no one is
satisfied with a more circumscribed audience than that very
indeterminate abstraction "the public," and men find a vent
for their opinions not in talk, but in "copy." We read the

"Athenæum" askance at the tea-table, and take notes from the "Philosophical Journal" at a soirée; we invite our friends, that we may thrust a book into their hands, and presuppose an exclusive desire in the "ladies" to discuss their own matters, "that we may crackle the 'Times'" at our ease.   In fact the evident tendency of things to contract personal communication within the narrowest limits makes us tremble lest some further development of the electric telegraph should reduce us to a society of mutes, or to a sort of insects, communicating by ingenious antennæ of our own invention.   Things were far from having reached this pass in the last century; but even then, literature and society had outgrown the nursing of coteries, and although many *salons* of that period were worthy successors of the Hôtel de Rambouillet, they were simply a recreation, not an influence.   Enviable evenings, no doubt, were passed in them; and if we could be carried back to any of them at will, we should hardly know whether to choose the Wednesday dinner at Madame Geoffrin's, with d'Alembert, Mademoiselle de l'Espinasse, Grimm, and the rest, or the graver society which, thirty years later, gathered round Condorcet and his lovely young wife.   The *salon* retained its attractions, but its power was gone; the stream of life had become too broad and deep for such small rills to affect it.

A fair comparison between the French women of the seventeenth century and those of the eighteenth would, perhaps, have a balanced result, though it is common to be a partisan on this subject.   The former have more exaltation, perhaps more nobility of sentiment, and less consciousness in their intellectual activity — less of the *femme auteur*, which was Rousseau's horror in Madame d'Epinay; but the latter have a richer fund of ideas — not more ingenuity, but the materials of an additional century for their ingenuity to work upon. The women of the seventeenth century, when Love was on the wane, took to Devotion, — at first mildly and by halves, as English women take to caps, and finally without compromise; with the women of the eighteenth century, Bossuet and Massillon had given way to Voltaire and Rousseau; and when youth and beauty failed, then they were thrown on their own moral strength.

M. Cousin is especially enamoured of the women of the seventeenth century, and relieves himself from his labors in philosophy by making researches into the original documents which throw light upon their lives. Last year he gave us some results of these researches in a volume on the youth of the Duchesse de Longueville; and he has just followed it up with a second volume, in which he further illustrates her career by tracing it in connection with that of her friend, Madame de Sablé. The materials to which he has had recourse for this purpose are chiefly two celebrated collections of manuscript: that of Conrart, the first secretary to the French Academy, — one of those universally curious people who seem made for the annoyance of contemporaries and the benefit of posterity; and that of Valant, who was at once the physician, the secretary, and general steward of Madame de Sablé, and who, with or without her permission, possessed himself of the letters addressed to her by her numerous correspondents during the latter part of her life, and of various papers having some personal or literary interest attached to them. From these stores M. Cousin has selected many documents previously unedited; and though he often leaves us something to desire in the arrangement of his materials, this volume of his on Madame de Sablé is very acceptable to us, for she interests us quite enough to carry us through more than three hundred pages of rather scattered narrative, and through an appendix of correspondence in small type. M. Cousin justly appreciates her character as "un heureux mélange de raison, d'esprit, d'agrément, et de bonté;" and perhaps there are few better specimens of the woman, who is extreme in nothing, but sympathetic in all things; who affects us by no special quality, but by her entire being; whose nature has no *tons criards,* but is like those textures which, from their harmonious blending of all colors, give repose to the eye, and do not weary us though we see them every day. Madame de Sablé is also a striking example of the one order of influence, which woman has exercised over literature in France ; and on this ground, as well as intrinsically, she is worth studying. If the reader agrees with us he will perhaps be inclined, as we are, to dwell a little on 'the chief points in her life and character.

Madeline de Souvré—daughter of the Marquis of Courtenvaux, a nobleman distinguished enough to be chosen as governor of Louis XIII. — was born in 1599, on the threshold of that seventeenth century, the brilliant genius of which is mildly reflected in her mind and history. Thus when in 1635 her more celebrated friend, Mademoiselle de Bourbon, afterwards the Duchesse de Longueville, made her appearance at the Hôtel de Rambouillet, Madame de Sablé had nearly crossed that table-land of maturity which precedes a woman's descent towards old age. She had been married, in 1614, to Philippe Emanuel de Laval-Montmorency, Seigneur de Bois-Dauphin, and Marquis de Sablé, of whom nothing further is known than that he died in 1640, leaving her the richer by four children, but with a fortune considerably embarrassed. With beauty and high rank, added to the mental attractions of which we have abundant evidence, we may well believe that Madame de Sablé's youth was brilliant. For her beauty we have the testimony of sober Madame de Motteville, who also speaks of her as having " beaucoup de lumière et de sincérité," and in the following passage very graphically indicates one phase of Madame de Sablé's character : —

" The Marquise de Sablé was one of those whose beauty made the most noise when the Queen came into France. But if she was amiable, she was still more desirous of appearing so ; this lady's self-love rendered her too sensitive to the regard which men exhibited towards her.   There yet existed in France some remains of the politeness which Catherine de' Medici had introduced from Italy, and the new dramas, with all the other works in prose and verse, which came from Madrid, were thought to have such delicacy, that she (Madame de Sablé) had conceived a high idea of the gallantry which the Spaniards had learned from the Moors.

" She was persuaded that men can, without crime, have tender

sentiments for women — that the desire of pleasing them led men to
the greatest and finest actions, roused their intelligence, and inspired
them with liberality, and all sorts of virtues; but, on the other hand,
women, who were the ornament of the world, and made to be served
and adored, ought not to admit anything from them but their respect-
ful attentions. As this lady supported her views with much talent and
great beauty, she had given them authority in her time ; and the number and consideration of those who continued to associate with her,
have caused to subsist in our day what the Spaniards call *finezas.*"

Here is the grand element of the original *femme précieuse*,
and it appears further, in a detail also reported by Madame
de Motteville, that Madame de Sablé had a passionate admirer in the accomplished Duc de Montmorency, and appar- .
ently reciprocated his regard ; but discovering (at what period
of their attachment is unknown) that he was raising a lover's
eyes towards the Queen, she broke with him at once. " I have
heard her say," tells Madame de Motteville, " that her pride
was such with regard to the Duc de Montmorency, that at
the first demonstrations which he gave of his change, she refused to see him any more, being unable to receive with satisfaction attentions which she had to share with the greatest
princess in the world." There is no evidence, except the un-
trustworthy assertion of Tallement de Réaux, that Madame
de Sablé had any other *liaison* than this ; and the probability
of the negative is increased by the ardor of her friendships.
The strongest of these was formed early in life with Mademoiselle Dona d'Attichy, afterwards Comtesse de Maure ; it
survived the effervescence of youth, and the closest intimacy
of middle age, and was only terminated by the death of the
latter in 1663. A little incident in this friendship is so characteristic in the transcendentalism which was then carried
into all the affections, that it is worth relating at length.
Mademoiselle d'Attichy, in her grief and indignation at Richelieu's treatment of her relative, quitted Paris, and was about
to join her friend at Sablé, when she suddenly discovered
that Madame de Sablé, in a letter to Madame de Rambouillet,
had said that her greatest happiness would be to pass her

life with Julie de Rambouillet, afterwards Madame de Montausier. To Anne d'Attichy this appears nothing less than
the crime of *lèse-amitié*. No explanations will appease her;
she refuses to accept the assurance that the offensive expression was used simply out of unreflecting conformity to the
style of the Hôtel de Rambouillet, that it was mere *galima-
tias*. She gives up her journey, and writes a letter, which
is the only one Madame de Sablé chose to preserve when, in
her period of devotion, she sacrificed the records of her youth.
Here it is : —

" I have seen this letter in which you tell me there is so much *gali-
matias*, and I assure you that I have not found any at all. On the
contrary, I find everything very plainly expressed, and among others,
one which is too explicit for my satisfaction — namely, what you have
said to Madame de Rambouillet, that if you tried to imagine a perfectly happy life for yourself, it would be to pass it all alone with
Mademoiselle de Rambouillet. You know whether any one can be
more persuaded than I am of her merit; but I confess to you that that
has not prevented me from being surprised that you could entertain a
thought which did so great an injury to our friendship. As to believ-
ing that you said this to one, and wrote it to the other, simply for the
sake of paying them an agreeable compliment, I have too high an esteem for your courage to be able to imagine that complaisance would
cause you thus to betray the sentiments of your heart, especially on a
subject in which, as they were unfavorable to me, I think you would
have the more reason for concealing them, the affection which I have
for you being so well known to every one, and especially to Mademoiselle de Rambouillet, so that I doubt whether she will not have been
more sensible of the wrong you have done me, than of the advantage
you have given her. The circumstance of this letter falling into my
hands has forcibly reminded me of these lines of Bertaut : —

'Malheureuse est l'ignorance,
Et plus malheureux le savoir.'

" Having through this lost a confidence which alone rendered life
supportable to me, it is impossible for me to take the journey so much
thought of. For would there be any propriety in travelling sixty miles
in this season, in order to burthen you with a person so little suited to
you, that, after years of a passion without parallel, you cannot help

thinking that the greatest pleasure of your life would be to pass it
without her? I return, then, into my solitude, to examine the defects
which cause me so much unhappiness, and unless I can correct them, I
should have less joy than confusion in seeing you."

It speaks strongly for the charm of Madame de Sablé's
nature that she was able to retain so susceptible a friend as
Mademoiselle d'Attichy in spite of numerous other friendships, some of which, especially that with Madame de Longueville, were far from lukewarm — in spite too of a tendency
in herself to distrust the affection of others towards her, and
to wait for advances rather than to make them. We find
many traces of this tendency in the affectionate remonstrances addressed to her by Madame de Longueville, now
for shutting herself up from her friends, now for doubting
that her letters are acceptable. Here is a little passage from
one of these remonstrances, which indicates a trait of Madame
de Sablé, and is in itself a bit of excellent sense, worthy the
consideration of lovers and friends in general: "I am very
much afraid that if I leave to you the care of letting me
know when I can see you, I shall be a long time without
having that pleasure, and that nothing will incline you to
procure it for me; for I have always observed a certain lukewarmness in your friendship after our *explanations,* from
which I have never seen you thoroughly recover; and that
is why I dread explanations, for however good they may be
in themselves, since they serve to reconcile people, it must
always be admitted, to their shame, that they are at least the
effect of a bad cause, and that if they remove it for a time
they *sometimes leave a certain facility in getting angry again,*
which, without diminishing friendship, renders its intercourse
less agreeable. It seems to me that I find all this in your
behavior to me; so I am not wrong in sending to know if
you wish to have me to-day." It is clear that Madame de
Sablé was far from having what Saint-Beuve calls the one
fault of Madame Necker, absolute perfection. A certain ex-
quisiteness in her physical and moral nature was, as we shall

see, the source of more than one weakness; but the perception of these weaknesses, which is indicated in Madame de
Longueville's letters, heightens our idea of the attractive
qualities which, notwithstanding, drew from her, at the sober
age of forty, such expressions as these: "I assure you that
you are the person in all the world whom it would be most
agreeable to me to see, and there is no one whose intercourse
is a ground of truer satisfaction to me. It is admirable that
at all times, and amidst all changes, the taste for your society
remains in me; and, *if one ought to thank God for the joys
which do not tend to salvation*, I should thank him with all my
heart for having preserved that to me at a time in which
he has taken away from me all others."

Since we have entered on the chapter of Madame de Sablé's weaknesses, this is the place to mention what was the
subject of endless raillery from her friends — her elaborate
precaution about her health, and her dread of infection, even
from diseases the least communicable. Perhaps this anxiety
was founded as much on æsthetic as on physical grounds, on
disgust at the details of illness as much as on dread of suffering; with a cold in the head or a bilious complaint, the exquisite *précieuse* must have been considerably less conscious
of being "the ornament of the world," and "made to be
adored." Even her friendship, strong as it was, was not
strong enough to overcome her horror of contagion; for when
Mademoiselle de Bourbon, recently become Madame de
Longueville, was attacked by small-pox, Madame de Sablé for
some time had not courage to visit her, or even to see Mademoiselle de Rambouillet, who was assiduous in her attendance
on the patient. A little correspondence, *à propos* of these circumstances, so well exhibits the graceful badinage in which
the great ladies of that day were adepts, that we are tempted
to quote one short letter.

Mademoiselle de Rambouillet to the Marquise de Sablé.

Mademoiselle de Chalais [*dame de compagnie* to the Marquise] will
please to read this letter to Madame la Marquise, *out of* a draught.

MADAME, — I do not think it possible to begin my treaty with you too early, for I am convinced that between the first proposition made to me that I should see you, and the conclusion, you will have so many reflections to make, so many physicians to consult, and so many fears to surmount, that I shall have full leisure to air myself. The conditions which I offer to fulfil for this purpose are, not to visit you until I have been three days absent from the Hôtel de Condé [where Madame de Longueville was ill], to choose a frosty day, not to approach you within four paces, not to sit down on more than one seat. You may also have a great fire in your room, burn juniper in the four corners, surround yourself with imperial vinegar, with rue and wormwood. If you can feel yourself safe under these conditions, without my cutting off my hair, I swear to you to execute them religiously; and if you want examples to fortify you, I can tell you that the Queen consented to see M. Chaudebonne, when he had come directly from Mademoiselle de Bourbon's room, and that Madame d'Aiguillon, who has good taste in such matters, and is free from reproach on these points, has just sent me word that if I did not go to see her, she would come to me.

Madame de Sablé betrays in her reply that she winces under this raillery, and thus provokes a rather severe though polite rejoinder, which, added to the fact that Madame de Longueville is convalescent, rouses her courage to the pitch of paying the formidable visit. Mademoiselle de Rambouillet, made aware, through their mutual friend Voiture, that her sarcasm has cut rather too deep, winds up the matter by writing that very difficult production, a perfectly conciliatory yet dignified apology. Peculiarities like this always deepen with age; and accordingly, fifteen years later, we find Madame D'Orleans, in her "Princesse de Paphlagonia," — a romance in which she describes her court, with the little quarrels and other affairs that agitated it, — giving the following amusing picture, or rather caricature, of the extent to which Madame de Sablé carried her pathological mania, which seems to have been shared by her friend the Countess de Maure (Mademoiselle d'Attichy). In the romance, these two ladies appear under the names of Princesse Parthénie and the Reine de Mionie.

" There was not an hour in the day in which they did not confer together on the means of avoiding death, and on the art of rendering themselves immortal. Their conferences did not take place like those of other people; the fear of breathing an air which was too cold or too warm, the dread lest the wind should be too dry or too moist — in short, the imagination that the weather might not be as temperate as they thought necessary for the preservation of their health, caused them to write letters from one room to the other. It would be extremely fortunate if these notes could be found, and formed into a collection. I am convinced that they would contain rules for the regimen of life, precautions even as to the proper time for applying remedies, and also remedies which Hippocrates and Galen, with all their science, never heard of. Such a collection would be very useful to the public, and would be highly profitable to the faculties of Paris and Montpellier. If these letters were discovered, great advantages of all kinds might be derived from them, for they were princesses who had nothing mortal about them but the *knowledge* that they were mortal. In their writings might be learned all politeness in style, and the most delicate manner of speaking on all subjects. There is nothing with which they were not acquainted: they knew the affairs of all the states in the world, through the share they had in all the intrigues of its private members, either in matters of gallantry, as in other things on which their advice was necessary, either to adjust embroilments and quarrels, or to excite them, for the sake of the advantages which their friends could derive from them, — in a word, they were persons through whose hands the secrets of the whole world had to pass. The Princess Parthénie [Madame de Sablé] had a palate as delicate as her mind; nothing could equal the magnificence of the entertainments she gave; all the dishes were exquisite, and her cleanliness was beyond all that could be imagined. It was in their time that writing came into use; previously, nothing was written but marriage contracts, and letters were never heard of; thus it is to them that we owe a practice so convenient in intercourse."

Still later, in 1669, when the most uncompromising of the Port Royalists seemed to tax Madame de Sablé with lukewarmness that she did not join them at Port-Royal-des-Champs, we find her writing to the stern M. de Sévigny:
" En vérité, je crois que je ne pourrois mieux faire que de tout quitter et de m'en aller là. Mais que deviendroient ces

frayeurs de n'avoir pas de médicines à choisir, ni de chirur-
gien pour me saigner ? "

Mademoiselle, as we have seen, hints at the love of delicate
eating, which many of Madame de Sablé's friends numbered
among her foibles, especially after her religious career had
commenced. She had a genius in *friandise*, and knew how
to gratify the palate without offending the highest sense of
refinement. Her sympathetic nature showed itself in this as
in other things ; she was always sending *bonnes bouches* to
her friends, and trying to communicate to them her science
and taste in the affairs of the table. Madame de Longueville, who had not the luxurious tendencies of her friend,
writes : " Je vous demande, au nom de Dièu, que vous ne
me prépariez aucun ragoût. Surtout, ne me donnez point de
festin. Au nom de Dieu, qu'il n'y ait rien que ce qu'on peut
manger, car vous savez que c'est inutile pour moi ; de plus,
j'en ai scruple." But other friends had more appreciation
of her niceties. Voiture thanks her for her melons, and
assures her that they are better than those of yesterday ;
Madame de Choisy hopes that her ridicule of Jansenism will
not provoke Madame de Sablé to refuse her the receipt for
salad ; and La Rochefoucauld writes : " You cannot do me a
greater charity than to permit the bearer of this letter to
enter into the mysteries of your marmalade and your genuine
preserves, and I humbly entreat you to do everything you
can in his favor. If I could hope for two dishes of those
preserves, which I did not deserve to eat before, I should be
indebted to you all my life." For our own part, being as far
as possible from fraternizing with those spiritual people who
convert a deficiency into a principle, and pique themselves
on an obtuse palate as a point of superiority, we are not inclined to number Madame de Sablé's *friandise* amongst her
defects. M. Cousin, too, is apologetic on this point. He
says : —

" It was only the excess of a delicacy which can be really understood,
and a sort of fidelity to the character of *précieuse*. As the *précieuse*
did nothing according to common usage, she could not dine like an-

other. We have cited a passage from Madame de Motteville, where Madame de Sablé is represented in her first youth at the Hôtel de Rambouillet, maintaining that woman is born to be an ornament to the world, and to receive the adoration of men. The woman worthy of the name ought always to appear above material wants, and retain, even in the most vulgar details of life, something distinguished and purified. Eating is a very necessary operation, but one which is not agreeable to the eye. Madame de Sablé insisted on its being conducted with a peculiar cleanliness. According to her, it was not every woman who could with impunity be at table in the presence of a lover; the first distortion of the face, she said, would be enough to spoil all. Gross meals, made for the body merely, ought to be abandoned to *bourgeoises*, and the refined woman should appear to take a little nourishment merely to sustain her, and even to divert her, as one takes refreshments and ices. Wealth did not suffice for this; a particular talent was required. Madame de Sablé was a mistress in this art. She had transported the aristocratic spirit, and the *genre précieux*, good-breeding, and good taste, even into cookery. Her dinners, without any opulence, were celebrated and sought after."

It is quite in accordance with all this, that Madame de Sablé should delight in fine scents, and we find that she did; for being threatened, in her Port Royal days, when she was at an advanced age, with the loss of smell, and writing for sympathy and information to Mère Agnès, who had lost that sense early in life, she receives this admonition from the stern saint: "You would gain by this loss, my very dear sister, if you made use of it as a satisfaction to God, for having had too much pleasure in delicious scents." Scarron describes her as

"La non pareille Bois-Dauphine,
Entre dames perle très fine;"

and the superlative delicacy implied by this epithet seems to have belonged equally to her personal habits, her affections, and her intellect.

Madame de Sablé's life, for anything we know, flowed on evenly enough until 1640, when the death of her husband threw upon her the care of an embarrassed fortune. She found a friend in Réné de Longueil, Seigneur de Maisons, of

whom we are content to know no more than that he helped
Madame de Sablé to arrange her affairs, though only by
means of alienating from her family the estate of Sablé; that
his house was her refuge during the blockade of Paris, in
1649; and that she was not unmindful of her obligations to
him, when subsequently her credit could be serviceable to
him at Court. In the midst of these pecuniary troubles came
a more terrible trial, — the loss of her favorite son, the brave
and handsome Guy de Laval, who, after a brilliant career in
the campaigns of Condé, was killed at the siege of Dunkirk,
in 1646, when scarcely four-and-twenty. The fine qualities
of this young man had endeared him to the whole army, and
especially to Condé, had won him the hand of the Chancellor
Séguire's daughter, and had thus opened to him the prospect
of the highest honors. His loss seems to have been the most
real sorrow of Madame de Sablé's life. Soon after followed
the commotions of the Fronde, which put a stop to social
intercourse, and threw the closest friends into opposite ranks.
According to Lenet, who relies on the authority of Gourville,
Madame de Sablé was under strong obligations to the Court,
being in the receipt of a pension of two thousand crowns; at
all events, she adhered throughout to the Queen and Mazarin,
but being as far as possible from a fierce partisan, and given
both by disposition and judgment to hear both sides of the
question, she acted as a conciliator, and retained her friends
of both parties. The Comtesse de Maure, whose husband was
the most obstinate of *frondeurs*, remained throughout her
most cherished friend, and she kept up a constant correspondence with the lovely and intrepid heroine of the Fronde,
Madame de Longueville. Her activity was directed to the
extinction of animosities, by bringing about marriages between the Montagues and Capulets of the Fronde, — between
the Prince de Condé, or his brother, and the niece of Mazarin, or between the three nieces of Mazarin and the sons
of three noblemen who were distinguished leaders of the
Fronde. Though her projects were not realized, her conciliatory position enabled her to preserve all her friendships

intact; and when the political tempest was over, she could assemble around her, in her residence in the Place Royal, the same society as before. Madame de Sablé was now approaching her twelfth lustrum; and though the charms of her mind and character made her more sought after than most younger women, it is not surprising that, sharing as she did in the religious ideas of her time, the concerns of "salvation" seemed to become pressing. A religious retirement, which did not exclude the reception of literary friends or the care for personal comforts, made the most becoming frame for age and diminished fortune. Jansenism was then, to ordinary Catholicism, what Puseyism is to ordinary Church-of-Englandism in these days; it was a *récherché* form of piety unshared by the vulgar; and one sees at once that it must have special attractions for the *précieuse*. Madame de Sablé then, probably about 1655 or 1656, determined to retire to Port Royal, not because she was already devout, but because she hoped to become so; as, however, she wished to retain the pleasure of intercourse with friends who were still worldly, she built for herself a set of apartments, at once distinct from the monastery and attached to it. Here, with a comfortable establishment, consisting of her secretary, Dr. Valant; Mademoiselle de Chalais, formerly her *dame de compagnie*, and now become her friend; an excellent cook; a few other servants; and for a considerable time a carriage and coachman; with her best friends within a moderate distance, she could, as M. Cousin says, be out of the noise of the world without altogether forsaking it, preserve her dearest friendships, and have before her eyes edifying examples, — "vaquer enfin à son aise aux soins de son salut et à ceux de sa santé."

We have, hitherto, looked only at one phase of Madame de Sablé's character and influence, that of the *précieuse*. But she was much more than this: she was the valuable, trusted friend of noble women and distinguished men; she was the animating spirit of a society whence issued a new form of French literature; she was the woman of large capacity and

large heart, whom Pascal sought to please, to whom Arnauld
submitted the Discourse prefixed to his Logic, and to whom
La Rochefoucauld writes: "Vous savez que je ne crois que
vous êtes sur de certains chapitres, et surtout sur les replis
du cœur." The papers preserved by her secretary, Valant,
show that she maintained an extensive correspondence with
persons of various rank and character; that her pen was
untiring in the interest of others; that men made her the
depositary of their thoughts, women of their sorrows; that
her friends were as impatient, when she secluded herself,
as if they had been rival lovers, and she a youthful beauty.
It is into her ear that Madame de Longueville pours her
troubles and difficulties, and that Madame de la Fayette
communicates her little alarms, lest young Count de St. Paul
should have detected her intimacy with La Rochefoucauld.[1]
The few of Madame de Sablé's letters which survive show
that she excelled in that epistolary style which was the specialty of the Hôtel de Rambouillet: one to Madame de Montausier, in favor of M. Périer, the brother-in-law of Pascal,
is a happy mixture of good taste and good sense; but
amongst them all, we prefer quoting one to the Duchesse
de la Tremouille. It is light and pretty, and made out of
almost nothing, like soap-bubbles.

" Je crois qu'il n'y a que moi qui face si bien tont le contraire de ce
que je veux faire, car il est vrai qu'il n'y a personne que j'honore plus
que vous, et j'ai si bien fait qu'il est quasi impossible que vous le puis-
siez croire. Ce n'estoit pas assez pour vous persuader que je suis in-
digne de vos bonnes grâces et de votre souvenir que d'avoir manqué
fort longtemps à vous écrire ; il falloit encore retarder quinze jours à
me donner l'honneur de répondre à votre lettre. En vérité, Madame,
cela me fait parôitre si coupable, que vers tout autre que vous j'aimeroix
mieux l'être en effet que d'entreprendre une chose si difficile qu'est celle

---

[1] The letter to which we allude has this charming little touch: "Je
hais comme la mort que les gens de son age puissent croire que j'ai des ga-
lanteries. Il semble qu'on leur parait cent ans des qu'on est plus vieille
qu'eux, et ils sont tout propre à s'étonner qu'il y ait encore question des
gens."

de mo justifier. Mais je me sens si innocento dans mon âme, et j'ai tant d'estime, do respect, et d'affection pour vous, qu'il me semble que vous devez le connôitre à cent lieues de distanco d'ici, encore que je no vous dise pas un mot. C'est ce quo me donno le courage de vous écrire à cette heure, mais non pas ce qui m'en a empêché si longtemps. J'ai commencé a faillir par force, ayant eu beaucoup de maux, et depuis je l'ai faite par honte, et je vous avoue quo si je n'avois à cette heure la confiance quo vous m'avez donnée en me rassurant, et celle quo je tire de mes propres sentimens pour vous, je n'oserois jamais entreprendre de vous faire souvenir de moi ; mais je m'assure que vous oublierez tout, sur la protestation quo je vous fais de ne mo laisser plus endurcir en mes fautes et do demeurer inviolablement, Madame, votre, &c."

Was not the woman, who could unite the ease and grace indicated by this letter, with an intellect that men thought worth consulting on matters of reasoning and philosophy, with warm affections, untiring activity for others, no ambition as an authoress, and an insight into *confitures* and *ragoûts*, a rare combination ? No wonder that her *salon* at Port Royal was the favorite resort of such women as Madame de la Fayette, Madame de Montausier, Madame de Longueville, and Madame de Hautefort, and of such men as Pascal, La Rochefoucauld, Nicole, and Domat. The collections of Valant contain papers which show what were the habitual subjects of conversation in this *salon*. Theology, of course, was a chief topic ; but physics and metaphysics had their turn, and still more frequently morals, taken in their widest sense. There were "Conferences on Calvinism," of which an abstract is preserved. When Rohault invented his glass tubes to serve for the barometrical experiments in which Pascal had roused a strong interest, the Marquis de Sourdis entertained the society with a paper entitled, "Why water mounts in a glass tube." Cartesianism was an exciting topic here, as well as everywhere else in France ; it had its partisans and opponents, and papers were read, containing "Thoughts on the opinions of M. Descartes." These lofty matters were varied by discussions on love and friendship, on the drama, and on most of the things in heaven and earth, which the philosophy of

6

that day dreamt of. Morals — generalizations on human affections, sentiments, and conduct — seem to have been the
favorite theme ; and the aim was to reduce these generalizations to their briefest form of expression, to give them the
epigrammatic turn which made them portable in the memory.
This was the specialty of Madame de Sablé's circle, and was
probably due to her own tendency. As the Hôtel de Rambouillet was the nursery of graceful letter-writing, and the
Luxembourg of " portraits " and "characters," so Madame de
Sablé's *salon* fostered that taste for the sententious style, to
which we owe, probably, some of the best *Pensées* of Pascal,
and, certainly, the Maxims of La Rochefoucauld. Madame
de Sablé herself wrote maxims, which were circulated among
her friends ; and, after her death, were published by the Abbé
d'Ailly. They have the excellent sense and nobility of feeling, which we should expect in everything of hers, but they
have no stamp of genius or individual character ; they are,
to the Maxims of La Rochefoucauld, what the vase moulded
in dull, heavy clay is to the vase which the action of fire has
made light, brittle, and transparent. She also wrote a treatise on Education, which is much praised by La Rochefoucauld and M. d'Andilly, but which seems no longer to be found ;
probably it was not much more elaborate than her so-called
"Treatise on Friendship," which is but a short string of
maxims. Madame de Sablé's forte was evidently not to write
herself, but to stimulate others to write, — to show that sympathy and appreciation which are as genial and encouraging
as the morning sunbeams. She seconded a man's wit with
understanding, one of the best offices which womanly intellect has rendered to the advancement of culture ; and the
absence of originality made her all the more receptive
towards the originality of others.

The manuscripts of Pascal show that many of the *Pensées*,
which are commonly supposed to be raw materials for a great
work on religion, were remodelled again and again, in order
to bring them to the highest degree of terseness and finish,
which would hardly have been the case if they had only been

part of a quarry for a greater production. Thoughts which are merely collected as materials, as stones out of which a building is to be erected, are not cut into facets, and polished like amethysts or emeralds. Since Pascal was from the first in the habit of visiting Madame de Sablé at Port Royal, with his sister Madame Périer (who was one of Madame de Sablé's dearest friends), we may well suppose that he would throw some of his jewels among the large and small coin of maxims, which were a sort of subscription-money there. Many of them have an epigrammatic piquancy, which was just the thing to charm a circle of vivacious and intelligent women: they seem to come from a La Rochefoucauld who has been dipped over again in philosophy and wit and received a new layer. But whether or not Madame de Sablé's influence served to enrich the *Pensées* of Pascal, it is clear that but for her influence the "Maxims" of La Rochefoucauld would never have existed. Just as in some circles the effort is, who shall make the best puns (*horribile dictu!*) or the best charades, in the *salon* of Port Royal the amusement was to fabricate maxims. La Rochefoucauld said, " L'envie de faire des maximes se gagne comme le rhume." So far from claiming for himself the initiation of this form of writing, he accuses Jacques Esprit, another *habitué* of Madame de Sablé's *salon*, of having excited in him the taste for maxims, in order to trouble his repose. The said Esprit was an academician, and had been a frequenter of the Hôtel de Rambouillet. He had already published "Maxims in Verse," and he subsequently produced a book called " La Fausseté des Vertus Humaines," which seems to consist of Rochefoucauldism become flat with an infusion of sour Calvinism. Nevertheless, La Rochefoucauld seems to have prized him, to have appealed to his judgment, and to have concocted maxims with him, which he afterwards begs him to submit to Madame de Sablé. He sends a little batch of maxims to her himself, and asks for an equivalent in the shape of good eatables: "Voilá tout ce que j'ai de maximes; mais comme je ne donne rien pour rien, je vous demande un potage aux carottes, un ragoût de mouton," &c. The taste and the talent enhanced each other, until at last La Rochefoucauld began to be conscious of his pre-eminence in the circle of maxim-mongers, and thought of a wider audience. Thus grew up the famous "Maxims," about which little need be said. Every one is now convinced, or professes to be convinced, that as to form, they are perfect, and that as to matter, they are at once undeniably true and miserably false; true as applied to that condition of human nature in which the selfish instincts are still dominant, false if taken as a representation of all the elements and possibilities of human nature. We think La Rochefoucauld himself wavered as to their universality, and that this wavering is indicated in the qualified form of some of the maxims; it occasionally struck him that the shadow of virtue must have a substance, but he had never grasped that substance; it had never been present to his consciousness.

It is curious to see La Rochefoucauld's nervous anxiety about presenting himself before the public as an author; far from rushing into print, he stole into it, and felt his way by asking private opinions. Through Madame de Sablé he sent manuscript copies to various persons of taste and talent, both men and women, and many of the written opinions which she received in reply are still in existence. The women generally find the maxims distasteful, but the men write approvingly. These men, however, are for the most part ecclesiastics, who decry human nature that they may exalt divine grace. The coincidence between Augustinianism, or Calvinism, with its doctrine of human corruption, and the hard cynicism of the maxims, presents itself in quite a piquant form in some of the laudatory opinions on La Rochefoucauld. One writer says: "On ne pourroit faire une instruction plus propre à un cate-chuméne pour convertir à Dieu son esprit et sa volonté . . . . Quand il n'y auroit que cet escrit au monde et l'Evangile je voudrois être chrétien. L'un m'apprendroit à connoistre mes miséres, et l'autre à implorer mon libérateur." Madame de Maintenon sends word to La Rochefoucauld, after the publication of his work, that the "Book of Job" and the "Maxims" are her only reading.

That Madame de Sablé herself had a tolerably just idea of La Rochefoucauld's character, as well as of his maxims, may be gathered not only from the fact that her own maxims are as full of the confidence in human goodness which La Rochefoucauld wants, as they are empty of the style which he possesses, but also from a letter in which she replies to the criticisms of Madame de Schomberg. "The author," she says, "derived the maxim on indolence from his own disposition, for never was there so great an indolence as his; and I think that his heart, inert as it is, owes this defect as much to his idleness as his will. It has never permitted him to do the least action for others; and I think that, amidst all his great desires and great hopes, he is sometimes indolent even on his own behalf." Still she must have felt a hearty interest in the "Maxims," as in some degree her foster-child, and she must also have had considerable affection for the author, who was lovable enough to those who observed the rule of Helvetius, and expected nothing from him. She not only assisted him, as we have seen, in getting criticisms, and carrying out the improvements suggested by them, but when the book was actually published, she prepared a notice of it for the only journal then existing — the "Journal des Savants." This notice was originally a brief statement of the nature of the work, and the opinions which had been formed for and against it, with a moderate eulogy, in conclusion, on its good sense, wit, and insight into human nature. But when she submitted it to La Rochefoucauld he objected to the paragraph which stated the adverse opinion, and requested her to alter it. She, however, was either unable or unwilling to modify her notice, and returned it with the following note : —

" Je vous envoie ce que j'ai pu tirer de ma teste pour mettre dans le ' Journal des Savants.' J'y ai mis cet endroit qui vous est le plus sensible, afin que cela vous fasse surmonter la mauvaise honte qui vous fit mettre la préface sans y rien retrancher, et je n'ai pas craint de le mettre, parce que je suis assurée que vous ne le ferez pas imprimer, quand même le reste vous plairoit. Je vous assure aussi que je vous serai plus obligée, si vous en usez comme d'une chose qui servit à vous pour le corriger ou pour le jeter au feu. Nous autres grands auteurs, nous sommes trop riches pour craindre de rien perdre de nos productions. Mandez-moi ce qu'il vous semble de ce dictum."

La Rochefoucauld availed himself of this permission, and " edited" the notice, touching up the style, and leaving out the blame. In this revised form it appeared in the "Journal des Savants." In some points, we see, the youth of journalism was not without promise of its future.

While Madame de Sablé was thus playing the literary confidante to La Rochefoucauld, and was the soul of a society whose chief interest was the *belles lettres*, she was equally active in graver matters. She was in constant intercourse or correspondence with the devout women of Port Royal, and of the neighboring convent of the Carmelites, many of whom had once been the ornaments of the Court; and there is a proof that she was conscious of being highly valued by them, in the fact that when the Princesse Marie-Madeline, of the Carmelites, was dangerously ill, not being able or not daring to visit her, she sent her youthful portrait to be hung up in the sick-room, and received from the same Mère Agnès, whose grave admonition we have quoted above, a charming note, describing the pleasure which the picture had given in the infirmary of "Notre bonne Mère." She was interesting herself deeply in the translation of the New Testament, which was the work of Sacy, Arnauld, Nicole, Le Maître, and the Duc de Luynes conjointly, Sacy having the principal share. We have mentioned that Arnauld asked her opinion on the Discourse prefixed to his "Logic," and we may conclude from this that he had found her judgment valuable in many other cases. Moreover, the persecution of the Port Royalists had commenced, and she was uniting with Madame de Longueville in aiding and protecting her pious friends. Moderate in her Jansenism, as in everything else, she held that the famous formulary denouncing the Augustinian doctrine, and declaring it to have been originated by Jansenius, should be signed without reserve, and, as usual, she had faith in conciliatory measures; but her moderation was no excuse for inaction. She was at one time herself threatened with the necessity of abandoning her residence at Port Royal, and had thought of retiring to a religious house at Auteuil, a village near Paris. She did, in fact, pass some summers there, and she sometimes took refuge with her brother, the Commandeur de Souvré, with Madame de Montausier, or Madame de Longueville. The last was much bolder in her partisanship than her friend, and her superior wealth and position enabled her to give the Port Royalists more efficient aid. Arnauld and Nicole resided five years in her house; it was under her protection that the translation of the New Testament was carried on and completed, and it was chiefly through her efforts that, in 1669, the persecution was brought to an end. Madame de Sablé co-operated with all her talent and interest in the same direction; but here, as elsewhere, her influence was chiefly valuable in what she stimulated others to do, rather than in what she did herself. It was by her that Madame de Longueville was first won to the cause of Port Royal; and we find this ardent, brave woman constantly seeking the advice and sympathy of her more timid and self-indulgent, but sincere and judicious friend.

In 1669, when Madame de Sablé had at length rest from these anxieties, she was at the good old age of seventy, but she lived nine years longer — years, we may suppose, chiefly dedicated to her spiritual concerns. This gradual, calm decay allayed the fear of death, which had tormented her more vigorous days, and she died with tranquillity and trust. It is a beautiful trait of these last moments, that she desired not to be buried with her family, or even at Port Royal, among her saintly and noble companions, — but in the cemetery of her parish, like one of the people, without pomp or ceremony.

It is worth while to notice that, with Madame de Sablé,

as with some other remarkable French women, the part of her life which is richest in interest and results is that which is looked forward to by most of her sex with melancholy, as the period of decline. When between fifty and sixty, she had philosophers, wits, beauties, and saints clustering around her; and one naturally cares to know what was the elixir which gave her this enduring and general attraction. We think it was, in a great degree, that well-balanced development of mental powers which gave her a comprehension of varied intellectual processes, and a tolerance for varied forms of character, which is still rarer in women than in men. Here was one point of distinction between her and Madame de Longueville; and an amusing passage, which Saint-Beuve has disinterred from the writings of the Abbé St. Pierre, so well serves to indicate, by contrast, what we regard as the great charm of Madame de Sablé's mind, that we shall not be wandering from our subject in quoting it.

" I one day asked M. Nicole what was the character of Madame de Longueville's intellect; he told me it was very subtle and delicate in the penetration of character; but very small, very feeble, and that her comprehension was extremely narrow in matters of science and reasoning, and on all speculations that did not concern matters of sentiment. For example, he added, I one day said to her that I could wager and demonstrate that there were in Paris at least two inhabitants who had the same number of hairs, although I could not point out who these two men were. She told me I could never be sure of it until I had counted the hairs of these two men. Here is my demonstration, I said: I take it for granted that the head which is most amply supplied with hairs has not more than 200,000, and the head which is least so has but one hair. Now, if you suppose that 200,000 heads have each a different number of hairs, it necessarily follows that they have each one of the numbers of hairs which form the series from one to 200,000; for if it were supposed that there were two among these 200,000 who had the same number of hairs, I should have gained my wager. Supposing, then, that these 200,000 inhabitants have all a different number of hairs, if I add a single inhabitant who has hairs, and who has not more than 200,000, it necessarily follows that this number of hairs, whatever it may be, will be con-

tained in the series from one to 200,000, and consequently will be
equal to the number of hairs on one of the previous 200,000 inhabitants. Now as, instead of one inhabitant more than 200,000, there
are nearly 800,000 inhabitants in Paris, you see clearly that there
must be many heads which have an equal number of hairs, though I
have not counted them. Still Madame de Longueville could never
comprehend that this equality of hairs could be demonstrated, and
always maintained that the only way of proving it was to count
them."

Surely, the most ardent admirer of feminine shallowness
must have felt some irritation when he found himself arrested
by this dead wall of stupidity, and have turned with relief
to the larger intelligence of Madame de Sablé, who was not
the less graceful, delicate, and feminine because she could
follow a train of reasoning, or interest herself in a question
of science. In this combination consisted her pre-eminent
charm : she was not a genius, not a heroine, but a woman
whom men could more than love ; whom they could make
their friend, confidante, and counsellor, — the sharer, not of
their joys and sorrows only, but of their ideas and aims.

Such was Madame de Sablé, whose name is, perhaps, new
to some of our readers, so far does it lie from the surface of
literature and history. We have seen, too, that she was only
one amongst a crowd — one in a firmament of feminine stars
which, when once the biographical telescope is turned upon
them, appear scarcely less remarkable and interesting. Now
if the reader recollects what was the position and average intellectual character of women in the high society of England
during the reigns of James the First and the two Charleses, —
the period through which Madame de Sablé's career extends,
— we think he will admit our position as to the early superiority of womanly development in France, and this fact, with
its causes, has not merely an historical interest : it has an
important bearing on the culture of women in the present
day. Women become superior in France by being admitted
to a common fund of ideas, to common objects of interest
with men ; and this must ever be the essential condition at

once of true womanly culture and of true social well-being. We have no faith in feminine conversazioni, where ladies are eloquent on Apollo and Mars; though we sympathize with the yearning activity of faculties which, deprived of their proper material, waste themselves in weaving fabrics out of cobwebs. Let the whole field of reality be laid open to woman as well as to man, and then that which is peculiar in her mental modification, instead of being, as it is now, a source of discord and repulsion between the sexes, will be found to be a necessary complement to the truth and beauty of life. Then we shall have that marriage of minds which alone can blend all the hues of thought and feeling in one lovely rainbow of promise for the harvest of human happiness.

MARGARET FULLER.

O UR prediction as to the rich harvest of American biography that is now ripening finds a beautiful fulfilment in the "Memoirs of Margaret Fuller Ossoli." Reading this book after Carlyle's "Life of Sterling," we are reminded, by their similarity of subject and authorship, as well as by their simultaneous preparation, that it is "the same spirit which ✓ worketh all in all." There is a noticeable resemblance between these two gifted beings: their studies, aspirations, endeavors, and influence were of a similar nature; they had the same unsettled career and the same premature end. But Margaret Fuller had a deeper, stronger, richer life, and wielded a mightier power over her companions and contemporaries. If her aim was not higher, it was clearer; and what she aimed at she accomplished. It is not, however, in contrast with Sterling, but in the midst of her friends, that we must view her. Considering the remarkable influence she exercised over the circle which ultimately acknowledged her as its ruling spirit, we are at a loss whether to regard her as the parent or child of New England transcendentalism. Perhaps neither the one nor the other. It seems to have been a movement on the part of different minds, as spontaneous and independent in each as it was simultaneous in all, — a movement flowing from the undying vernal impulse of nature. It was essentially an intellectual, moral, and spiritual regeneration ; a renewing of the whole man; a kindling of his aspirations after full development of faculty and perfect symmetry of being. Then followed the fruits of this spirit, — faith, hope, and love; self-sacrifice, mutual sympathy, fellowship, and earnest endeavor. "Thus, by mere attraction of affinity," says Mr. Channing, "grew together the brotherhood of the 'like-minded,' as they were pleasantly nicknamed by outsiders and by themselves, on the ground that no two were of the same opinion." Of this sect Margaret Fuller was the priestess. In conversation she was as copious and oracular as Coleridge, brilliant as Sterling, pungent and paradoxical as Carlyle; gifted with the inspired powers of a pythoness, she saw into the hearts and over the heads of all who came near her; and, but for a sympathy as boundless as her self-esteem, she would have despised the whole human race! Her frailty, in this respect, was no secret either to herself or her friends. She quizzed them and boasted of herself to such an excess as to turn disgust into laughter, — yea, so right royally did she carry herself that her arrogance became a virtue, worshipful as the majesty of the gods! Yet along with all this there was much self-scrutiny; and underneath it all much womanly tenderness, which ripened and mellowed till, after all, few women were more womanly than Margaret Fuller. "Very early," she says, "she perceived that the great object of life was to grow;" and with rare courage she put no check even upon the growth of her infirmities, convinced, no doubt, that it required only a corresponding growth of some other qualities to constitute them her glory and her crown. That supplementary growth subsequent events tended to foster. The two sides of her more mature character — the tender and the strong — were harmonized and tested by the peculiar position into which she was thrown during her sojourn at Rome, at the time of the Revolution. We have not space to explain our allusions to those who have not read, or do not intend to read, these Memoirs for themselves; but in indicating our general opinion of her character, we must say that from the time she became a mother till the final tragedy when she perished with her husband and child within sight of her native shore, she was an altered woman, and evinced a greatness of soul and heroism of character so grand and subduing that we feel disposed to extend to her whole career the admiration and sympathy inspired by the closing scenes. While her

reputation was at its height in the literary circles of Boston
and New York, she was so self-conscious that her life seemed
to be a studied *act*, rather than a spontaneous growth ; but this
was the mere flutter on the surface. The well was deep, and
the spring genuine ; and it is creditable to her friends, as well
as to herself, that such at all times was their belief.

We have already spoken of her in connection with Sterling.
Both have found kindred spirits to write their biographies ;
but Emerson and his colleagues must yield to Carlyle in
mastery of the pencil. The "Life of Sterling," though made
up of fragments and reminiscences, is a finished portrait.
But the "Memoirs of Margaret Fuller" is a book of reminiscences merely. No attempt is made at symmetry of form or
color ; nor are even the outward events of her life presented
in their consecutive order. Something like an appropriation
of periods and localities seems to have been prearranged, but
not attended to ; and according to the caprice of the writer's
memory you are carried hither and thither, backwards and
forwards, over the scenes of her history. A little more attention to chronology and geography would have mended the
matter considerably, and made the mechanism of the narrative as good as the material. "Memoirs," then, — memo-
randa, — not a life, yet full of life and full of thought, —
these volumes will be read and prized by all truth-loving,
sympathetic souls.

GEORGE FORSTER.

WE do not know a more touchingly tragical history than that of George Forster, who closed in so·lonely and wretched a manner that life which, as a boy, he began so dazzlingly; leaping, when yet in his teens, into startling fame, and winning the lively interest of all Europe as the companion of Cook, and the recounter of his second expedition to those blessed isles of the Southern Sea. Other lives have been more violently checkered, or rent by abrupter incidents; but the web of none has been so altogether spun with the threads of straitened penury and grinding distress. It is curious to observe the course of lives: there are some whose very accidental adventures are pitched into such wondrous tune with their owners' tempers, that fancy might stray to the thought of a moulding destiny designing their career from womb to death, — lives the turns and meetings of which strike so into their tendencies, that they foster them, whether for weal or woe, as it were out of necessity, and beyond any aid or power of repression of their own. Doubtless, when closely viewed, the mystery proves to be only that such souls, endowed with lively quickness, seize on everything akin to their promptings, while dullards stumble blindly on their way, and mysterious destiny resolves itself into a goodly dose of enterprise. There are other lives which offer analogies more worthy of consideration: the lives of the children of their age, showing its sum total in their thoughts and doings as the blood and type of family come out in its offspring; the chance adventurers, who are transformed and diverted to their own purposes and feelings, as deluges turn to flooded lakes or rivers, according to the nature of the country that takes them in. Such men exist at all times; for times are the work of men, and in the summary of the man we learn to know mankind. George Forster was one of these. All his thoughts and doings are the utterings of that strange eighteenth century; as a boy turned into a mighty traveller suiting his age's spirit of inquiry, he remains his whole life long an eager, restless wanderer, an Ishmaelite on the face of his century, ever seeking and peering on to a brighter future; his temper is marked by that simple and undoubting trust in new perfections and coming certainties, with a credulous leaning to all novel and hidden truths, prevalent in his age, when man awoke to belief after centuries of slumber; his heart is honest and generous, his spirit eager, and freed from all he considers prejudice, — allowing itself to soar into regions, the subtle air of which is too rare to live in; a sufferer by his father's unbridled humors, in married life not slightly tried, and if not wholly wrecked then, saved only by a lifeboat of most thorough eighteenth-century build; renowned as a sailor round the world, and as the man who had brought to Europe knowledge of friendly savages, and who could, from personal acquaintance, describe new realms of nature and mankind to the sickened age yearning for fancied archetypes of man and the world; — all these characteristics give a special zest to poor George Forster's life. In short, we see mirrored in his history the whole painful lot and social shackling of a man of science of those days in Germany, and how a thinking and feeling mind became drifted athwart them into perilous rapids and breakneck eddies; we see a man gifted with the highest abilities and soundest learning, strong in spirit and heart, moreover privileged with a hold on the tastes of the public from the very nature of his fame, — we see this man, in spite of his advantages, doomed to toil his whole life long beneath a weight of trammels, unable to find the hand that might drag him out of the choking mudsloughs of rotten petty courts, until at last he topples over the mighty chasm of the French Revolution. To the English public he is wholly unknown, — to that of his own country, by a freak of destiny, he was until lately only notorious; for while straitened circumstances deprived his fine intellect of that repose, as necessary to its nurture as light and space are to a tree to enable it to put forth perfect fruit, the peculiarities of his political adventures exposed him to an ill wind which blasted his memory. Almost all Forster's writings partake of a fragmentary nature and hasty slightness of design, which were imparted to them of a necessity from the enforced circumstances of their production. They are mostly essays, contributed regularly to journals, or prefaces to translations of travels, undertaken at the bidding of publishers; but as soon as we look at them, we perceive a fund of learning, lively feeling, and suggestive thought set forth in wording so full of natural charm, that we at once guess a mind of no common power to be at work here. Twice only in the course of his hard-working life did he get respite enough to be able to undertake a connected production, — the first time, when, hardly past his boyhood, he wrote that account of his voyage with Cook, which at once made his name known all over the world; the second time, just before the close of his career, when he began, but did not finish, his journey through Brabant and England. The two volumes he accomplished are his most perfect literary work, and show what would have been the fulness of Forster. Here is a mass of thoughtful observation and rich suggestion. The whole tone and scope of his writing were wholly different from the abstractness and vagueness from which no German thinker of his day was free; it had the life of reality about it, and his truthful feeling and keen eye made him so lively an expounder of nature, that his method and style were the chosen model of Humboldt, as Forster's example was his first incentive to scientific exploration.

The youth he had spent in his country had accustomed his mind to the ways of public life, and imparted to it habits of practical thought, which impregnated his whole being, and distinguished him for readiness of bearing amidst the dim haziness of his countrymen. His turn of mind found in the study of natural science the only nurture which the arid social system of Germany left for it; but as soon as the great French Revolution loosened the stoniness in which he had been bound, the promptings of his nature made him strike at once into the genial soil of politics. In truth, the quickenings of his mind were those that stamp the citizen; he was public-spirited in the true sense of the word; and bred in self-governing England, accustomed to public enterprise and rule, he stood before his countrymen, in the delicately organized manifoldness of his constitution, in the sparkle of his renown, and in charm of writing, like a prophet whose words, passing their understanding, were coarsely maligned. Therefore people's minds turned away from Forster until, when after near half a century the growth of enlightenment stirred up feelings of independence, men found that in him they had possessed one whose sound and patriotic aspirations had been altogether calumniated, and who combined the qualities of a noble intellect with the virtues of the citizen.

It is the interesting history of this man that Heinrich König recounts in a book undertaken under the inspiration of times in many respects akin to those of his hero, and written with a most intimate knowledge of the scenery of the story's plot. For many years he has studied every detail, however petty, of German history of the end of the last century; and before he entertained any thought of this book, he had already written a novel on the Revolution of Mayence, which is a wonderfully accurate picture of the times, and the close researches for which had made him intimately acquainted with many parts of Forster's life.

George Forster was born on the 26th November, 1754, at the poor village of Nassenhuben, near Danzig, where his father, whose Christian names were John Reinhold, was the Calvinistic minister. He had been driven to this calling by his father, who had been highly displeased on learning that his son, while a student at Halle, had taken the liberty to desert the law for medicine and the natural sciences, in which

7

he had made considerable progress. It thus happened that
he was, as it were, turned off cramped from the very starting-
post, and all through life's race he limped. Though ever an
honest Protestant, science was more his love than theology,
and the straits of his position chafed his temper to that iras-
cibility which afterwards so marred his good and sterling
parts. His son, who amidst all his trials never laid aside a
most dutiful bearing towards him, strikes off the following
sketch of him once in a letter to Jacobi: —

" My father is, in every respect, a useful man for the sciences, —
possessed of solid learning, choice reading, and book-lore, besides being
a good naturalist, antiquary, and also theologian, although the last
study does not occupy him any more, nor can it interest him scientifi-
cally, as I think. His warmth, hot temper, and eager battling for
his ideas, have done him immeasurable harm, as it is also his misfortune that he does not know, and never will know, mankind, — always
suspicious and credulous exactly there where he should not be so."

We can fancy the quarrelsome divine plagued by his boor-
ish parishioners in the midst of his study of Buffon, and flying into whims of wrongs under the friction of such daily
worries. The living was not a fat one, while his family —
for he early married a cousin — was the contrary of meagre ;
seven children required feeding, and the means to do so were
not ready at hand. Under these circumstances the elder
Forster, with his hankering for the sciences and his discontent with his parish, jumped at an offer made to him by the
Russian Government to inspect and report on the new colo-
nies founded on the banks of the Volga. Taking his son
George, then eleven years old, with him, he spent the summer of 1765 in performing the journey and returning to St.
Petersburg ; in the autumn he handed in his report, the matter of which is said to have been so good as to have given the
Empress suggestions for her great code of laws. His blus-
tering temper, however, which often proved his worst enemy,
closed his promising career in Russia ; and he spent the winter in St. Petersburg, urging obstinate claims for recompense

and imperturbably refusing to accept the offers made. During this time his wants drove him to the shifts of a translator,
in which he called his boy to his aid, who was following the
course of lessons at the high-school, and who thus early was
broken in to his life-long drudgery of an overworked literary
hack. At last the priest-sage gave vent to his anger with
the Russian Government, and left St. Petersburg with the
satisfaction of having at least had his will, if not the very
sum of money, and none other than that which he had made
his mind up to have. But if St. Petersburg and the Russias
were well behind him and his son, it was not very clear what
land lay ahead. The good Christians of Nassenhuben had
provided themselves, during their high-priest's gaddings
about on the Volga, with some ghostly vice-regent, who seems
to have been unwilling to give up his realm on his lord's
advent; and so John Reinhold, who perhaps rather liked the
chance, conscious of his real acquirements and sphere of action, took the sudden resolve to seek his fortune in England,
and, without even visiting his wife or family, sailed thither
with his son. They sturdily fought off the dreariness of the
voyage, lengthened by storms, with the study of English; and
soon after their arrival, the father's solid scientific knowledge
having gained him the good-will of many distinguished men
in London, he was appointed teacher of natural history at an
educational institution for dissenting clergymen, at Warrington in Lancashire. George was apprenticed to a Russian
merchant named Lewin; but the sedentary application of this
life so pulled the youth down, that when, on his mother and
sisters' arrival, he escorted them to Warrington, his father
became alarmed at his favorite child's looks, and kept him
by him. George was thus brought back to the study of the
natural sciences under his father's immediate influence; and
as the latter soon embroiled himself, as usual, with his supe-
riors, while the wants of his large family caused him to feel
sorely pinched in his resources, the son had to put himself
into the family traces, and help sturdily to keep the household van going. We find him, therefore, not only combining

the parts of scholar and teacher, learning botany and zoölogy from his restless father, and teaching French and German in a neighboring school to those who ought to have been his playfellows, but the poor youth's strength was still further strained by continual translations of foreign books of travels into English. Thus early was the boy brought to encounter those hardships of life whose freaks, in spite of his bold struggle, it was never his lot to be able to say that he was freed from. From this time of his life a story remains which is told by all his biographers, as foreshadowing in its small burden the haphazards which so often befell him, and the temper with which he took them. The pygmy professor's road to his lecture-chair lay past a pastry-cook's savory stall of sweet cakes, and the tale of this temptation ended as temptations will end when brought to bear on lively flesh and blood; the savor tingled through his veins, till, wholly rapt by its witchery, he swallowed as many cakes as he could cram. The cook, however, like a crafty worldly cook, only considered his pies' sweetness as the means of barter; and before their taste was off poor George's lips, the horror of dunnery and dismay of debt cut short his relish. Shame made him skulk along back ways; but the sharp cook's twinkling eyes would flash on him still, until his little heart burst forth its bitter distress in a fervent prayer, when, lo! on crossing the next fence on his hiding by-path, his eye caught sight of a guinea embedded in a horse's tread, and, having run to pay his debts, he bought with the remainder a gilt thimble for his sister. Painful troubles and dribbling windfalls of luck are indeed the tissue of his whole life; but if a lowness of spirit did come over him for a season in his gloomy times, one sunny ray was ever enough to lighten his heart and make it beat high and bold.

Under all these circumstances, and with the peculiar keen temper of Dr. John Reinhold Forster, it will be easily believed that he clutched at the sudden offer to accompany Cook as naturalist on his expedition. He only bargained to be allowed to take with him his son, then seventeen years of age; and so hurried was their departure that only nine days intervened between decision on the journey and embarkation. The history of this voyage is known to most persons. At that time all Europe eagerly watched its result; for since the discovery of America, no geographical riddles had so whetted its curiosity as those of the great Southern Sea. The fashionable idyllic sentimentalism of those times, so fostered by the hothouse breathings of B. de St. Pierre and Rousseau, was fascinated by the gentle savages and peaceful virgin isles of whose reality Cook's first voyage had given the certainty; and all the smirking skirmishers of enlightenment were on the eager look-out for new and startling confirmation of their yearning dreams. How the many and large views of nature such a journey brought with it must have impressed the quick mind of young Forster, already so given to a wandering, shifting life, can be easily conceived. The driest man could not have met with such a chance at such an age of his life without learning from it somewhat which lasted for the remainder of it. George Forster bore away with him that largeness of views on nature and man which so nobly marked his thoughts in all stages of his life; he got his mind enriched with a tender, yet a large and manly sense of nature's beauty, whose healthy freshness contrasted as vividly with the mawkish feeling of those times as a peasant girl's ruddy cheek with a painted face; but he also bore away from these three roving years a hankering after travel which never left him, and to which, under the weight of trouble, he was too apt to give himself up, as the drinker grasps at his dram, while the seeds of lasting illness were laid in his body by an attack of scurvy.

The enjoyment of these pleasures was somewhat marred by painful embarrassments arising from fresh outbursts of his father's wild temper, which chafed at the discipline of a man-of-war, entailing on the commander the necessity of severe measures to repress his mutinous freaks. The youth himself was, however, a favorite with Cook; and the language in which he speaks of him in a biographical sketch, written

many years later, shows how thoroughly he knew the worth
of that daring seaman's character. But when, on the return
of the expedition, the Doctor, with headstrong stubbornness,
ran foul of the Admiralty itself, George was dragged into the
quarrel, or from filial love rushed into it to a degree which
had a lasting influence. It seems that the elder Forster had
not fully understood the meaning of his engagement with
the Government, according to which no account of the voyage was to be published before the official one: the Admiralty, therefore, stopped the publication of a work he was
preparing; and in consequence of the fiery naturalist's per-
sistence in contesting its right to do so, it proceeded to an act
which seems harsh, and might have maddened many a quieter
man so laden with troubles, who saw his hopes of gain vanish, and nothing before him but poverty, debts, and a starving family, — it despoiled him of any share in the proposed
Government publication. The blow was a desperate one.
Yet even now the old man could not curb his temper ever so
little, or matters would still have come to run more smoothly :
George himself says as much in a letter of later date, although at all times he held his father to have been unjustly
and most cruelly treated. As no mention of his own name
had been made in the engagement with Government, he
balked the Admiralty's precautions (probably at his father's
desire) by writing himself an account of the voyage, — a pro-
ceeding which at the time exposed him to much abuse, and
poisoned the quarrel beyond remedy. In this work the journey and the countries visited are described with simple truth,
and a color which shows how thoroughly his soul had become
impregnated with the sunny warmth of the tropics. The
artlessness of the account has a charm which carries the
reader away, and is sufficient proof that, although the father
looked over the scientific description of animals and flowers,
the bulk of the work is entirely George's own. The success
of the book was great; the author's name became at once
well known, and the poor family garrets in Percy Street were
enlivened by the hail of many a foreigner, anxious to see the

lucky travellers who had, beyond doubt, beheld and been in the happy South Sea Isles. It was on the occasion of such a pilgrimage that George was first brought together with a young German physician, whose name was Sömmering. He had come over to England to attend its medical schools; and that attraction which had drawn him unto his renowned countrymen grew quickly into the tightest bonds of friendship with the younger of them, fastened by kinship in studies, and probably also by ties of masonic brotherhood, which then, and for many years after, largely took hold of their minds in that alchemistic form under which it so mightily swayed the thought of Europe of that century.

The proceeds of the book were, unfortunately, small in money; starvation daily haunted the wretched dwelling, barely staved off by petty gifts from a friend, or some German princeling, coaxed into dribbling forth scanty alms by a present of South Sea rarities; the sale of the latter also came to an absolute standstill, and the Admiralty was deaf to the roar of claims, till at last hard-hearted creditors came down on the forlorn family, and bore away its mainstay and pillar, and dreary King's Bench shut on the chafing Doctor. It was indeed a bleak and starving future which George had then to look upon, — his father imprisoned and no prospect of relief, his mother sick and his sisters weak and helpless, while he himself was racked by continued ill-health maiming the sinews of his good-will to work. He soon had to yield to the conviction that in England there was no chance of obtaining aid; so, with the one thought of straining his utmost nerve for his parents, he turned himself to his native country, from which sundry cheers of fellow-feeling had at times gladdened the wretchedness of Percy Street. Making up, therefore, a bale of dried plants and other specimens of natural history, in the hope some continental museums might buy them, he, whose name was then trumpeted forth as the foremost of explorers, embarked at Harwich, to cross to Holland as an anxious pedler and seeker of alms. Nothing can be more touching than to read in his letters to his parents his grief at their sorrows, and his unflinching trust in Providence: —

"I am well and fresh" (he writes to his father), "resigned, and full of trust that God will not forsake us; he has often proved his exceeding goodness, and will deliver us out of our present evil chances and hardships, which have weighed us down for these last years. I submit to all trials with the firm trust that they are meant for our best, and believe that, while I leave everything to the ordaining of the most perfect Being, I act neither unrighteously nor forwardly if I beseech him daily for the peace and earthly welfare of us all; for also here on earth we can reach to a certain pitch of happiness, and why, then, should we not pray for it?"

In these words we meet with two thoughts, which are the groundwork of Forster's belief and lively trust in the happy ending of all chances, which, through every distress, kept him from continued hopelessness, yet never stiffened into dull fatalism, and a strong religious feeling, full of devout yearnings, but with an inborn loathing of all strained asceticism.

Though he was received by the learned men of Holland with the most flattering kindness, and every sort of civil attention was paid him, he soon saw that he could have no hopes of bettering his family by any help from that country. In his letter to his mother he pours out the sorrow of his heart: —

"My hopes to dispose of something here have been driven to the winds. There is, in plain speaking, no possibility of doing so. I am in the hands of Almighty God, and yield myself to his ordaining. Before me I see nothing but darkness; but let his will be done. Amen! Oh, alas, my poor heart! I can write no more. . . . The thought on mine in England has given me many a troubled moment. Are you well, dearest mother? — are you at all at rest? Does God send you comfort and courage in the tribulation which you have to undergo? Has no new need befallen our sorely pressed house?"

Driven on by such painful thoughts, George hastened to Germany, reproaching himself with the slightest delay. At Dusseldorf, then renowned for its galleries of art, he was, however, waylaid by Jacobi, who, with enthusiastic kindness,

as soon as hè heard of the famed traveller's arrival, wrote him
before daybreak a pressing invitation to spend a whole day
with him. Forster was fascinated by the society he was
introduced to, and that spell in Jacobi's bearing which had
ravished Goethe with delight. One of the lords of the German commonwealth of letters, the bosom friend of Goethe
and of its chief leaders, whom he loved to gather around him
at his country-seat at Pempelfort, he enthralled the loving
temper of young Forster by the welling forth of his speech,
which he would let flow in the full stream of enthusiasm.
Forster found himself transferred, as it were by a wizard's
wand, into the very midst of the choicest spirits of Germany,
while the charm of Jacobi's kindly hospitality soothed his
aching heart like balm. The latest poems of Goethe ; snatches
from "Woldemar," which Jacobi was then writing ; freshly
received letters from the stars of literature, — were the treats
which, during four days, were thrust on Forster, spiced by
the touching kindness of his host and his sisters ; he tore
himself from Dusseldorf, enraptured with his new friends.
"Such people as these we shall not meet again on our whole
journey," was his exclamation to Alexander von Humboldt,
when, twelve years later, on their trip to England, they
turned out of their way to visit Jacobi.
　Cassel was the goal of his immediate expectations. He
had hopes that the new Landgrave, Frederick II., who partook
of the fashionable taste for dallying with enlightenment, provided it could be done cheaply, might be tempted to gain a
man of his father's fame for his new high-school. This sovereign, who, during his father's lifetime, had forsaken his
Protestant faith and ancestral views in politics, had, since his
accession to his states, calmed the lively fears of the old
servants of his house by steadily settling down into all the
good old family ways. Although remaining a Catholic himself, he swore, as a true son of Hesse, to the maintenance of
Protestantism in his country ; and, quitting forthwith the
Austrian Court, with which while heir apparent he had been
unmindful enough of his blood to flirt, he left off all new-

fangled whims, to the delight of his gray-haired ministers,
ruling as his father had ruled before him, to the comfort of
himself and the fattening of his exchequer, which he shrewdly
enriched by selling twenty-two thousand true Hessians to
England for £7,000,000. If the sum seemed large, it also
appears that the Landgrave had many calls for it. But
George soon saw his hopes vanish afresh; the whole of the
funds allotted for the mental enlightenment of such Hessians
as were not gaining it in another way in America, had been
sunk in a parcel of rubbishy marbles, which were their
owner's joy and pride. A sum that might have freed the
starving traveller from King's Bench, and have allowed him
and his family to live at Cassel, could not possibly be made
forthcoming; but, in its stead, his Highness deigned to
admit George to a gracious audience in his statue gallery,
and insisted on his delaying his filial researches till after the
next sitting of his Academy of Antiquities, at which he accordingly held a discourse ; and at last the Landgrave not only
accepted a copy of the father's books, but even strained his
poverty to the disbursing of a gift of fifty louis, besides thrust-
ing on the unwilling son the appointment of professor of
natural history at the University of Cassel, with the dazzling
salary of seventy pounds. It is touching to read how anxiously
Forster debated with his conscience, whether he would be
justified in accepting anything for himself as long as he had
not achieved that relief for his parents which he had set out
to seek ; and when at last he did accept, it was with the express understanding that he should be allowed certain months
of absence, wherein he might bring his endeavors to a satisfactory result. At Göttingen he made acquaintances which
afterwards ripened into friendship, — especially that of
Heyne; and he wrote a letter to his father — who he evidently feared might misinterpret his proceedings — in which
he tried to enliven his gloom by the friendly greetings of the
leading members of that University ; but such kindly wishes
were all he reaped, both here and at Berlin, with the excep-
tion of a pittance of one hundred louis from the Prince of

Dessau, bestowed in a warm-hearted manner, and coupled with the promise to use his influence in England with the Admiralty, to obtain some recompense, which, however, proved vain. Such painful disappointments did not allow Forster to begin his stay at Cassel, in the spring of 1779, with a light heart; and his correspondence reveals his writhing efforts to burst his father's prison bars, when, in the forlorn midnight of this gloom, a hidden hand all of a sudden thrust comfort and freedom on the wretched family. The masonic lodges of Germany, at the call of the Duke of Brunswick, their grand-master, paid the father's debts, while the chair of natural history at Halle was to provide for his maintenance. True, however, to his self-willed temper, he nearly marred his own luck; for he could not for a long while be brought to give up the character of a victim, and insisted on his just claims, spurning what he deemed a dishonorable compromise, till the earnest entreaties of his family and the smarting reminiscences of imprisonment at last softened his resolve. If this happy event freed George's mind from a load of care, the spring of his spirits was now still further braced by a new piece of luck. Sömmering, the brother of his heart, — he to whom in the heyday of betrothal he wrote, "Love itself yields to the bond of soul which links me to thee," — obtained the professorship of anatomy at Cassel, by dint of sundry diplomatic wiles which his eager friend suggested to him; for the Landgrave had snatched up the crotchet, that only Frenchmen knew the science, and it wanted no little knack to master his whims. With such intercourse to encourage him, he set to his duties with eagerness, employing his leisure hours with a translation of Buffon, to the account of which were put sundry trips to the library of Göttingen, which were perhaps suggested, if the whole truth were known, by other promptings than those of absolute literary research. Nor was the society of Cassel wanting in interest; besides many men of more or less distinction who were attached to its high-school, it counted the illustrious historian, Johannes von Müller, amongst its residents, between whom and Forster an intimacy sprang up; so that, had it not been for other discomforts, he might have contentedly endured the petty worries of Court attendance; for the Landgrave regarded his University, with its staff, as his toys, and Forster found, on promotion to the inspectorship of a most threadbare cabinet of natural history, that he shared with the statue gallery the honor of being his Highness's chief entertainer. But the want of money, the canker of his life, soon made its gnawings felt. The pittance of his salary, and the loss by shipwreck of all his little property on its way from England, had made it impossible for the famished youth to start his establishment, however frugally, without a loan the cost of which shackled him like a galley-chain. Jacobi, with whom he kept a close correspondence, in which he poured forth his sorrow into his kind and sympathetic heart, had already of himself devised how to help his friend to ease, by procuring for him the administratorship of the proposed new customs board for the Duchy of Berg, intending to pay from his own purse the required security of thirty thousand thalers, when his hopes were disappointed by the abandonment of the whole plan. He now, therefore, on hearing of his friend's straits, came forward at once with his generous feeling, and thrust on him a loan of twenty-five pistoles in so brotherly a manner, that Forster was forced to yield all misgivings about its acceptance. But this sum was far from enough to insure him from further difficulties. In consequence of the miserable resources of the University, he found himself obliged to provide books at his own outlay, and, in spite of convulsive attempts at thriftiness, debt dogged him like a spectre. "Fy! fy! I can't get a book to look at here, unless I buy it," he writes to Jacobi. "Cassel is a perfect wilderness, as regards new books, for the annual sum allotted for procuring such for the Prince's library does not amount to £60." Under such circumstances it is easy to feel that alchemistic notions, if once allowed to be at all entertained, must have involuntarily lured him on with absorbing temptations.

Freemasonry, in the garb of Illumination and Rosicrucian-
ism, at that time had largely laid hold of the mind of Germany. Its many interturnings are not easy to unravel
through the mazes of its stealthy course ; but in every court
and in every high-school its high-priests were then to be
found, — for the catholic tone of its mystic language had
charms for the most varied tempers, — and thus, at the dawn
of the sunrise of modern science, we see the smouldering
embers of the alchemist's nightly furnaces flare through the
breadth of the land once more into flame, fanned by the
adroit breathings of jugglers on that vein of faith which ran,
as it were, in irony so fully through an age boastful that the
amulet of enlightenment shielded it from reach of dupery
and superstition. The Rosicrucians were especially devoted
to this scientific dressing up of mysticism ; and the possibility of finding prime matter endowed with the virtues of an
universal medicine and the transmutation of metals was seriously entertained by men of learning, and its research followed by many. We know that both the Forsters were keen
freemasons ; and a letter from George to Heyne informs
us that it was through masonry that he became intimately
acquainted with the Rosicrucians. Sömmering, his bosom
friend, had joined the brotherhood, which counted amongst
its active members most of the leading professors of Cassel ;
and even the great Johannes von Müller had allowed the
shrewd twinkle of his keen sight to be hoodwinked for the
nonce. Eagerly and fervently did these associates stimulate
each other in the prosecution of what they held to be the
great work, conjointly with their brethren spread on the surface of the globe. At this time an event happened which
startled the scientific world, and the tidings of which were
caught up with nervous eagerness by the brethren of Cassel.
The witheringly sarcastic Lichtenberg, that keen intellect the
bolts of whose wit loved to split the very heart of humbug,
seriously communicated to his friend Forster trustworthy
accounts of transmutations of metals by Dr. Price, in England, in the presence of competent witnesses. The doings

of this man were, indeed, such as to attract general attention. A member of the Royal Society, and a wealthy practitioner in Guildford, he believed or professed to have discovered a powder able to change silver or mercury into gold; and after two years spent in doubt (as he averred) whether to publish or keep secret his discovery, he spoke of it to some friends, one of whom was Grose the antiquary, and to whom he even showed proofs of his skill. Success emboldened him to lay aside his fears, so that during several months of the year 1782 he exhibited before anybody who chose to visit him at Guildford, evidence of his power to change mercury into gold and silver by means of certain white and reddish powders; and at last, on the 30th of May of that year, he produced an ingot of silver weighing two ounces, which he offered as a present to the King. All this he described in a pamphlet, containing numerous testimonials signed by unexceptionable witnesses, — amongst them Lords Onslow, King, and Palmerston. On the demand, however, of the Royal Society, that its fellow should renew his marvels before a chosen board, Price refused to do so, on the ground that he had exhausted his stock of philosopher's powder, the preparation of which required much time; and that, as a Rosicrucian, he was bound to maintain the secrets of the craft. Finding, however, that by such excuses his credit was thoroughly shaken, he retired, in January, 1783, to his laboratory at Guildford, announcing that he would be back in London in a month; and, having first prepared a large decoction of laurel juice and written his will, he shut himself up in his study, when six months passed by before the world again heard of him. The Royal Society, at the end of that time, received an invitation to visit him in a body on a certain day; but when, instead of the whole society, he saw but one or two of his colleagues arrive, he was so stung at the contempt shown for him and his discovery, that, entering his closet, he destroyed himself with the poison he had prepared. Before the melancholy end happened, the announcement of Price's success excited the greatest interest; and was not Forster's heart made to leap with a fevered heat, when the hope of escape from poverty seemed to be visibly beckoning to him ? It is nowhere clearly stated how far he allowed himself to be practically inveigled into great loss of time. Forster acknowledges in letters, and König supposes, that both he and Sömmering melted away much useful money in their Rosicrucian crucibles. It was not, however, a greedy want of gold which had been our friend's snare; his heart, in mysticism, was noble as in everything else. The mystic piety of language and the cosmogonic professions of the society had enticed his religious feeling and his inquiring mind. In letters to Sömmering, he prays that the Spirit of Jesus might lead them in holiness, forbearance, and love; and in the following extract from a letter, written to his bride after his breaking off with all secret brotherhoods, will be found a picture of his hopes and delusions : —

"You know that I was a dreamy enthusiast; but few people could be aware how far I was one, and to what degree I had allowed myself to be carried away, for I held it as a duty to keep it hidden. I have believed everything. The conviction that those who had misled me into this faith were morally bad *themselves*, opened my eyes. I thought, then, that I saw the whole pile of this fabric of faith resting on the point of a needle, which on inquiry I found to be itself rusted and crumbling. I was like one who awakes from a heavy dream, and finds that he has escaped danger of death. . . . Nothing is more intoxicating for one so vain as I was, as to look upon the great interlinkings in the plan of creation; to be drawn near to God, — viewing, as it were, through him to read and overlook that universe in concentration which seems to lie before us in disorder that baffles understanding ; to be the familiar of the world of spirits, — one's self a little demigod, whole lord of the creation ; and to know all, even the yet hidden powers of nature ; — all this by the easiest means in the world, through boundless seraphic love of the most perfect Being, intimate communion in spirit with him, self-denial in the highest degree, a forsaking of all vanity, continued ascetic intercourse with him, and a contemplative as well as practical spying by experiments into nature, &c. From such a height as this, the fall, as can be foreseen, was far from soft."

It is the greatest proof of Forster's healthy soundness, that when he did wake to the self-knowledge of his trance, it was to renewed strength, — as illness cleanses a strong body of a surfeit of bad humors. He wished himself joy that he had thrown off such a change of dreaminess before his thirtieth year; and, taking up his studies with no loss of true enthusiasm, he zealously tried to lessen the heap of debt which his mistakes had probably helped to pile up, by renewed translations and active contributions to literary journals. He, who by the chances of his early life had seemed to have been born at once to manhood, had proved how all must pay Nature's debts, and, having cheated her of his childishness in his teens, she had exacted from his manhood payment of her calls. But now Forster the *man* was born, and he was a goodly and a noble man. "The past is behind me," he says in the letter last quoted, "and I still retain a burning desire to arrive at the best possible insight of what we call truth, which my nature is able to arrive at."

In spite, however, of this sturdy spirit, Cassel and all belonging to it had become loathsome to him. The remembrance of his errors was there continually thrust upon his thoughts, and all social enjoyment poisoned by Sömmering's trouble of mind, who, a true comrade to the last, had left at the same time with him the brotherhood which they had entered together, but bore away so trembling a fear of the wrath of its fellows, that it haunted his every step, and kept such a hold of his mind, even until his death in 1830, that when Forster's widow was preparing his letters for publication in 1829, Sömmering not only refused to contribute those in his keeping, but entreated her, even by threats, not to broach a hint, in her sketch of her husband's life, as to any connection with secret societies. Against such daily wrong of life neither learned dissertations on the bread-fruit and other points of natural history, nor translations of books of travels, proved sufficient antidotes; and he who had already feverishly exclaimed that a great journey alone could restore him to usefulness, can be well believed to have felt quickenings of joy at the sudden chance of removal to a new world. He was offered the professorship of natural history at Wilna in Poland, and accepted it, not merely on his own hasty promptings, but by the counsel of such wary friends as Lichtenberg and Heyne. The conditions were, in fact, such as might have tempted many a literary man : besides a fair salary, a sum was settled for correspondence and the purchase of specimens of natural history, while the flattering language of the Primate Poniatowsky's letter was backed by subscriptions which freed him from his liabilities at Cassel, and provided for his travelling outlay. Thus, at a moment when the atmosphere of Cassel choked his manly vigor, luck seemed to shower on him the very windfall befitting his wants ; and with the good cheer with which he had formerly run to buy his sister a thimble with the chance sovereign that saved him from his boyish scrapes, he now leapt forward to snatch the happiness which seemed to be beckoning him.

Happiness this time appeared to him in the guise of a young girl of twenty. During his visits to Göttingen he had learnt to know Theresa Heyne, and had been struck by her feeling disposition and artless liveliness. She had been brought up in early youth at a distance from home ; and a freedom of carriage, thus contracted from habit, was increased by the enthusiasm of her temperament, while daily intercouse with the distinguished men who frequented her father's house fostered a feverish liking for all which partook of intellectual superiority and excellence. Her feelings with regard to Forster are told by herself in the following words, written when the reflection of age threw its clear, steady light upon the dark eddies of her life : —

"The girl had seen Forster repeatedly on his visits to Göttingen during his stay at Cassel ; and the most heartfelt regard, which lasted till his death, gave her trust in him, while compassion for the forlorn position which awaited him in lonely Poland, hearty feeling, youthful spirit, and pride, spurred her to share the stern lot of the famed man ; and thus she gave Forster the preference over other prospects."

8

A certain easily fanned rapture, and something which partook of a love of frolic, were therefore, in truth, rather the spurs of her resolve than a thorough love passion. George, on his part, with his susceptibility and generous feeling, was strongly drawn to the lively girl; and although the kindly old father, with his wary forethought, would not allow himself to be edged into express sanction of the marriage, as long as Forster's worldly means were so doubtful, the eager girl soon dragged his good-will into a tacit understanding that the wedding should come off as soon as Polish pledges proved trustworthy; and he started for his new home with the consciousness of being betrothed. He passed through Vienna on his way; when, what with the flow of his spirits at this the heyday of his life, when he saw gloom and error behind him, while happiness and ease were awaiting him in the future, and what with the flattering attention paid him by high and low, his delight was such, that his letters overflow with enthusiastic praise of that capital, which for a long while remained the Elysian paradise of his fancy. The Emperor Joseph received him in his closet, with his well-known friendliness, and on dismissing him, after much talk, foretold him laughingly that he would not long stay in the wilderness of Poland; while invitations from the mighty Kaunitz, and choice meetings at the house of the celebrated Countess Theresa Thum, whose pride and joy it was to gather together the picked spirits of Vienna, showed in what esteem the traveller was held by all.

The first impression of Polish bleakness was indeed gloomy, and he owns that what he saw on crossing the frontier filled his soul with dismay, although he had tuned his expectations down to the lowest pitch. The rawness of October weather fretted his sickly frame, which always suffered cruelly from cold and damp; while all the endless discomforts of jolted travel through fathomless roads, and lodging at filthiest hovels, crowded on him, yet revelling in the fresh memory of Vienna.

At Grodno he found himself in the very heart of the life

and Court of Poland. The first free diet which had met since many years, was then holding its sittings there; and the mean huts and filthy lanes of the so-called city were thronged by the motley crush of Polish aristocracy, from the King and magnificent magnates with their dazzling followings, down to the equally haughty peasant nobles swaggering about with their big swords (the badge of their rank), while they floundered through the mammoth sloughs of mire in huge boots lined with dirty straw, in their proud disdain of the effeminacy of stockings and linen. Amongst the higher classes, however, he found many persons possessed of much elegant culture, which was, moreover, set off by a lordly hospitality, in which they vied with each other to show how highly they valued the gain of so noteworthy a man to their country. The King's sister, commonly called Madame de Cracovie, because her deceased husband, Marshal Branicki, had been Castellan of Cracow, received him with the most marked kindliness, and presented him herself to her brother, whom he often saw in the familiarity of her evening meetings. That worn-out lover of the great Catherine, by whose bounty he had been pensioned with the royalty of Poland, had a mind whose dainty and over-refined taste delighted in the society of literary men, and Forster experienced the courtesy of his bearing, while the assurances of good-will which he gathered from the King and Primate for himself and the University encouraged his hopes for the future. It was, therefore, with pleasurable feelings that he continued his journey in November, on the closing of a diet with the unwonted open-handedness and even flow of which the Government expressed itself delighted, though Forster writes that not a day passed but the Marshal of the Lower House smashed sundry staves of office in trying to allay uproar.

The first acquaintance with Wilna did not discourage him. It was true that "the cabinet of natural history proved not only a child in its cradle, but not even a fine child, while the library was most meagre;" but then he had the assurance that their wants were acknowledged, and would be made good. The University, as most of the schools in Poland, had been founded by the Jesuits, in consequence of whose suppression the whole system of education was being remodelled. His lodging was in the old palace of the Order, and, though wretchedly bleak and bare, he comforted himself by comparing it with those of his fellow-teachers, and by the readiness with which such changes as he asked for were granted. Many of the Jesuits remained attached to the high-school as laymen ; and although he arrived by no means well disposed towards them, — having been fully warned by the great Jesuit-croaker, Nicolai, against their wiles, — his first letters speak the praise of their unselfish behavior, so that he even utters his conviction that the Jesuits of Wilna, at least, do not deserve the suspicion under which their brethren generally labor. The difficulties of his position showed themselves immediately on entering upon his duties, when he had to deliver his lectures in Latin; for though a master in German style, and able to write English and French with wonderful correctness, Latin composition was a labor which cost him " an everlasting time ; " while the unwonted tongue hampered his speech, which was at all times highly embarrassed in the professor's chair, although its flow in conversation was astounding. But athwart the wintry cloudiness of his horizon there was the light of his love to cheer him on ; so, sturdily attacking the hardness of the Polish tongue, he hotly tried to overcome all bars between himself and happiness. The winter was thus employed by him in preparations for his marriage, which was fixed for the summer; and so engrossed was his mind in this one thought, that at first he overlooked how sundry impediments were being slyly thrown in the way of his university career. The fears he felt for Theresa's comfort in the dreary banishment of Wilna were laughed at by her eager temper, and her lively fancy rejoiced at the prospect of hardships to be overcome ; in spite of which Forster's tender care for her ease would not rest content with any but a home of such snugness, that the nakedness of Polish shops and the dull sloth of Polish workmen could not

be got to fit it up, and in the warmth of his heart he launched
into the outlay of getting furniture and servants from abroad.
Forster always had a love for household comfort which was
above his means, and is startling in a man of so roving a turn
of mind. He would have spent lordly incomes had he possessed them; and with all his zeal for thriftiness, the close
spirit of reckoning was not in him. Not that he had a bent
for squandering, but with his scientific occupations he could
never resist the purchase of books, charts, and instruments;
and his only taste which could be chid as partaking of ex-
travagance was this love of snugness, which, from repeated
change of dwelling, brought heavy pulls on his purse. So
little did any fondness for show enter into this. liking, that
to save money for it he even refused himself horses, which,
according to Polish ideas of respectability, were nearly as
necessary household articles as clean linen with us. As all
such bits of economy were, however, altogether insufficient
to mend the hole made in his income, he restlessly sought
means of repairing it, and at last decided on perfecting himself in the study of medicine. There was a great want of
physicians in the country, and the skill of such as there were
was eagerly sought and richly paid by noble Poles, who
seemed to have pinned their faith in health on the multitude
of doctors; for we are told that as soon as anything like ailing was felt, the sick man called all the leeches together he
could lay hold of, when he himself would preside, and ad-
judge their debate. With feverish looking forward to spring
and happiness, he thus fretted through the dreariness of his
first Polish winter in utter loneliness and daily worry; for, as
time wore on, he saw that none of the pledges made to him
were kept, while painful rheumatisms and weakened eyesight, brought on by climate, racked his poor body, until, at
the very moment of his start on his longed-for journey, a
putrid fever laid him for several weeks on a sick-bed, and
threatened to cut short his life in its bloom. Convalescence,
like all other things, is helped by a stout heart; thus, as soon
as the crisis was surmounted, his eagerness quickened his

recovery, so that he reached Göttingen in August, 1785; and, having been married in the beginning of the following month, he hastened back with his wife to his bleak banishment.

Henceforth Forster's household was the sanctuary wherein alone, during the remaining two years of his stay in Poland, he found refuge from endless teasing and annoyance. If fancy rather than thorough love had made Theresa become his wife, acquaintance with her husband at all events at first confirmed and increased her good opinion of him. Forster always maintained in his daily bearing so chaste a delicacy that his widow declares never to have seen him guilty of an unseemly outburst; and this overwrought unwillingness to ruffle her peace of mind was such, that he never brought himself to unfold his many straits to her, until this very silence produced the misunderstanding which it had been meant to avoid. Thus, while in his generous fear lest she should not be fully aware of the lot she was encountering, he had always dwelt much on the privations awaiting her in Poland, this nice feeling had kept him from alluding to the pet home he had prepared; so that the young woman was quite rapt with joy to find so snug a dwelling on her arrival at Wilna. It was, in truth, not more than they wanted; for beyond it they found no comfort. If Cassel was loathsome, yet how grand was it when compared with the Polish University, which had not even one bookseller. Intercourse with the world was slow and difficult; he could not often even hear of new books, much less get a sight of them; so that his letters to Lichtenberg piteously beg for the crumbs which might be swept from the fulness of his literary table. The want of all congenial society was the bitterest hardship to him; for the revels of the Lithuanian nobles had no charms, and his Jesuit fellows, on closer knowledge, had come out in their true light. Having failed in their stealthy stalking for the father and mother's souls, they hoped to net that of George's first-born child; but their wiles were roughly torn by a gruff sally, "that, as baptism must be, it should be done according to Calvinism," and henceforth their friendship was

at an end. The turmoils of the State and the ill-will discovered to be borne to the University by the Primate, who even
applied its funds to the one of Cracow, abashed his trust in
promised improvements which would have enabled him to
make himself practically useful; yet every time that in a fit
of anguish he eagerly jumped at a chance of escape from this
forlorn banishment, he was quickly dragged back by the feeling of its impossibility. By agreement he had bound himself to serve for eight years, in consideration of the payments
whereby he had been freed from his Cassel debts; and no
literary labor in his present wilderness, obliged as he was to
buy at great expense every book he might require, could
ever enable him to pay off this loan. Thus was there nothing for him but patience, rendered doubly irksome by continued attacks of painful illness. His courage, nevertheless,
never flagged for any length of time; and as soon as health
buoyed up his good cheer, his letters showed him even dwelling on the advantages of his abode in Poland.

" The experience which I have gained through this change of residence has been dearly bought, but is withal worth much; I was
obliged to see black against white, that I might know what white
was. I owe it to my journey hither that I am aware of the full worth
of many things, and chiefly of friendship. My mind has also obtained
much growth and enlightenment which I should not have gained by
staying at Cassel. Oh ! a good shove, which thrusts us all at once out
of the centre wherein we have long been resting, or in which we have
been moving around our own pivot, gives us so thorough a shaking
that one gets to espy countless new things in one's self and others. . . .
Here, at all events, I can become wise through my faults, in perfect
peace, for I can commit my faults and mend them unperceived. I look
at Wilna as my caterpillar's case,   I am bound for eight years, after
that come my wings, and the perfect insect will follow its destination."

He even produced, besides sundry translations, two little
works which deserve notice, to the writing of which he devoted himself so assiduously, that long before daybreak he
sat at his desk, and his health began to suffer from the strain.
The one was a dissertation on " The Human Race," intended

as an answer to an essay by Kant on the same subject, in which mistaken statements had been made about the South Sea Islanders. The dogmatic boldness with which the metaphysician laid down the law in matters of science displeased Forster, who in general had little liking for speculative philosophy, and even called Kant, in a private letter, "the archsophist and arch-scholastic of the age." In this dissertation, which is written with great moderation, he maintained the existence of distinct races of men, though he did not deny their belonging to one kind. The other work was a "Life of Cook," already alluded to, the dedication of which was graciously acknowledged by the Emperor Joseph — a fact rendered highly remarkable by the broad freedom of thought running through the whole book, which contains, as in a summary, the political faith which guided Forster's future conduct. It has often been noticed, that there is not a single passage in any of the French writers of the eighteenth century, which shows any foreknowledge of the revolution which was coming over their country, although many travellers (amongst them Goldsmith) foretold it; but there is no man whose prophecies can vie in clearness with those of Forster. As early as 1782, he exclaimed in a letter to his father, "Europe seems to be on the point of a fearful overthrow;" and in a remarkable fragment amongst his writings, the precise date of which is not known, the following striking words occur: —

"We stand at the close of the century; this universal longing for change in our present forms, for relief from our many defects, the searching hither and thither, this revolt of reason against political pressure, this supremacy of understanding over feeling, these educational institutions for the rearing of sensible machines, these convulsive clutchings of faith at miraculous powers beyond the realm of understanding, this struggle between enlightenment and religion, this universal leavening, — herald a new teacher and a new doctrine."

Yielding to his heart's ever warm interest in his fellow-beings' weal, he had been steadily growing in his age's political thought, so that it was ever engrossing the better part of his mind; and while, therefore, it is not wonderful that in 1787 he should have arrived at writing as he then did, it is most wonderful that the head of the Holy Roman Empire should have nodded approbation to such words as these : —

" Human infallibility is disappearing before the dawn of knowledge. Tolerance and freedom of conscience proclaim the victory of reason, and make the way for freedom of the press and free search into all those relations which, under the name of truth, are of value to man. Lastly, luxury and industry are giving new worth to life; the arts are attaining the height of perfection and simplicity; observation and experience are enlarging and combining all knowledge, and all political powers are tending to an equality; in short, it is, or is about to be, the season of flowering."

It is well to recollect these words in connection with Forster's after life; for they prove how he was not then whirled away by a sudden puff of rapture, but obeyed the long-flowing stream of his thoughts.

Early one morning in the month of June, 1787, Forster was disturbed at his desk by the entry of a Russian naval officer, who, presenting him with a letter from the ambassador, Stackelberg, made the startling announcement that he had full power to settle all terms, if he would agree to accompany a voyage of discovery in the Southern Ocean. What a leap for Forster from dreariest banishment into the very Eden of dreams ! The open-handedness of the Russian Government removed all difficulties about the repayment of his loans, and an ample salary was assigned to him, as also a pension for his wife in the event of his death; while his delight with luck was raised in the highest pitch by the promised companionship of Sömmering, whom the Empress immediately appointed physician to the expedition, on Forster's recommendation ; and as soon as ever he had brought his affairs to a close, he hastened away, traversing with six post-horses the space between Poland and Göttingen, which he reached on the 16th September. His hopes were fated to meet with a sad dash : the outbreak of the Turkish war caused the voyage to be laid aside for the present; and as Forster would not accept an appointment at St. Petersburg just after his escape from Polish winters, he was turned adrift on the world with a year's salary, but free from debt, so that, though pleasant visions had come to nought, he yet blessed the wondrous luck which alone had been able to snatch him from Poland and set him down in the heart of Europe. A vague chance of employment in the Philippine Isles also proved vain, and is only worth remembering for a letter he wrote with a description of himself, which shows that practical matters had so laid hold of his attention that he held himself to be more fitted for affairs than for science proper, while he thought himself free from the usual prejudices of "learned men, who, having small knowledge of the world, seldom understood how to fit their theories and hypotheses on to the real business of life."

While Forster was thus anxiously looking around him for some opening suitable to his wants, his attention was drawn to the electoral city of Mayence, where his old friend Johannes von Müller had just vacated the librarianship, on promotion to be the Elector's private secretary, while the prospect of the society of Sömmering, who had for several years taught anatomy there, was a most powerful attraction. By the counsel of friends he went thither, that his presence might draw attention to him; and, having been presented to the Elector by Müller, his appointment was decided on with a speed unwonted for the lazy sluggishness of spiritual courts. The salary was small; but then there was the advantage of a central position, which the portly Elector, with sly shrewdness, pointed out to him when, throwing open the casement of his closet, he showed him the view over the Rhine and its rich banks, asked him to compare it with Poland, and went on to reckon the cheapness of provisions, — backing the whole with promise of regular payment.

It is as well shortly to describe the soil into which Forster was now transplanted; for it was owing to its nature that his life took the turn it did. The ancient German Empire was dying the death of corruption, and the very death-slumbers of its elders were being broken in upon by forward heirs ; foremost among whom was Prussia, who, like a night-mare, bestrode and pinched them, even at the point of death. Everywhere there was silent dissolution of the powers that had been ruling, while popular spirit and enlightenment as yet only flitted here and there through the land, like the will-o'-the-wisps that flicker about churchyards. German Courts lay lazily bedded in a woof of wiles and tricks whose toils entangled the strength of the whole land, out of whose rich-ness it had been spun for the enjoyment of a few sly cozen-ers. In looking at their doings and lives, so fevered and so bloated, one might think them creations banded by spells to a hectic existence, and who could not but fade away as soon as the healthy air of truth stole upon their pampered being. The time-honored See of Mayence, with whose spiritual elec-torate was coupled the arch-chancellorship of the empire, as it had ever been one of the chief pleasure-haunts of the lusti-ness of Rhenish prelacy, so was it in its decay the hotbed of corruption. The predecessors of the reigning Elector had, like the Emperor Joseph, partaken of the reforming fashion of his time, and had foolishly thought that the worn-out body might be quickened again into youth. The Elector — simple, good-natured man, the chief feature of whose temper was kindly trustful feeling, and a fondness for plain burgher-like life — forsook the wonted pomp of a high prince of the empire, to follow the bent of his homely likings. Instead of having courtly feasts, he not only mingled in the holiday gambols of the citizens, but he forfeited the indulgence of his courtiers, who with shrugs would have winked at these whims of a sovereign, by his harmful meddling in the olden habits of the State. Saints were curtailed of their dues, monkish trickery was checked ; and when, in 1773, the Jesuits were suppressed by the Pope, Eusmerich Joseph seemed like a man who felt a load off his chest, and launched forth into plans for setting up sound schools in his lands. The Jesuit party was, however, not crushed, though beaten ; and on the

Elector's suspicious death in the following year, before he had time to carry out all his plans, they carried by a push the election of Canon Erthal as his successor. Shrewd, ambitious, and thoroughly worldly, he had graduated in the schools of courtly diplomacy, where he had acquired that varnish whereby poor wits can for a time pass themselves off as minds of superior stuff. As the party had worked the strong Catholic feeling of the population, the new Elector began his reign with a mighty show of piety and devotion that edified the mob, but which were laid aside for more congenial pastimes, as soon as their need was less apparent; the banqueting halls of the archiepiscopal pleasure palaces rang with the revelry of feasts, the spice of whose cheer was set off by ribald wit.

"The Prince's spirit of thrift was changed into the wantonest court pomp, pious cant into voluptuous sensuality, and church zeal into a little freethinking. Instead of evening devotions, a late hour brought with it a refined supper for a knot of chosen fellows, to which sometimes artists and witty heads were admitted. The knee-cushions remained as footstools, before the pleasure-couches brought from Paris and London. Foot-washings and layings on of hands had been withdrawn (who knows with what ceremonies) into the innermost chambers of the castle of St. Martin, beyond the whispering Rhine and the gaze of the public. Father Goldhagen's theological discussions had been exchanged for talk with Heinse about his novel, 'Ardinghelle;' in the room of the Deacon's service in the Missal, Madame de Coudenhoven read Voltaire's 'Pucelle,' and the 'Lettres Persanes' to her French-talking friend, herself so clothed that the listener could easily attach himself to the visible instead of the edifying, and kiss the fair reader himself, in lieu of the gospels formerly offered by the Deacon." [1]

Altogether, as far as bedding and nursing will go, the reverend prelate, Erthal, should have been snugly off in this world, — well fed, softly bedded, and gently cherished by two willing damsels; so that when the stately Coudenhoven found that she palled on his old heart, her charity loved to find her cousin Ferette at hand as a safe cordial to warm it.

[1] "Haus und Welt," vol. ii. p. 14.

Around this foul carcase as the main pier of this Augean stable, the inmates of its stalls stood ranged and grouped. The throng was choicely noble ; for the utmost that was given to a burgher in Mayence was the gift of a clerkship. The nobility was, however, far from being all on an equality within itself, and the highest class, whose string of ancestors enabled them to stand the tests required for canonries, looked down as haughtily on their lower fellows as those again on the mob of burghers at large ; while besides, and above all hereditary rank, there was the consecration of holy orders, whereby, first, only even the highest-born nobility became entitled to share fully the fatness of the State. Gluttony, wassailing, and a greedy craving for rich prebends, were the main qualities of these servants of the Church ; and it was well when, in the revelry of their drinking-bouts over flagons of old Rhenish, which in summer time they loved to hold in the pleasure-grounds of their lordly abbeys scattered along the stately river's banks, their wanton humor would be content with such harmless freaks as wagering whether this or that lady's calves could be encircled by the ribbons of their gold canon's crosses.

Yet were there some men amongst them who, athwart all this overcoat of fashionable dross, were not without stuff, and who learned, in the shifts and wiles of this evil haunt, that great skill in statecraft which enabled them to juggle the world at large. Thus Forster found here Stadion, who, from a gay and enterprising canon, became one of the leading ministers of Austria ; while the master of modern statesmen, Prince Metternich, took his first lesson in cunning in this high school of human worthlessness. High above these in nobleness of nature, as in the splendor of his birth, but so hampered by the contradictions between his position and his likings, that he never mastered their difficulties, and thus through life had an awkward hesitation in his public conduct which looked almost like wilful trimming, was Dalberg, Bishop of Erfurt, coadjutor and expected successor of the Elector ; but who afterwards, under Napoleon, became Duke of Frankfort, and died as Bishop of Ratisbon. His love of letters was great; and so zealously had he devoted his fine intelligence to study, especially of metaphysics, that his works ranked him amongst his country's leading writers, while his position and prospects caused him to be looked to, by such men as Schiller, as the coming Lorenzo de' Medici of Germany. Everything without the circle of nobility was held to be mob; and at most a sort of half recognition was now and then extended as a favor to the professors, though never so far as to admit them with their wives to the houses of the aristocracy. The mass of burghers and the country people were inert, listless, and stolid, and their dull faint-heartedness was frightened as soon as they caught themselves but grumbling at a tax — their only idea of the State; but in Mayence itself there were a few citizens whose Rhenish light-mindedness had been unwittingly rapt by the political freethinking of the professors. These latter were, indeed, a body by themselves, whose opinions, probably whetted by daily grinding against the world around, were so wholly at variance with its whole creed, that in their compactness they looked like a set of pioneers thrust forward into the enemy's country in advance of the coming revolution. This circle was the only one which offered Forster any chance of society. The old Jesuit party, which had already declaimed often against the Protestant Johannes von Müller, looked with no friendly eyes on the new librarian; and such was the bigoted feeling fomented against everything that came from him, that his bare proposal to sell the duplicate copies of books was met by the cry that desecration was threatening the work of the fathers, every single book gathered by whom deserved being treasured as a relique. In truth, as far as public enterprise was concerned, there was nothing gained by change from Poland; for the Elector and his Court, like a host of locusts, ate up the wealth of the land in their lavish luxury, while the jealous ill-will of the Jesuit swarms stifled every undertaking which smacked of enlightenment or free thought. Mayence, therefore, had no resources beyond the

society of a few friends, foremost amongst whom was Sömmering, and its position in the heart of Germany. The
neighborhood of Dusseldorf reawakened the intimacy with
Jacobi, which had slacked in distant Poland, while the literary activity of Heyne spurred Forster to share it by becoming a regular contributor to the "Göttingen Advertiser,"
and the kindly old man's fatherly love filled that gap in his
heart which had been made by his wilful sire's estrangement.
How this last came about is not plainly stated: occasional
letters passed between them from time to time, and those of
the son are marked by the most reverential respect; but time
and distance had accomplished a work which it is wonderful
that so headstrong a temper had not brought about long
ago.

The family-ghost, poverty, showed itself in the household
as soon as its tent had been pitched on the banks of the
Rhine. Although he had been urged by the Elector to give
lessons in natural history, the best of reasons stayed his
doing so — for no pupils were to be found; and his duties as
librarian were easy, since the fifteen thousand works which
formed the boasted fifty thousand volumes of the library,
were stowed away in a lumber-room beyond reach or use.
Thus he found his literary activity arrested at every turn by
an impassable slough of sluggishness; and as his desultory
writings barely sufficed to enable him to live from hand to
mouth, his mind reverted to his favorite plan of a History of
the Geographical Discoveries in the Southern Seas, and a
Flora of its Islands; when, as no German publisher could
defray such an undertaking, he turned his thoughts to England. His old claim on the Admiralty presented itself as an
incentive to a plan, the travel of which already allured his
roving turn; and so, having obtained three months' leave of
absence, he started, in the end of March, 1790, with Alexander von Humboldt, on a trip, in the course of which they
passed through Brabant to England, and on their way home
took a hasty look at Paris, then in the glory of its new-won
freedom. It is an interesting connection which thus brings

together the famed explorer Forster, in the evening of his renown as traveller, with the youth of that man who was to carry out scientific journeying and research to the furthest limit that has yet been reached by one man; and thus what seemed to the partakers thereof but the heedless chatting of a pleasure trip, takes for us the look of world-important intercommunings between two souls, the burden of which yet rings in our ears through the clear-spoken words of the aged seer.   A private pupil — a certain Mr. Thomas Brand — was the only pecuniary advantage brought by the journey, beyond a crowd of vivid impressions; for he had seen the two chief events on which the attention of Europe was fastened. In England he had attended Warren Hastings's trial, where he had heard and beheld all the oratory and the genius of the country; while in Paris he had looked on the pageantry of its strange liberty, in the enthusiastic preparations for the great feast of the Champs de Mars.   The result he gave to the world in his "Views of the Rhine and Brabant;" a work which, written in the gloomiest period of his life, is a masterpiece of racy writing, both as regards clearness of wording as well as the ease with which an array of deep thought is marshalled.   "I tell you I hold your 'Views' to be one of the best books in our language," is the opinion pronounced by Lichtenberg.

Forster's household had been hitherto his stronghold, wherein he defied all evil chances; but now this also began to fail him.   The story is a strangely painful one, and of such woven intricacy as to be almost beyond unravelling, for never was there any show of strife; and this not from a cloaking guardedly worn against the world's insight, because, wondrously enough, the tightest friendship and esteem continued between husband and wife, when by the flight of that happy contentment which springs from love, the once cheerful homestead had been left bare and lonely.   The truth seems that the warmth of Forster's temper, which had never known the sprightliness of boyhood, was mellowed to an even glow, less fitted for love's frenzy than for steady friendship, against which the fluttering heart of the woman mauled itself as a bird against its cage's bar, until, all forlorn, and innerly bruised and bleeding, the kindly nursing bestowed by a chance passer-by was taken with thankfulness. That passer-by was ready at hand in Huber, Secretary to the Saxon Mission, a slim, simpering, scrofulous fellow, whose rather petty powers of mind were akin to his body's slightness; a man, the intertwinings of whose life with that of Forster, and the upshot thereof, remind one how, as well as the eagle, the reptile by crawling reaches the pyramid's summit. With the feverish trembling of sickly nervousness he tells us himself that he always felt the want of something to close his day, "so that on going to bed the last sounds might not be wanting to him as in unfinished accords." Possessed of that painful perseverance which is often found in small minds, he had wormed himself into the intimacy of Forster's home by dint of painstaking; and so anxious had he been for this acquaintance, especially for that of the wife, from the accounts he had heard of her, that, having learnt to know George on his first visit to Mayence, his nervous impatience drove him to meet him at Frankfort on his coming with his wife; and in a letter which marks the sickly anxiety with which he watched himself, he tells his delight that the interview went off well, "because desire to please strangers often gave his bearing something wavering and unsteady." So insignificant a man would never have enthralled the love of a spirited woman like Theresa, had not her loneliness made her feel herself drawn towards one who wholly merged his existence and feelings in her. There was no forethought on the part of any one in this business. Forster's large soul knew not what was meant by jealousy; and, moreover, in accordance with his own and his age's philosophy, he favored close friendships as a duty, so that when the cautious Sömmering, before his marriage, once expressed some dislike of a freedom in Theresa's bearing towards men, he answered that every sympathetic quickening of her heart gave him pleasure, and that he felt himself happy every time she heartily loved some one whom he believed to be good and noble. "I hate everything which bars freedom, everything which hinders a seed or bud from sprouting," are his words in an early letter to her. His honest soul, all glowing with fellow-feeling and steady devotion, had no inkling how such thoughts might get twisted by others; for his own healthy being was free from any sickly taint.

The household straits, together with Forster's overwrought reserve about them, daily brought fresh worries, more and more inflaming a covert misunderstanding, which found its chief food in that very silence beneath which it was foolishly thought to stifle its quickenings. Huber appeared, on the occasion of these embarrassments, as the beam that propped the tumbling homestead; for while his simpering feeling had a charm for Theresa under the circumstances of her situation, he not only actually helped Forster in the toils of translation, but, from his many connections with leading publishers and literary journals, was enabled to be in many ways of real service to him. It was, therefore, in that state of inner strife which is brought about by want of happiness, that during her husband's absence the wife was, as it were, thrust to rest herself in Huber, who naturally redoubled his nursing care, sanctioned, as it was, by Forster's knowledge thereof; while, on the other hand, Theresa's undisturbed attention fastened itself more and more on his devotion until it came out to her sight in striking relief against the dim canvas of household disappointment. Thus Forster returned from England after failure in his hopes, while the irresistible temptations of books and charts had largely added to the heavy outlay of his journey, to find that he had lost the greatest blessing of his life, — the peace of a loving home. His exceeding delicacy probably never allowed him to broach his knowledge of his loss to his wife, but henceforth regard carefully maintained the chastity of a bond which hitherto had been the happy delight of love. Probably, had Sömmering been at a distance, the facts of this strange misunderstanding would be somewhat laid bare in the letters that then

would have passed between the two; but as it is, there is
nothing in the affectionate correspondence with Heyne which
hints that the father had the least inkling of his children's
unhappiness. Forster shrouded the barrenness of his home
from every one, fighting, with a brave heart, the throng of
his painful disappointments and the ever-growing load of
poverty and debt. Once only, in a letter to Jacobi, after
speaking of efforts to obtain relief from his embarrassments,
he added : —

"Call it weakness, or an insurmountable artlessness, that I could
not break myself from some expressions which have caused you anxiety — or, as it is better to touch all the cords of my heart, which set
it a-going, excuse the sallies of peevishness, spleen, and sadness there-
with, that I have moments when another sort of misfortune lets me
feel still more deeply the oppressiveness of my circumstances."

Happiness had gone from him ; yet in the midst of his sad
loneliness, how deeply touching is it to see the thoughtful
care for the peace of mind of those about him, which is revealed by the following prayer in another letter to Jacobi,
wherein he had been dwelling on his gloomy prospects : —

"One thing I beg of you, if you touch on this point in your letter,
then do so on a separate bit of paper. Whatever I have to suffer, I
like to suffer alone; and as your dear letters are that which we all
love to snatch at, I could wish that no one who is dear to me but
myself should find anything in them which might cause anxiety and
pain."

The household was not the only thing which had changed :
time had borne Mayence itself along with it. The great world-
drama in France was progressing in its mighty working; and
all Europe was watching it, some with hearty sympathy,
others with hatred and fear. The Elector and his pampered
courtiers, too rotten at heart to be quickened into a manly
outburst of hate, kept shooting from over their cups a
shower of wit-bolts at King Mob. Soon a throng of noble ex-
iles began to crowd the neighborhood of the Rhine, who loved
rather to eat goodly messes in other men's homes than to try

to save their own; and great was the soul's delight of the
Electoral Court that chance should allow them to fawn in
daily intimacy on so high and illustrious a brood. The town
and country were literally overrun by boastful runaways, in
pandering to whose whims it was felt to be an honor to squan-
der the exchequer; and the general ill-will at these new-
comers, which was powerfully fomented in the first instance
by the dearness of food, was heightened into exasperation by
the swaggering effrontery of their behavior. While every
branch of the administration was neglected and its hard-
working servants were being starved, every fund and re-
source of the country was drained to its uttermost farthing
that the Electoral Court might not be stinted in its pomp.
The Prince de Condé was splendidly lodged, with his mistress, the Princesse de Monaco, in the Episcopal Palace of
Worms, which belonged to the Elector; and on Comte d'Ar-
tois' visit to Mayence, his private household was defrayed
by the impoverished principality at a daily cost of £200.
Wherever money could be found, it was laid hold of by the
clutches of the pilfering Court; and thus about a million of
florins, which belonged to the University, out of the sale of
church lands, were swallowed up in gormandizing and riot.
Nor did the Elector even reap hearty thankfulness from the
beggars whom he was thus stripping himself bare to clothe
and feed; for while in public they showered on him the titles
of father and protector till they made the dulled blood of his
head tingle with delight, as soon as his back was turned the
graceless crew would nickname him Sir Upstart, and Mon-
sieur l'Abbé de Mayence. Meanwhile the tide of German
politics was rising, and rapidly bearing away the little
princes who were unguardedly disporting themselves in its
heavy swell. There was a mighty plotting of statecraft
going on between Austria and Prussia; and the Elector of
Mayence was puffed up and full of importance, for he had
been admitted to look on in that innermost closet where the
secretest designs were being concocted by wily heads, too
glad to buy with a little flattery a cat's-paw willing to pick

for them the burning brands out of the fire. As he found
his old ministers too awkward to handle such nice devices, he
procured from Vienna Baron Albini as a master in statesman-
ship, and bestowing on him the title of Grand Chancellor,
with a salary befitting his high dignity, he trustfully had
himself launched, under his steering, upon the sea of political machination. The first fruits of such superior guidance
was the glorious honor of holding Liège at a cost of three
millions of florins, as a conqueror, with the Mayence army,
as soon as the two heads of the empire decided that German
troops should quash the revolutionary movement in that
bishopric. This army was of a piece with the whole fabric
of the State; for while it barely counted three thousand ill-
appointed and worse-fed soldiers, its army list counted no less
than twelve noble and richly paid generals. But when the
coronation of the new Emperor Francis had come off at Frankfort, which the Elector, of course, attended with the pomp
and state befitting his high rank, then it was that the flock of
princely brains there assembled and laboring in the birth-
throes of subtlest State thought, accepted the invitation to
the hospitable retreat of Mayence as best suited to their
deep councillings; and its sovereign gloated with delight at
seeing himself the pivot around which the princes of Europe
moved. Never had anything been beheld like the endless
changes of dazzling revelry which followed on each other
during the stay of princes and statesmen, so that it was a
wonder at what time they snatched bare minutes for those
cunning designs which it was whispered were being woven
in a poor hut, away from din and distraction, on the shrouded
islet of Weissanau. At last the high-born wiseacres were
delivered, and the printing-presses of the Court published
the Duke of Brunswick's famous manifesto. "These are the
men whose measures one is told to approve of," Forster exclaimed. "That man is happy who has found a nook whence
he can quietly look on the mad turmoil."

The French Revolution could not otherwise than powerfully interest one who was so alive to the welfare and doings

of his fellow-beings. His letters to Heyne show how closely
he watched its course, and that, keenly aware of its blemishes, he yet ever felt such sympathy for its struggles that
he would become quite enraged at the fashion of overlooking
its world-meaning in the flippant judgments currently passed
upon it after flurried glances at some of its wild incidents.
So, on the occasion of a book full of abuse of everything connected with France, he exclaimed : —

" Mr. Girtaner is impassioned for the old system, because, under
the new constitution, he received sundry digs between the ribs on the
14th July, in the Champs de Mars. Who taught him the wrong
conclusion that a democratic crowd is not just the same sort of crowd
as any other? Had he stood on the scaffolding which fell in on the
occasion of the rejoicings of the Dauphin's birth, and had he sprained
his toe or finger, he would have written an apology of regicide."

Injustice and selfishness were things so hateful to him,
that his soul could never desist from battling against them ;
and the daily sights and haps of his Mayence life were such
as to be always stirring up his otherwise peace-loving heart.
Not that he was minded to preach overthrow and change in
Germany ; over and over again he utters his belief, in letters,
that public feeling and enlightenment were yet a century or
two behind a want of political freedom, so that he bewails
the blindness of princes, who, by wilful goadings, hasten an
unseasonable discharge of ill-humors, which thus must burst
forth with the acrid pungency of unripeness. Heyne, whose
thoroughly humane feeling was being constantly shocked by
the wanton temper of German aristocracy, but whose character partook of a certain painful caution, kept hovering about
his outspoken son-in-law with timid hints and prudent coun-
sels. It is amusing to see how the old man is surprised into
expressing his heart's joy at every fine burst of public feeling in France ; and how again, in his next letter, frightened
at his own daring, he pours out a string of saws meant to
quench the fire of revolutionary enthusiasm. Already, while
Forster was writing his " Views," Heyne had given vent to

his fears as to how he would treat the political and religious considerations which would be suggested by the events of the countries he described, and Forster had felt so discouraged by his exceeding timidity, that he had given himself much trouble to explain away the meaning of his warnings. Soon after this, however, he was thrown into a mightier fit of alarm, on hearing that his son-in-law was translating a work of Brissot's, of which he had written a review for the " Göttingen Advertiser," in language which had attracted such attention that the name of its author had been repeatedly asked. In the trouble of his mind he posted off a letter of earnest warning as to the consequences likely to ensue from so rash an undertaking, when Forster answered as follows : —

" I am not translating Brissot, and never thought of doing so. There is as much aristocratizing going on in my house as there is spoken on the other side ; and as for myself, I certainly belong as little to the *enragés* of the one party as of the other. It is this very fairness which is hateful to all the fools and rogues who have espoused a party. . . . How should I tumble on the thought of wishing to preach an overthrow which I myself do not desire, but rather hold to be so great a mishap for Germany, that I make every effort to ward it off, and on this account chiefly blame all the lying reviewers, who only embitter the public by their partiality, inasmuch as they give themselves the appearance as if it must needs trust them on their word. . . . I can remain silent, but I cannot write against my insight and conviction."

While such feelings animated him with regard to the great movement going on everywhere around, his own private circumstances were getting more and more engulfed in gloom. His courage bore gallantly up against his adversity as long as health lasted; for in the end of 1790 he wrote that he felt the courage of a lion in him. His literary labors at this period brought his latterly somewhat forgotten name with fresh vividness to the memory of the general public. Besides his " Views," which he wrote in such sunny moments as he could snatch, he translated the Sanscrit drama, " Sacontala," from Sir W. Jones's English version. This glowing flower, picked from the tropical garden of Indian poetry, excited such intense interest in Germany, that Goethe, in an epigram, styled it the embodiment of all beauty. All this was, however, far from enough to shield him from the embarrassments which kept tormenting him from without, while at home there was cold comfort, to all which trouble there came besides the rack and wear of bodily sickness, and at last the sorrow of losing his youngest child, a boy to whose growth and training he had fondly looked forward. "The whole year through I have ceaselessly worked with iron application and great strain of mind. My powers are worn out, my body is incapable of any more exertion, my mind is palsied, and I have the gloomiest prospect before me for the winter and coming year. It is as if all my hopes should run to water, — nothing succeeds; the more I work, the more I hope to earn, so much the more do things come to nought in my hands; and now I stand empty-handed, unable to work as hitherto, and yet in a position that I cannot make the two ends meet in my housekeeping without a continuation of my former application." In vain he would recur to his proposed work on the "Botany of the South Sea," for which, when last in England, he had launched into the outlay of having the drawings colored by skilled artists: there was no one who would pay for the work. "I could find a publisher in Germany, but none who would pay me. Fruitlessly do I look about me for a Mæcenas amongst our magnates and princes, who would pay with a couple of hundred louis for being paraded in a dedication as the protector of the work, and becoming immortal in the world of science." Soon after these sad bewailings, in a letter written late in 1791, it was the mockery of his lot, that just when they were too late, two chances were thrown to him, which a little earlier might have proved the cables of his rescue from shipwreck. Prospects of enlarged activity were opened to him in Mayence by the sudden decision of the Elector to assign the Jesuit church to the library, while on the death of the Professor of Natural History, his salary was added to Forster's pay. On the other hand, a man of the highest standing and name, unexpectedly put himself in friendly communication with him. Amongst his literary jobs, he had received from the well-known Berlin publisher, Voss, the commission to write an account of the events of 1790, with an especial view to the part played in them by the Prussian statesman, Herzberg, between whom and Pitt he wished a parallel to be drawn. Herzberg, the old minister of Frederick the Great, and at that moment pretty much out of favor at the Court of his successor, felt himself too much interested in this work not to wish that an account bearing the name of such an author and publisher should be trustworthy. He wrote Forster a letter, marked by honorable esteem, in which, after sending him some printed documents, he offered, if the manuscript were communicated to him, to look through it, and see that its statements were historically true, "as the King had positively forbidden him to make known a collection of State Papers he had prepared, and which would have thrown much light on these events." Forster thankfully accepted the offer; and Herzberg expressed himself highly satisfied with his exposition of his ministry. Before this business had, however, gone thus far, Mayence had been occupied by the French, and Forster had embarked in the new state-vessel, as he thought, beyond possibility of an honorable return. Herzberg wrote him, through Voss, a letter in which he expressed his hope that Forster would continue a well-intentioned Prussian, and accompanied it not only with a batch of books having reference to the history of the said times, but also with the silver medal of the Berlin Academy (of which Forster was a member and Herzberg curator), and sent him a considerable sum of money. It is plain that the statesman, who knew of Forster's embarrassed circumstances, thought that he might by these means save a man, whose worth and abilities he had learnt to know, from following a path which he believed would lead to his destruction. Forster thought he saw an attempt at bribery, and wrote the following answer, at a time when he was smarting under the direst want: —

"If I understand aright the wish that I should remain a good Prussian, it is a suggestion wholly incompatible with my principles, and with that love of freedom spoken out in so many of my writings, although certainly with some caution, because of despotism. I was born in Polish Prussia, an hour's distance from Danzig, and left my birthplace before it came under Prussian rule. Thus far, therefore, I am no Prussian subject. I have lived as a man of science in England, have made a voyage round the world, and, furthermore, have tried to impart my poor knowledge at Cassel, Wilna, and Mayence. Throughout my life I have always tried to be a good citizen; and wherever I was, I worked for the bread I received. *Ubi bene ibi patria* must remain the motto of the man of science; and it must also remain that of the free man, who must meanwhile live isolated in lands which have no constitution. If to be a good Prussian means as much as when one is in Mayence under French lordship, to wish for a speedy peace and recovery from all the ills of war, then I am a good Prussian as I am a good Turk, Chinese, Moor; but if it means that I am to deny in Mayence my well-known principles — that I should not rejoice at its having a free constitution — that, being called upon, I should not help to work for it — that in a time of fermentation and crisis, when one must absolutely take a decision, I should either remain undecided, or should try to talk over the people of Mayence, that they had better keep their old outrages than be free with the French, — if then to be a good Prussian, means to take principles which never were mine, and which are, not to keep in view the weal of the inhabitants of Prussia, but the weal of the Cabinet, the Court, the ghost-seers of Mayence, then one asks me to do something for which I should deserve to be strung up on the next lamp-post. You will understand now, that it is my most pressing duty wholly to renounce the offered advances of money — although I never was so poor as now, and have become poorer through disappointed hopes. I would rather that every wretchedness came over me, than that I should become untrue to my principles. How could I take, under such circumstances, an advance of . . . dollars, when I would scorn half a million as a bribe?"

Yet had Herzberg only known Forster some few months earlier, and had he by such means entered that sphere of business and historical writing into which he only got this late peep, how different might his end have been! The throng of princes and statesmen had left Mayence behind them in the progress of their crusade; and the sultriness of suspense had followed on riotous revelry; for the nobility was daily awaiting tidings how the revolutionary snake had been scotched by their lucky brethren who were happy partakers of the great royal pageant. As thus hope and good cheer were in the hearts of all the swarm, and their boastful trust knew no bounds, a fearful blow came upon their rejoicings. Custine had suddenly passed the Rhine at Spiers, and was in full march on Mayence, having thoroughly beaten the Electoral troops under Colonel Winkelmann, an officer of such excellent sentiments that the bare words of freedom and the rights of man were enough to send him into a fit of raving. It was as if a pack of wild beasts had been suddenly let loose on a tea-party; the whole nobility of Mayence thought of nothing but to snatch up as much of their wealth as they could carry, and betake themselves with it beyond the Rhine. It was an endless bustle and trooping by day and night across the bridge and through the town gates: laden skiffs covered the river, and the roads were blocked with every sort of cart and wagon; while runaways on foot and horse hurried along in selfish haste to their hiding-places, thoughtless of all but their own safety. It is said that two hundred thousand florins were spent in means of transport out of the town in these few days. The Elector scurried into the town, to take a glimpse at it, but left it again secretly, after dark, on the day of his arrival, in well-closed chariots, with his mistress and his jewels, having first seen that his arms were well erased from his carriage-panels, after which he bethought himself of duly naming Chancellor Albini as Regent. The treasures of the churches were also packed up and got safely out of the town; and then the High Chancellor called the burghers (in truth, the only inhabitants who remained) to a meeting, at which he urged them not to lose courage, but, abiding by the town, to defend it to the last, and, addressing them as his brethren, read a proclamation, forbidding flight and removal of goods, on pain of

severest punishment. The fraternal title, we are told, so
dumfoundered the burgher brains, that a rough journey-
man unwittingly gave vent to his astonishment by a thun-
dering rap of his big fist on the table, accompanied by a
monstrous oath ; when, just as brotherly affection was about
to make them all strike into that stream of bravery let loose
by the Chancellor, an ill-timed meddler dashed this flow of
mind by the shout that their most gracious brother, the
Chancellor, in his heavily laden chariot, had just safely passed
the gates. His Excellency General von Gymnich, Master-
General of the Ordnance, swore loudly he would defend the
town *to his last shirt ;* and truly endless was the clatter and
the bustle of warlike preparations during the next few days.
The burgher-guard were even under arms ; all horses were
put in requisition to drag artillery, and the full-dressed generals of the Mayence army inspected the raising of batteries
by panting citizens, who were praying God to put a speedy
end to such troubles, before worse came of them. Now and
then a bit of news would come how Custine had advanced
another march ; and once the sight of a cloud of dust sent
such a thrill of fear through the town, that the garrison
nearly crushed itself to atoms in scampering across the
bridge on the Rhine ; until, on the 19th of October, the
French arrived bodily under the walls of Mayence, and sum-
moned the town to surrender ; when General von Gymnich
gathered his splendidly clad brother generals about him,
amongst them the Elector's relative, Count Hatzfeldt, to
consider in council whether they should desert or defend the
town. To desert was the decision they quickly came to; so,
having bargained that each officer should be allowed to take
away a horse out of the Elector's stable, while he himself
received six famous cream-colored steeds, his Excellency-in-
Chief rode over to the opposite bank with the proud bearing of
one who had worthily taken care of his master's dearest interests ; and, having received each officer's pledge to restore his
animal to its owner, he hastened to present himself, his horses,
and his report, at Erfurt, whither his sovereign had retired.

It was no wish to abet French conquest which made Forster remain in Mayence. His post was there; the world without was all strange to him, and offered him no home which he could make for in these troubles; and while his duty and his interests both told him to stay, his generous mind was, moreover, deeply shocked at the selfishness of the higher classes, and of every one connected with the Government. The very last act of the Elector was to pilfer and bear away with him the saving fund of widows and orphans, so that Forster could well exclaim, " The last quivering of despotism is one more piece of unrighteousness, which calls to Heaven for vengeance." He determined, therefore, to abide events, — a resolve in which he was strengthened at the time by Theresa's good cheer and encouragement. So active a mind, with its love of practical employment, could not, however, remain long without being drawn into the eddy which was spinning around him; and thus his great knowledge of French made him the University's natural spokesman with Custine, on the occasion of its being threatened with loss of funds by new decrees concerning tithes and dues. In those days events marched rapidly; and while the memory of the Elector, in his distant retirement, or from the selfish abandonment of everything by him and his own, had faded in a few weeks, as if years had elapsed since his departure (so that all believed, come what might, the old Government at least could not return), every day brought with it new situations, which not only loudly called on a man of Forster's knowledge and parts to seize as a duty the occasion thrust on him, of warding ill from off his fellow-citizens, but which often, from the nature of their complications and his peculiar position, pointed him out as the man who could alone unravel and straighten them. Thus, from being his fellow-professors' champion for their dues and rights, he came to have to do with the equitable allotment of the demands of the French Commissariat, until step by step he was drawn into being the heart and soul of the new administration, and, on the appointment of a provisional government, allowed himself to be named one of its nine

members. His motives are manfully stated in a letter to
Heyne, whose fears at his son-in-law's conduct were becoming
excessive.

" It is the duty of every honest inhabitant, I think, to take thought,
when called upon to do so, for the ease and property of the inhabitants
in general ; for, let Mayence come into whose hands it may, it must
always be pleasing to the sovereign of the day to have a country
which is not exhausted, and which is in the enjoyment of its resources.
I have no other principle of action, and this one is as simple as it is
true. No one will deny that if the people of Mayence can become
free on this occasion, they would be great fools not to become so, and
they really seem possessed of enough sound sense to do it."

This step was final ; it tore almost all his ties of friendship; and even Sömmering was so overcome with fear and
horror, that, turning away from one who loved him so dearly,
he henceforth would have no further knowledge of him.
Traitor and low designer were the names showered upon him ;
and the Duke of Brunswick's remark, on hearing of Forster's
doings, was astonishment that one who had so many means
of earning a livelihood should have sought a rebel's calling !
Yet if Forster proved wrong in his political belief, he shared
his mistake with many keen thinkers ; for even the shrewd
Johannes von Müller, initiated as he was into all the springs
and workings of German statecraft, gave it as his opinion,
on a hasty visit to Mayence for matters of private business
(where he was beset by hundreds of doubtful burghers seeking to steady their minds by the wisdom of so deep an ora-
cle), that under the circumstances they would do best to
rally round the republican Government. In the midst of
the bustle of convening the assembly which was to decide
whether Mayence would become independent or not, affairs
without the walls grew dark and threatening.

The French had been driven back from Frankfort, and
the allies were hovering about the town. Business now
overwhelmed Forster; his fluent French made him necessary everywhere, and, after working all day in offices, he

had to take the chair of an evening in the Jacobin Club,
while the editorship of a journal left him not a spare moment to himself. It was in the turmoil of such troubled
times, when every day the look-out became more and more
threatening, that he determined Theresa should no longer
encounter the risks of his lot. She had been entirely deprived of society by the universal emigration (Huber, as
Saxon agent, had been forced to leave the town), and hardships which would formerly have excited her romantic temper, now only tended to depress it; so it was decided that
Thomas Brand, the English pupil, should take her to Strasburg, where she was to reside with good Jacobin friends of
her husband. Thus was the knot of Forster's marriage
noiselessly untied, although it is certain that neither husband nor wife was fully aware that they were then un-
loosening it so completely forever. Much deep and earnest
thought had Forster held within himself as to what it was
his honest duty to do for his wife's happiness; that secret
about Huber weighed upon him, in spite of his philosophy;
yet, seeing himself and the ship of his household becoming
more and more engulfed in an eddy, he wished to see his
wife at least landed beyond its reach; and thus this severing
was, in truth, a renunciation on his part. Huber soon after
vowed that as long as he lived Theresa should never suffer
want, and, forsaking his diplomatic calling, — advancement in
which was barred by his well-known friendship for the Jaco-
bins,— he went to Switzerland, whither she had gone from
Strasburg with her children. Strange to say, a happier and a
better understanding between all three was the immediate result of this unwonted settlement. Forster had lost much, but
he had won a devoted friendship which, freed from the re-
straint of late doubt and fear, now revealed itself in its full
strength; and his letters show how at this time, at least, it
did not enter his thoughts that the new order of things would
cut him off from personal intercourse with his wife; while
she again manifests the liveliest sympathy and interest in his
career, and fully approves of his pursuing it. In truth, this

is one of the most wonderful complications woven out of the smallest and pitiablest misunderstandings with the highest and noblest self-denial, so that it passes comprehension how they could be dovetailed together; and not least strange is the artless bearing and true childlike affection shown by all the sharers in this odd union.

It was time for women to get out of Mayence when Theresa left. Merlin de Thionsville, Haussmann, and Rewbell arrived from Paris, as commissioners, when all doubt as to the future constitution of the country was laid aside. Endless was now the racket of Forster's daily life; and especially was he worried by the labor of presiding at the club sittings, which were violently disturbed by unseemly brawls. Then were there also patriotic banquets, followed by long-winded orations, so that he might well groan over the part he was made to go through; yet his health was wonderfully borne up by excitement, until a four hours' bath of snow and sleet, on the solemn planting of the tree of freedom on the 4th of January, nearly ended the patriot's days. The loss of so useful a man was borne impatiently; so no sooner was he able to move than he was made to travel through the country districts, as Government Commissioner, to watch the elections of deputies for the Constituent Assembly of Mayence, — an office which brought him into collision with the nobles on their estates. The Union was voted at once, when Forster, with two other citizens, was sent to bear to the Convention the decree which he himself had drawn up. So little did he foresee, in the eagerness of that hour, how events were upon the point of turning, that he expected to be back before the end of three weeks, and even neglected to take any care for his books and papers. On the 30th of March he was admitted to the bar of the Convention, where he was received with the enthusiastic cheers of that France to which he was sent as the spokesman of its new brethren, although one short week was sufficient to prove how unstable and tottering was the Union he heralded.

The allied armies had crossed the Rhine the day before

Forster's departure, and since then had advanced upon the
town, so as to invest it completely.   Under such circumstances, return was for the present out of the question; so
to shift for himself as he best could in the heaving surf
of Paris, on the pittance of eighteen assignat livres a day,
was all the look-out left to him, and he tried to make it
as cheery a one as good-will would allow.   A large world
suited Forster's temper; the many shiftings of his early
life had given him habits of largeness, and there was in
the nature of Paris and its world-movement abundance to
fasten and powerfully interest the peculiar tastes of his
mind.   Moreover, he came thither with a lively trust and
belief in the great Revolution, which the excitement of partisanship had worked up into passionate liking; and yet the
first impression of what he saw, when he began to sift and
order the crush of sight which thronged on him, was disappointment, which, in spite of himself, stole with clammy
chill over his boiling enthusiasm.   He saw the ugly under-
workings of parties and of party-chiefs, and his gossamer
visions threatened absolutely to fade away at the strong
glare of Paris light.   "The only thing still wanting, after
all I have suffered of late, is to have the conviction forced
on me, that I have offered up my best strength to a monster,
and have worked with honest zeal for a cause with which no
one else will work honestly, and which is a cloak for the
maddest passions."   Forster's political faith, and keen glance
into the workings of men and times, were, however, far too
steady to be shaken or blinded by any sudden gust.   He had
become enamored of the Revolution for herself; and through
the throng of low suitors who had jostled and dragged her
along into the filth of their debaucheries, his eye, disregard-
ing the harlotry of foisted fashion, dwelt ever lovingly on
the beauty with which she had been born.   Thus, while
goaded to despair by the excesses and horrors of the violent
party, he yet proclaimed himself a Jacobin, because he saw
in extreme measures the State's only safeguard against a return of old abuses.   " I do not deny that the men of the

10

Mountain often show themselves from a disadvantageous and impolitic side; but they seem withal to be freer from prejudice than the others, and, beyond doubt, they have more power and decision." Thus Forster remained true to his convictions, — for with him they were the clear light of belief, which no chance storm could lastingly trouble, for he knew that, in the heaven of his world, certain seasons must have passing storms, and that the big darkness was but the shadow which must come along with the mighty lightning that would clear the firmament.

Eighteen paper livres a day (of which a hundred went to make one gold louis) were slender rations to fatten on, especially for a man who found himself unable to pick up any scrap of means for himself, being yet so thorough a stranger in the wild chaos he had got into, that, in spite of all his efforts, he could pitch on no standing ground whatsoever in its rocking whirligig. Affairs in Mayence grew daily worse; for not only were a hundred ducats put upon his outlawed head, about which he could afford to joke from his Paris garret, but what was infinitely more alarming, a thorough rain of shells and cannon-balls had been hurled upon the town, great part of which, and especially of his own neighborhood, had been burned; while, even if his house escaped destruction, there was small chance that he would be able to recover his papers, which he had so thoughtlessly forgotten to stow away. Without his papers he was like a palsied man pilfered of his crutches; for his hopes of active employment in the service of France did not wear a promising look. All France was then bustling about Paris and the office haunts of the ministers; and unless a man had big shoulders, and a strong will to make others afraid of him, there was small likelihood for his luck in picking up anything. Lebrun, Minister of Foreign Affairs, had indeed received him in a friendly manner, and he had the justest claims on the State for whose benefit he had risked and lost his all; yet, if such hopes were worth aught, their value was as yet to come, and so far not even in sight.

"After so many years' hard work, everything which I have undertaken for my advancement has failed, and I begin the world, as it were, afresh, without knowing how or wherewith, as cut off from all Europe and overladen with debt. I am here without means, without any support, and almost without prospects. I have pledged myself to accept everything which may be offered to me. Scientific merit, and even the skill of the man of business, are now of no avail here. Whoever floats uppermost sits at the helm, until the next man, being the strongest for the moment, dislodges him. In short, for the first time in my life, all my means prove utterly useless; and I stand as forlorn as a child which has not the strength to nourish itself."

This dreary view of his circumstances did not, however, long cast down his spirits. Summer always invigorated Forster; it was as if this season ever quickened the throb of his tropical heart; and so, as it came on, his courage began to plan designs which smacked of its temper and his roving disposition. He thought of studying Eastern languages, and of going to India for some years.

"If I could only scrape together £400 or £500, and were it only £300, I would learn Persian and Arabic, and go overland to India to gather new experience, and besides make my fortune as a physician in a few years. Wholly new objects, foreign sights, movement, occupation, discomfort, and even danger, — all this together, with the consciousness that I am busy in the enjoyment and pursuit of such human work as suits my powers, knowledge, and taste, must infallibly prove healing balm to my wounded feelings. I might stay away from four to six years, or still longer, and then return not yet too old to enjoy the end of my days in my children's arms; while, finding them happy, I should bring back to you a friend thankful for the fulfilment of your motherly duties."

Is not this the same old Forster, — good, generous, and never allowing himself to be long downcast? This last-spoken hope of seeing his wife and children remained bright through all his summer visions, although resignation had been steadily growing on him, so that he saw now clearly enough that it would not do for him to live in the neighborhood of Theresa, and any longings for such a life passed only like the death-quivers of his lone existence. The intimacy of their correspondence was extreme; it was a continual outpouring of friendliest love and sympathy, and he seemed but to feel the pains of his straitened circumstances in the palsy they brought on that helping hand he was always wishing to thrust to those he was so fond of. Even in his uttermost poverty he screwed together a little money for some present when a trusty opportunity of sending it offered; and the only occasion when his letters showed any displeasure with his wife, was when she chanced to lag behind his zeal and faith in the Revolution.

At times Lebrun threw out a sign which buoyed up his hope, and made him look nearer home than India for a beam whereon to float from drowning; until at last, in October, he really was named a French envoy, and was sent to Cambrai to negotiate an exchange of prisoners with the allied generals. On the very day of his appointment, the Angel of Blood had passed close by him with his sword. Lux, one of his two fellow-deputies from Mayence, and who had been the comrade of all his Paris penury, had been arrested that morning to be dragged before the revolutionary tribunal. The poor youth, crazed with admiration of Charlotte Corday's heroism, had loudly said that he would hold it as his highest honor to be doomed to share her death, and wrote an apotheosis of her, in which he proposed that a statue should be erected to her as greater than Brutus. Nor was the mission itself a pleasant and comfortable thing, whatever visions friends abroad made to themselves of Forster's mightiness; in truth, the Republican Envoy was wofully off in every way, worried by the dullest of business, which during three months he in vain tried to see make some progress, without a friend or an amusement to cheer weary days, while he ruefully shivered in a reeking garret (and even there in his wretched bed he was robbed of comfort by hosts of vermin), for the measure of wood cost one hundred and twenty livres, and, as he says himself, " he did not understand the art of swelling his income of three thousand into forty thousand livres." Still

this mission may well be put down amongst the lucky windfalls of his life; for at this time Paris was at the highest
pitch of its mistrust of foreigners, and but for his absence,
Forster would hardly have escaped suspicion, with his open,
outspoken honesty, and his intimate connection with poor
Lux, who, when brought before the tribunal and in prison,
bore himself like one rapt with frenzy, and at last leapt up
the steps of the scaffold as lightly as if they led to a bri-
dal chamber.

It is very noteworthy what calm, unruffled courage Forster shows during all these sad times; it is as if the thought
of danger to himself never crossed him for an instant; and
from his garret at Arras (whither the approach of the allies
had driven him rather hastily from Cambrai), as from the
heart of Paris, he looks unflinchingly on the terrible things
going on around him, and passes his judgment as quietly
and unguardedly on men and matters as if he himself
were wholly beyond their power and reach. There is literally not one word in his correspondence which betrays the
thought that he might be drawn down by the wild eddy he
was so close to. The only uneasiness which worried him
was the uncertainty of his prospects, by which he found himself kept in continued fever; for while he saw that his foreign origin and sturdy independence were stumbling-blocks
in the way of employment, the absence of his papers and
books rendered him unable to undertake any literary labor.
Yet with all this his brave spirit was not abashed; and indeed at this period of his life he seemed to have been animated with unwonted courage. In the outer world there
was only one spot for him where he hoped to find soothing
comfort; and daily, on returning from long, lonely walks
along the poplar-edged canals of Flanders, his mind spinning
with schemes for the future, the perusal of Theresa's letters,
or chafing disappointment when his expectation of such
was balked, made him turn with impassioned longing to the
thought of once more seeing her and his children. The difficulty was great; for even if he could find the requisite money,

public mistrust was ever watching the goings and comings on the frontier, and Forster in his peculiar position could easily come to be denounced as a traitor who held intercourse with the enemy's spies. Theresa was staying at Neufchâtel, which, being under Prussian supremacy, was forbidden ground to the outlaw. Yet for her to come over into France was even more dangerous than for Forster to break the decree of the Convention, which forbade any one to cross the boundaries without the Government's express permission. The first petty police-officer might cheaply show his zeal by laying hold of her as a skulking emigrant; while Huber, as an enemy's subject, could never be admitted.

About the middle of October, being at last relieved from his diplomatic functions, Forster moved heaven and earth in Paris to be able to obtain his wishes. It was resolved that Theresa should come with Huber to Travers, a poor village in the Jura, a few miles from the French frontier, whither Forster was to cross from Pontarlier. He obtained a loan of one thousand livres from an old Mayence friend. He reckoned on his official character to overcome any difficulties on the frontier, while he hoped to shield himself against the penalty of death which was attached to the transport of coin out of the country, by bringing back a paper in Huber's possession, which, written by Clermont Tonnerre, contained matters of high importance about General Luckner's supposed treason, and which, if subjected to inquiry, Forster would pretend to have been bought with the money he had, in truth, carried to his children. At last the arrangements were ready, and early in November he left Paris for Pontarlier. The chief of the frontier post proved a friendly man, who willingly agreed to help him as far as he could; so, riding across the snowy ridges of the Jura, he reached unobserved the appointed hamlet on a November morning. What passed between the three, — what overwhelming thoughts, what flashes of hope and pangs of disappointment, shot across their minds in those three days, when all the floodgates of their hearts were opened, and their fulness flowed so fast to choking, — there is no account; for how could any cunning words set forth such a throng of emotion ? It is a meeting worth thinking about. Forster seemed to his friends to have grown stouter in health, and his complexion appeared to have a freshness, which was probably but the flush of joyous excitement, while he also expressed himself pleased with what he saw. Thus did these few days fly past but too swiftly in the enjoyment of the highest and most heartfelt bliss, and the three were again torn asunder so suddenly and so rapidly that all was like a dream, had not the tingling throbs of memory continued to heave and flush their frames.

"I thank Heaven," he writes, the day after the separation, "that I have carried out coming to you; these three days have strengthened me for a long while, and have perhaps poised me rightly forever. I feel myself like Antæus, the son of Earth, who received new strength when he touched his mother. My courage to hold out is firmer and more decided, and my resignation (if I may so call it) to everything which may happen, has now no struggle more to overcome. We could still be happy, and live with and near each other some twenty or thirty years. As for our starving, that is out of the question; and the more so if we are together, and restrict ourselves to that which is simply necessary. Would that be any suffering *for us*, especially after all we have experienced, seen, and heard, — after all that happens and takes place about us? I can reckon that I shall always have an income of six thousand livres ; —could I only find four thousand for Huber, then I would pledge myself that we might live perfectly well in Paris. Why, it must go! Kiss my sweet children. How I scanned the mail-guard to-day who had seen them yesterday. Good-by."

Poor Forster ! who, reckoning on thirty years of happiness, had bare nine weeks of nether life allotted to him, and most of these to be passed in racking torments !

For a fortnight Forster still remained by himself at Pontarlier, — for what reason does not appear unless it were that he feared to leave the neighborhood of those he loved until want of money drove him away. The journey was made in

the wretchedest winter weather, so that he reached Paris in
sad plight, where he put up at the Hôtel des Patriotes Hol-
landais, in the Rue des Moulins. He had been attacked on
the way with rheumatic spasms in the chest, which, however,
yielded to remedies, and allowed him to run about Paris,
where, as he wrote, he found not a few new things. Chebot
and Bazire's imprisonment, which had just happened, were
startling tidings even in those days; while Danton's mighty
voice, after long silence, was beginning to let itself be heard
again within the walls of the Convention. Poor Chamfort,
the librarian, whom he had left dealing out books in the Rue
Richelieu, was lying in the Luxembourg prison, being carefully nursed of his razor-gashes that he might be reserved
for the guillotine, which, in the interval of his absence, had
been at work on many known heads, — amongst them, Man-
uel and Bailly and Egalité. Careless exposure to wintry
weather did him, however, fresh harm; for, on the 11th December, he had to write that for three days he had been
obliged to keep his bed, but that things were mending, and
before three other days were over he would be able to go out
again as usual. His old disease, the scurvy, brought on, in
the first instance, by the wet and cold he had encountered on
his journey, had taken the shape of rheumatic gout, and was
flying about his body, having been violently increased by his
careless neglect of precautions. Still gradually he began to
recover, though sleepless nights and exhausting torments
required a longer convalescence than the three days he had
been hopefully looking to as enough. With his inborn eagerness, at this time heightened by the lively spirit of enterprise which had come over him since his visit to Travers, he
forthwith went out as soon as ever he could, in cold and bitter weather; and so, having visited some friends on the evening of the 19th December, he found himself obliged to walk
home late at night, as no carriage could be found. The consequence was an immediate and violent return of his malady.
"I have fared ill in this undertaking. My chest became as
sore and tired as if a scraper had been passed over it; and

even now my whole inside is still one sore." Two days
later, however, he already wrote a more hopeful account; for
though so weak as to be unable to walk a hundred steps without violent coughing and faintness, while his joints were
painfully swollen, he yet declared himself without fear of the
consequences of his illness; and so duped were Theresa and
Huber by the cheerful tone of his letters, that, accustomed,
on the one hand, to know Forster continually ailing, while,
on the other, trustful in the healthy look he had at Travers,
they felt no serious alarm about his state. The improve-
ment announced in every letter would not come. The gouty
swellings spread more and more over the whole body, racking it with ceaseless torments, which baffled all soothing
medicines, though they did not overcome his sturdy courage. On the 4th January he wrote the following letter to
Theresa : —

"But a few lines from my bed of pain, that my darlings be not
without tidings. My sickness has now lasted thirteen days. I do not
shut an eye, and until this night I have always had more or less violent pain. Now it seems to be venting itself, — the fourth day after two
blisters. At the same time I have that fearful scorbutic flow of saliva
which I had at Mayence when your father came to see us. Danger
there is none. Strength exists still, although so lessened that my
recovery will be slow. Believe me, that in the account of my sickness there is neither a word too much nor too little. The pains have
left the stomach and bowels; they were the chief thing. You will
understand that I can do no work. I can only save myself. I cannot continue this scrawl, — therefore, only be without anxiety. I beg
of you, dear Huber, take care that our Theresa does not create herself
any fancies. It is true that I am very and painfully ill; but once
more — there is no danger. Your letters, my dear child, which I have
all received, have been a dear gift to me in my illness; be sure to
continue writing assiduously! We have everywhere been victorious
like lions; the Frankfort call has been full of augury. I am curious
to learn how public spirit will express itself on the other side of the
Rhine, now that the truth of the news is undoubted. Is it not true,
my children — a few words are better than nothing? I have no more
strength to write. Farewell! Guard yourselves against illness, —
kiss my darlings."

It was the last letter ever written by George Forster; and
with what a healthy flow of unaffected feeling does it teem,
and how thoroughly warm and lively is his heart's throb to
the last! He had a few friends who at first watched at his
bedside; but, becoming tired with waiting for his death, they
all of them forsook him, except one old messmate from Mayence. The gout by degrees conquered the body bit by bit,
until at five o'clock in the afternoon of the 12th January,
1794, the brave soul breathed its last. The Mayence friend
immediately informed Huber of what had happened in the
following words : —

" My tears announce to you, dear friend, a melancholy event.   Our
poor Forster is dead; he died in his room an hour ago of apoplexy,
after a long gouty illness.   I rendered him the last duties of a friend,
and closed his eyes. . . . Of the last hours of our poor dead friend I
can, in truth, say nothing, but that the proverb proved itself true : —

'Donec eris felix multos numerabis amicos,
Tempora si fuerint nubila solus eris.'

Ovid was quite right.   In the last eight days, as Forster's illness became more serious, all his many friends — French, Germans, Poles —
forsook him; I alone remained to succor him in his sufferings.   I seldom left him; and on the day of his death I was with him till four in
the afternoon.   At that time his illness did not yet threaten death ;
business called me away, and when I returned at five in the evening,
nature's struggle between existence and cessation had already begun,
and my poor friend was at the point of death.   The gout had got into
the chest, an apoplectic stroke came thereto, and his last words were
of his children.   Quiverings snapped the fetters of life ; his two watch-
men and myself were present at his last breath, and I then immediately
took care about the sealing up of all he had left behind him, and the
procès verbal which the juge de paix arranged."

Little indeed was it that he left behind him; for the journey to Travers had not yet been paid for, and even that little got frittered away by dishonest handling.   An ex-count —
at that time Citizen Joguet — thrust himself, with much show
and bustle of friendship, on Theresa, and offered, by his

influence and knowledge of Paris, to settle her husband's affairs, if she would furnish him with the authority to do so. What became of the man himself does not appear, beyond that he tried to turn to his own best possible advantage the trust which had been blindly reposed in his assurances. Theresa sent such of Forster's papers as he had with him in Paris, as a donation from his children to the Committee for Education, without ever receiving any acknowledgment, until, many years later, a friend of the family found a bundle of old papers in the lumber-room of the National Institute, and on scrutiny it proved to be the remains of this donation, which figured as a patriotic gift of the said citizen. So forsaken was the end of one who had begun life so dazzlingly. Hardly a word was spoken about his death; and if so, then was it mostly a curse, for pity was barely dared to be whispered. Sömmering, peevish and fretting at the chattels he had lost during the Mayence outbreak, started back from the very name of Forster as from the Evil One. Lichtenberg timidly bewailed that his married state imposed caution, so that all he could afford to do for his friend's memory was to *think* freely of him. Jacobi's delicate nature did not mingle in the low choir of hooters, but still he stood silently aloof; and, most shocking of all, the old father at Halle, in the mad frenzy of hoary age, belched forth a yell of outrage against his George, to have seen whom swing on the gallows he declared would have been the closing pleasure of his life. One man alone dared to weep openly for him, and tenderly he wept over his loss,—kindly old Heyne, who, in the fulness of his honest heart, cast aside all his caution and regard for consequences, to let its sorrow pour itself forth.

"Since yesterday's news, which has altogether confounded me" (he wrote to Huber on the 31st of January), "I cannot collect my thoughts. I cannot console myself for the loss of my Forster. Truly was he *my Forster*. I loved him beyond expression; so many feelings were mingled in him. His worth — ah! he will never be replaced for the world. The knowledge that was gathered in him will not soon again be found in one man. The noblest nature — the noblest heart; and for me ever the object of sorrow, of pity. I always thought of him with emotion; he deserved to be happy more than thousand others, and yet was never so, — was so deeply unhappy! It is as yet impossible for me to think that I am never to see him again! I shall never be able to forget him; always will he float before my eyes, — thou noblest, best man! What would I give for one hour which I might have conversed with him! Rest in peace, my dear, my cherished Forster!"

The man who had borne the name of Germany all over the world, whose writings were amongst the masterpieces of its language, whose feelings were so true and whose thought so national, that he first coined a thorough German word for public spirit (*gemeingeist*), — that man's memory was tracked and hunted down as of the vilest traitor; so that, nearly forty years after his death, his wife did not dare to publish his letters without prefixing an apology. Four months after Forster's death Theresa and Huber were married, and the remainder of their lives was at least happy and contented.

SILLY NOVELS BY LADY NOVELISTS.

SILLY Novels by Lady Novelists are a genus with many species, determined by the particular quality of silliness that predominates in them, — the frothy, the prosy, the pious, . or the pedantic. But it is a mixture of all these, a composite order of feminine fatuity, that produces the largest class of such novels, which we shall distinguish as the *mind-and-millinery* species. The heroine is usually an heiress, probably a peeress in her own right, with perhaps a vicious baronet, an amiable duke, and an irresistible younger son of a marquis as lovers in the foreground, a clergyman and a poet sighing for her in the middle distance, and a crowd of undefined adorers dimly indicated beyond. Her eyes and her wit are both dazzling; her nose and her morals are alike free from any tendency to irregularity; she has a superb *contralto* and a superb intellect; she is perfectly well dressed and perfectly religious; she dances like a sylph, and reads the Bible in the original tongues. Or it may be that the heroine is not an heiress, — that rank and wealth are the only things in which she is deficient; but she infallibly gets into high society, she has the triumph of refusing many matches and securing the best, and she wears some family jewels or other as a sort of crown of righteousness at the end. Rakish men either bite their lips in impotent confusion at her repartees, or are touched to penitence by her reproofs, which, on appropriate occasions, rise to a lofty strain of rhetoric; indeed, there is a general propensity in her to make speeches, and to rhapsodize at some length when she retires to her bedroom. In her recorded conversations she is amazingly eloquent, and in her unrecorded conversations amazingly witty. She is understood to have a depth of insight that looks through and through the shallow theories of philosophers, and her superior instincts are a sort of dial by which men have only to set their clocks and watches, and all will go well. The men play a very subordinate part by her side. You are consoled now and then by a hint that they have affairs, which keeps you in mind that the working-day business of the world is somehow being carried on; but ostensibly the final cause of their existence is that they may accompany the heroine on her "starring" expedition through life. They see her at a ball, and are dazzled; at a flower-show, and they are fascinated; on a riding excursion, and they are witched by her noble horsemanship; at church, and they are awed by the sweet solemnity of her demeanor. She is the ideal woman in feelings, faculties, and flounces. For all this, she as often as not marries the wrong person to begin with, and she suffers terribly from the plots and intrigues of the vicious baronet; but even death has a soft place in his heart for such a paragon, and remedies all mistakes for her just at the right moment. The vicious baronet is sure to be killed in a duel, and the tedious husband dies in his bed, requesting his wife, as a particular favor to him, to marry the man she loves best, and having already despatched a note to the lover informing him of the comfortable arrangement. Before matters arrive at this desirable issue our feelings are tried by seeing the noble, lovely, and gifted heroine pass through many *mauvais moments;* but we have the satisfaction of knowing that her sorrows are wept into embroidered pocket-handkerchiefs, that her fainting form reclines on the very best upholstery, and that whatever vicissitudes she may undergo, from being dashed out of her carriage to having her head shaved in a fever, she comes out of them all with a complexion more blooming and locks more redundant than ever.

We may remark, by the way, that we have been relieved from a serious scruple by discovering that silly novels by lady novelists rarely introduce us into any other than very

lofty and fashionable society. We had imagined that desti-
tute women turned novelists, as they turned governesses, because they had no other "lady-like" means of getting their
bread. On this supposition, vacillating syntax and improb-
able incident had a certain pathos for us, like the extremely
supererogatory pin-cushions and ill-devised nightcaps that
are offered for sale by a blind man. We felt the commodity
to be a nuisance, but we were glad to think that the money
went to relieve the necessitous, and we pictured to ourselves
lonely women struggling for a maintenance, or wives and
daughters devoting themselves to the production of "copy"
out of pure heroism, — perhaps to pay their husband's debts
or to purchase luxuries for a sick father. Under these impressions we shrank from criticising a lady's novel: her English might be faulty, but we said to ourselves her motives are
irreproachable; her imagination may be uninventive, but her
patience is untiring. Empty writing was excused by an
empty stomach, and twaddle was consecrated by tears. But
no! This theory of ours, like many other pretty theories,
has had to give way before observation. Women's silly novels, we are now convinced, are written under totally different
circumstances. The fair writers have evidently never talked
to a tradesman except from a carriage window; they have no
notion of the working-classes except as "dependants;" they
think five hundred a year a miserable pittance; Belgravia
and "baronial halls" are their primary truths; and they
have no idea of feeling interest in any man who is not at
least a great landed proprietor, if not a prime minister. It
is clear that they write in elegant boudoirs, with violet-col-
ored ink and a ruby pen; that they must be entirely indifferent to publishers' accounts, and inexperienced in every form
of poverty except poverty of brains. It is true that we are
constantly struck with the want of verisimilitude in their
representations of the high society in which they seem to
live; but then they betray no closer acquaintance with
any other form of life. If their peers and peeresses are im-
probable, their literary men, tradespeople, and cottagers are

impossible; and their intellect seems to have the peculiar impartiality of reproducing both what they *have* seen and heard, and what they have *not* seen and heard, with equal unfaithfulness.

There are few women, we suppose, who have not seen something of children under five years of age, yet in "Compensation," a recent novel of the mind-and-millinery species, which calls itself a "story of real life," we have a child of four and a half years old talking in this Ossianic fashion : —

" ' Oh, I am so happy, dear gran'mamma ! I have seen — I have seen such a delightful person; he is like everything beautiful, — like the smell of sweet flowers, and the view from Ben Lomond; — or no, *better than that,* — he is like what I think of and see when I am very, very happy ; and he is really like mamma, too, when she sings; and his forehead is like *that distant sea,*' she continued, pointing to the blue Mediterranean; ' there seems no end, — no end; or like the clusters of stars I like best to look at on a warm fine night. . . . Don't look so . . . your forehead is like Loch Lomond, when the wind is blowing and the sun is gone in; I like the sunshine best when the lake is smooth. . . . So now — I like it better than ever . . . it is more beautiful still from the dark cloud that has gone over it, *when the sun suddenly lights up all the colors of the forests and shining purple rocks, and it is all reflected in the waters below.*' "

We are not surprised to learn that the mother of this infant phenomenon, who exhibits symptoms so alarmingly like those of adolescence repressed by gin, is herself a phœnix. We are assured, again and again, that she had a remarkably original mind, that she was a genius, and "conscious of her originality," and she was fortunate enough to have a lover who was also a genius and a man of " most original mind."

This lover, we read, though "wonderfully similar " to her "in powers and capacity," was "infinitely superior to her in faith and development," and she saw in him " ' Agape,' — so rare to find, — of which she had read and admired the meaning in her Greek Testament ; having, *from her great facility in learning languages,* read the Scriptures in their original *tongues.*" Of course ! Greek and Hebrew are mere play to a heroine; Sanscrit is no more than *a b c* to her; and she can talk with perfect correctness in any language, except English. She is a polking polyglot, a Creuzer in crinoline. Poor men! There are so few of you who know even Hebrew; you think it something to boast of if, like Bolingbroke, you only "understand that sort of learning and what is writ about it;" and you are perhaps adoring women who can think slightingly of you in all the Semitic languages successively. But, then, as we are almost invariably told that a heroine has a "beautifully small head," and as her intellect has probably been early invigorated by an attention to costume and deportment, we may conclude that she can pick up the Oriental tongues, to say nothing of their dialects, with the same aerial facility that the butterfly sips nectar. Besides, there can be no difficulty in conceiving the depth of the heroine's erudition, when that of the authoress is so evident.

In "Laura Gay," another novel of the same school, the heroine seems less at home in Greek and Hebrew, but she makes up for the deficiency by a quite playful familiarity with the Latin classics, — with the "dear old Virgil," "the graceful Horace, the humane Cicero, and the pleasant Livy;" indeed, it is such a matter of course with her to quote Latin, that she does it at a picnic in a very mixed company of ladies and gentlemen, having, we are told, "no conception that the nobler sex were capable of jealousy on this subject. And if, indeed," continues the biographer of Laura Gay, "the wisest and noblest portion of that sex were in the majority, no such sentiment would exist; but while Miss Wyndhams and Mr. Redfords abound, great sacrifices must be made to their existence." Such sacrifices, we presume, as abstaining from Latin quotations, of extremely moderate interest and applicability, which the wise and noble minority of the other sex would be quite as willing to dispense with as the foolish and ignoble majority. It is as little the custom of well-bred men as of well-bred women to quote Latin in mixed parties; they can contain their familiarity with "the humane Cicero" without allowing it to boil over in ordinary conversation, and even references to "the pleasant Livy" are not absolutely irrepressible. But Ciceronian Latin is the mildest form of Miss Gay's conversational power. Being on the Palatine with a party of sight-seers, she falls into the following vein of well-rounded remark : —

"Truth can only be pure objectively; for even in the creeds where it predominates, being subjective, and parcelled out into portions, each of these necessarily receives a hue of idiosyncrasy, that is, a taint of superstition more or less strong; while in such creeds as the Roman Catholic, ignorance, interest, the basis of ancient idolatries, and the force of authority have gradually accumulated on the pure truth, and transformed it, at last, into a mass of superstition for the majority of its votaries; and how few are there, alas! whose zeal, courage, and intellectual energy are equal to the analysis of this accumulation, and to the discovery of the pearl of great price which lies hidden beneath this heap of rubbish."

We have often met with women much more novel and profound in their observations than Laura Gay, but rarely with any so inopportunely long-winded. A clerical lord, who is half in love with her, is alarmed by the daring remarks just quoted, and begins to suspect that she is inclined to free-thinking. But he is mistaken; when in a moment of sorrow he delicately begs leave to "recall to her memory a *dépôt* of strength and consolation under affliction, which, until we are hard pressed by the trials of life, we are too apt to forget," we learn that she really has "recurrence to that sacred *dépôt*," together with the tea-pot. There is a certain flavor of orthodoxy mixed with the parade of fortunes and fine carriages in "Laura Gay," but it is an orthodoxy mitigated by study of "the humane Cicero" and by an "intellectual disposition to analyze."

"Compensation" is much more heavily dosed with doctrine; but then it has a treble amount of snobbish worldliness and absurd incident to tickle the palate of pious frivolity. Linda, the heroine, is still more speculative and spiritual than Laura Gay, but she has been "presented," and has more

and far grander lovers; very wicked and fascinating women
are introduced, — even a French *lionne;* and no expense is
spared to get up as exciting a story as you will find in the
most immoral novels.   In fact, it is a wonderful *pot-pourri* of
Almack's, Scotch second-sight, Mr. Rogers's breakfasts, Italian
brigands, death-bed conversions, superior authoresses, Italian mistresses, and attempts at poisoning old ladies, the whole
served up with a garnish of talk about "faith and development" and "most original minds."   Even Miss Susan Barton, the superior authoress, whose pen moves in a "quick,
decided manner when she is composing," declines the finest
opportunities of marriage; and though old enough to be
Linda's mother (since we are told that she refused Linda's
father), has her hand sought by a young earl, the heroine's
rejected lover.   Of course, genius and morality must be
backed by eligible offers, or they would seem rather a dull
affair; and piety, like other things, in order to be *comme il
faut*, must be in "society," and have admittance to the best
circles.   •

"Rank and Beauty" is a more frothy and less religious
variety of the mind-and-millinery species.   The heroine, we
are told, "if she inherited her father's pride of birth and her
mother's beauty of person, had in herself a tone of enthusiastic feeling, that, perhaps, belongs to her age even in the
lowly born, but which is refined into the high spirit of wild
romance only in the far descended, who feel that it is their
best inheritance."   This enthusiastic young lady, by dint of
reading the newspaper to her father, falls in love with the
prime minister, who, through the medium of leading articles
and "the *résumé* of the debates," shines upon her imagination as a bright particular star, which has no parallax for her
living in the country as simple Miss Wyndham.   But she
forthwith becomes Baroness Umfraville in her own right, as-
tonishes the world with her beauty and accomplishments
when she bursts upon it from her mansion in Spring Gar-
dens, and, as you foresee, will presently come into contact
with the unseen *objet aimé.*   Perhaps the words "prime min-

ister" suggest to you a wrinkled or obese sexagenarian; but
pray dismiss the image. Lord Rupert Conway has been
" called, while still almost a youth, to the first situation which
a subject can hold in the *universe*," and even leading articles
and a *résumé* of the debates, have not conjured up a dream
that surpasses the fact.

" The door opened again, and Lord Rupert Conway entered. Evelyn gave one glance. It was enough; she was not disappointed. It
seemed as if a picture on which she had long gazed was suddenly instinct with life, and had stepped from its frame before her. His tall
figure, the distinguished simplicity of his air — it was a living Vandyke, a cavalier, one of his noble cavalier ancestors, or one to whom
her fancy had always likened him, who long of yore had with an Umfraville fought the Paynim far beyond the sea. Was this reality ? "

Very little like it, certainly.

By and by it becomes evident that the ministerial heart is
touched. Lady Umfraville is on a visit to the Queen at
Windsor, and, —

" The last evening of her stay, when they returned from riding, Mr.
Wyndham took her and a large party to the top of the keep, to see
the view. She was leaning on the battlements, gazing from that
' stately height' at the prospect beneath her, when Lord Rupert was
by her side.

" ' What an unrivalled view ! ' exclaimed she.

" ' Yes, it would have been wrong to go without having been up
here. You are pleased with your visit ? '

" ' Enchanted ! A Queen to live and die under, to live and die for ! '

" ' Ha ! ' cried he, with sudden emotion and with a *eureka* expression of countenance, as if he had *indeed found a heart in unison with
his own*."

The "*eureka* expression of countenance," you see at once
to be prophetic of marriage at the end of the third volume;
but before that desirable consummation, there are very com-
plicated misunderstandings, arising chiefly from the vindic-
tive plotting of Sir Luttrel Wycherley, who is a genius, a
poet, and in every way a most remarkable character indeed.
He is not only a romantic poet, but a hardened rake and a

cynical wit; yet his deep passion for Lady Umfraville has
so impoverished his epigrammatic talent, that he cuts an extremely poor figure in conversation. When she rejects him,
he rushes into the shrubbery and rolls himself in the dirt;
and on recovering, devotes himself to the most diabolical and
laborious schemes of vengeance, in the course of which he
disguises himself as a quack physician and enters into general practice, foreseeing that Evelyn will fall ill, and that
he shall be called in to attend her. At last, when all his
schemes are frustrated, he takes leave of her in a long letter,
written, as you will perceive from the following passage,
entirely in the style of an eminent literary man : —

" Oh, lady, nursed in pomp and pleasure, will you ever cast one
thought upon the miserable being who addresses you ? Will you
ever, as your gilded galley is floating down the unruffled stream of
prosperity, — will you ever, while lulled by the sweetest music, —
thine own praises, — hear the far-off sigh from that world to which I
am going ? "

On the whole, however, frothy as it is, we rather prefer
" Rank and Beauty " to the two other novels we have mentioned. The dialogue is more natural and spirited; there is
some frank ignorance and no pedantry ; and you are allowed
to take the heroine's astounding intellect upon trust, without
being called on to read her conversational refutations of
sceptics and philosophers, or her rhetorical solutions of the
mysteries of the universe.

Writers of the mind-and-millinery school are remarkably
unanimous in their choice of diction. In their novels there
is usually a lady or gentleman, who is more or less of a upas
tree; the lover has a manly breast; minds are redolent
of various things; hearts are hollow; events are utilized;
friends are consigned to the tomb; infancy is an engaging
period; the sun is a luminary that goes to his western couch,
or gathers the rain-drops into his, refulgent bosom; life is a
melancholy boon; Albion and Scotia are conversational epi-
thets. There is a striking resemblance, too, in the character
of their moral comments, such, for instance, as that " it is a

fact, no less true than melancholy, that all people, more or less,
richer or poorer, are swayed by bad example;" that "books,
however trivial, contain some subjects from which useful information may be drawn;" that "vice can too often borrow
the language of virtue;" that "merit and nobility of nature
must exist, to be accepted, for clamor and pretension cannot
impose upon those too well read in human nature to be easily
deceived;" and that, "in order to forgive, we must have been
injured." There is doubtless a class of readers to whom these
remarks appear peculiarly pointed and pungent; for we often
find them doubly and trebly scored with the pencil, and delicate hands giving in their determined adhesion to these hardy
novelties by a distinct *très vrai*, emphasized by many notes
of exclamation. The colloquial style of these novels is often
marked by much ingenious inversion, and a careful avoidance
of such cheap phraseology as can be heard every day. Angry
young gentlemen exclaim, "'T is ever thus, methinks;" and
in the half-hour before dinner a young lady informs her
next neighbor that the first day she read Shakspeare she
"stole away into the park, and beneath the shadow of the
greenwood tree devoured with rapture the inspired page of
the great magician." But the most remarkable efforts of the
mind-and-millinery writers lie in their philosophic reflections.
The authoress of " Laura Gay," for example, having married
her hero and heroine, improves the event by observing that
"if those sceptics, whose eyes have so long gazed on matter
that they can no longer see aught else in man, could once
enter with heart and soul into such bliss as this, they would
come to say that the soul of man and the polypus are not of
common origin or of the same texture." Lady novelists, it
appears, can see something else besides matter; they are not
limited to phenomena, but can relieve their eyesight by occasional glimpses of the *noumenon*, and are therefore naturally better able than any one else to confound sceptics, even
of that remarkable but to us unknown school, which maintains that the soul of man is of the same texture as the
polypus.

The most pitiable of all silly novels by lady novelists are what we may call the *oracular* species, — novels intended to expound the writer's religious, philosophical, or moral theories. There seems to be a notion abroad among women, rather akin to the superstition that the speech and actions of idiots are inspired, and that the human being most entirely exhausted of common sense is the fittest vehicle of revelation. To judge from their writings, there are certain ladies who think that an amazing ignorance, both of science and of life, is the best possible qualification for forming an opinion on the knottiest moral and speculative questions. Apparently, their recipe for solving all such difficulties is something like this : Take a woman's head, stuff it with a smattering of philosophy and literature chopped small, and with false notions of society baked hard, let it hang over a desk a few hours every day, and serve up hot in feeble English, when not required. You will rarely meet with a lady novelist of the oracular class who is diffident of her ability to decide on theological questions, who has any suspicion that she is not capable of discriminating with the nicest accuracy between the good and evil in all church parties, who does not see precisely how it is that men have gone wrong hitherto, and pity philosophers in general that they have not had the opportunity of consulting her. Great writers, who have modestly contented themselves with putting their experience into fiction, and have thought it quite a sufficient task to exhibit men and things as they are, she sighs over as deplorably deficient in the application of their powers. " They have solved no great questions ; " and she is ready to remedy their omission by setting before you a complete theory of life and manual of divinity, in a love story, where ladies and gentlemen of good family go through genteel vicissitudes, to the utter confusion of Deists, Pusey-ites, and ultra-Protestants, and to the perfect establishment of that peculiar view of Christianity which either condenses itself into a sentence of small caps or explodes into a cluster of stars on the three hundred and thirtieth page. It is true, the ladies and gentlemen will probably seem to you remarkably little like any you have had the fortune or misfortune to meet with for, as a general rule, the ability of a lady novelist to describe actual life and her fellow-men is in inverse proportion to her confident eloquence about God and the other world, and the means by which she usually chooses to conduct you to true ideas of the invisible is a totally false picture of the visible.

As typical a novel of the oracular kind as we can hope to meet with, is "The Enigma : a Leaf from the Chronicles of the Wolchorley House." The "enigma" which this novel is to solve, is certainly one that demands powers no less gigantic than those of a lady novelist, being neither more nor less than the existence of evil. The problem is stated, and the answer dimly foreshadowed on the very first page. The spirited young lady, with raven hair, says, "All life is an inextricable confusion;" and the meek young lady, with auburn hair, looks at the picture of the Madonna which she is copying, and — "*There* seemed the solution of that mighty enigma." The style of this novel is quite as lofty as its purpose; indeed, some passages on which we have spent much patient study are quite beyond our reach, in spite of the illustrative aid of italics and small caps, and we must await further "development" in order to understand them. Of Ernest, the model young clergyman, who sets every one right on all occasions, we read, that "he held not of marriage in the marketable kind, after a social desecration;" that, on one eventful night, "sleep had not visited his divided heart, where tumultuated, in varied type and combination, the aggregate feelings of grief and joy;" and that, "for the *marketable* human article he had no toleration, — be it of what sort or set for what value it might, whether for worship or class, his upright soul abhorred it, whose ultimatum, the self-deceiver, was to him THE *great spiritual lie,* 'living in a vain show, deceiving and being deceived;' since he did not suppose the phylactery and enlarged border on the garment to be *merely* a social trick." (The italics and small caps are the

author's, and we hope they assist the reader's comprehension.)
Of Sir Lionel, the model old gentleman, we are told that
"the simple ideal of the middle age, apart from its anarchy
and decadence, in him most truly seemed to live again, when
the ties which knit men together were of heroic cast. The
first-born colors of pristine faith and truth engraven on the
common soul of man, and blent into the wide arch of brotherhood, where the primeval law of *order* grew and multiplied
each perfect after his kind, and mutually interdependent."
    You see clearly, of course, how colors are first engraven on
the soul, and then blent into a wide arch, on which arch of
colors — apparently a rainbow — the law of order grew and
multiplied, each — apparently the arch and the law — perfect
after his kind ? If, after this, you can possibly want any
further aid towards knowing what Sir Lionel was, we can
tell you that in his soul "the scientific combinations of,
thought could educe no fuller harmonies of the good and the
true, than lay in the primeval pulses which floated as an
atmosphere around it ! " and that, when he was sealing a letter, "Lo ! the responsive throb in that good man's bosom
echoed back in simple truth the honest witness of a heart
that condemned him not, as his eye, bedewed with love,
rested, too, with something of ancestral pride, on the un-
dimmed motto of the family, — 'LOIAUTÉ.' "
    The slightest matters have their vulgarity fumigated out of
them by the same elevated style. Commonplace people would
say that a copy of Shakspeare lay on a drawing-room table ;
but the authoress of "The Enigma," bent on edifying periph-
rasis, tells you that there lay on the table "that fund of
human thought and feeling which teaches the heart through
the little name, 'Shakspeare.' " A watchman sees a light
burning in an upper window rather longer than usual, and
thinks that people are foolish to sit up late when they have
an opportunity of going to bed ; but, lest this fact should
seem too low and common, it is presented to us in the following striking and metaphysical manner : "He marvelled — as
a man *will* think for others in a necessarily separate person-

ality, consequently (though disallowing it) in false mental premise, — how differently *he* should act, how gladly *he* should prize the rest so lightly held of within." A footman — an ordinary Jeames, with large calves and aspirated vowels — answers the door-bell, and the opportunity is seized to tell you that he was a "type of the large class of pampered menials who follow the curse of Cain, — 'vagabonds' on the face of the earth, and whose estimate of the human class varies in the graduated scale of money and expenditure. . . . These, and such as these, O England, be the false lights of thy morbid civilization!" We have heard of various "false lights," from Dr. Cumming to Robert Owen, from Dr. Pusey to the Spirit-rappers, but we never before heard of the false light that emanates from plush and powder.

In the same way very ordinary events of civilized life are exalted into the most awful crises, and ladies in full skirts and *manches à la Chinoise*, conduct themselves not unlike the heroines of sanguinary melodramas. Mrs. Percy, a shallow woman of the world, wishes her son Horace to marry the auburn-haired Grace, she being an heiress; but he, after the manner of sons, falls in love with the raven-haired Kate, the heiress's portionless cousin; and, moreover, Grace herself shows every symptom of perfect indifference to Horace. In such cases, sons are often sulky or fiery, mothers are alternately manœuvring and waspish, and the portionless young lady often lies awake at night and cries a good deal. We are getting used to these things now, just as we are used to eclipses of the moon, which no longer set us howling and beating tin kettles. We never heard of a lady in a fashionable "front" behaving like Mrs. Percy under these circumstances. Happening one day to see Horace talking to Grace at a window, without in the least knowing what they are talking about, or having the least reason to believe that Grace, who is mistress of the house, and a person of dignity, would accept her son if he were to offer himself, she suddenly rushes up to them and clasps them both, saying, "with a flushed countenance and in an excited manner,"

"This is indeed happiness; for may I not call you so, Grace? — my Grace, — my Horace's Grace! — my dear children!" Her son tells her she is mistaken, and that he is engaged to Kate, whereupon we have the following scene and tableau : —

"Gathering herself up to an unprecedented height (!), her eyes lightening forth the fire of her anger, —

"'Wretched boy!' she said, hoarsely and scornfully, and clenching her hand, 'take then the doom of your own choice! Bow down your miserable head and let a mother's —'

"'Curse not!' spake a deep, low voice from behind; and Mrs. Percy started, scared, as though she had seen a heavenly visitant appear, to break upon her in the midst of her sin.

"Meantime Horace had fallen on his knees at her feet, and hid his face in his hands.

"Who, then, is she — who! Truly his 'guardian spirit' hath stepped between him and the fearful words, which, however unmerited, must have hung as a pall over his future existence; — a spell which could not be unbound, which could not be unsaid.

"Of an earthly paleness, but calm with the still, iron-bound calmness of death, — the only calm one there, — Katherine stood; and her words smote on the ear in tones whose appallingly slow and separate intonation rung on the heart like the chill, isolated tolling of some fatal knell.

"'He would have plighted me his faith, but I did not accept it; you cannot, therefore, — you *dare* not curse him. And here,' she continued, raising her hand to heaven, whither her large dark eyes also rose with a chastened glow, which, for the first time, *suffering* had lighted in those passionate orbs, — 'here I promise, come weal, come woe, that Horace Wolchorley and I do never interchange vows without his mother's sanction, without his mother's blessing!'"

Here, and throughout the story, we see that confusion of purpose which is so characteristic of silly novels written by women. It is a story of quite modern drawing-room society — a society in which polkas are played and Puseyism discussed; yet we have characters, and incidents, and traits of manner introduced, which are mere shreds from the most heterogeneous romances. We have a blind Irish harper, "relic of the picturesque bards of yore," startling us at a Sunday-school festival of tea and cake in an English village; we have a crazy gypsy, in a scarlet cloak, singing snatches of romantic song, and revealing a secret on her deathbed which, with the testimony of a dwarfish miserly merchant, who salutes strangers with a curse and a devilish laugh, goes to prove that Ernest, the model young clergyman, is Kate's brother; and we have an ultra-virtuous Irish Barney, discovering that a document is forged, by comparing the date of the paper with the date of the alleged signature, although the same document has passed through a court of law and occasioned a fatal decision. The "Hall" in which Sir Lionel lives is the venerable country-seat of an old family, and this, we suppose, sets the imagination of the authoress flying to donjons and battlements, where "lo! the warder blows his horn;" for, as the inhabitants are in their bedrooms on a night certainly within the recollection of Pleaceman X., and a breeze springs up, which we are at first told was faint, and then that it made the old cedars bow their branches to the greensward, she falls into this mediæval vein of description (the italics are ours) : —

" The banner *unfurled it* at the sound, and shook its guardian wing above, while the startled owl *flapped her* in the ivy; the firmament looking down through her 'argus eyes,' —

'Ministers of heaven's mute melodies.'

And lo! two strokes tolled from out the warder tower, and ' Two o'clock' re-echoed its interpreter below."

Such stories as this of " The Enigma " remind us of the pictures clever children sometimes draw " out of their own head," where you will see a modern villa on the right, two knights in helmets fighting in the foreground, and a tiger grinning in a jungle on the left, the several objects being brought together because the artist thinks each pretty, and perhaps still more because he remembers seeing them in other pictures.

But we like the authoress much better on her mediæval

stilts than on her oracular ones, — when she talks of the *Ich* and of "subjective" and "objective," and lays down the exact line of Christian verity, between "right-hand excesses and left-hand declensions." Persons who deviate from this line are introduced with a patronizing air of charity. Of a certain Miss Inshquine she informs us, with all the lucidity of italics and small caps, that "*function*, not *form*, AS *the inevitable outer expression of the spirit in this tabernacled age*, weakly engrossed her." And apropos of Miss Mayjar, an evangelical lady who is a little too apt to talk of her visits to sick women and the state of their souls, we are told that the model clergyman is "not one to disallow, through the *super* crust, the undercurrent towards good in the *subject*, or the positive benefits, nevertheless, to the *object*." We imagine the double-refined accent and protrusion of chin which are feebly represented by the italics in this lady's sentences! We abstain from quoting any of her oracular doctrinal passages because they refer to matters too serious for our pages just now.

The epithet "silly" may seem impertinent, applied to a novel which indicates so much reading and intellectual activity as "The Enigma;" but we use this epithet advisedly. If, as the world has long agreed, a very great amount of instruction will not make a wise man, still less will a very mediocre amount of instruction make a wise woman. And the most mischievous form of feminine silliness is the literary form, because it tends to confirm the popular prejudice against the more solid education of women. When men see girls wasting their time in consultations about bonnets and ball-dresses, and in giggling or sentimental love-confidences, or middle-aged women mismanaging their children, and solacing themselves with acrid gossip, they can hardly help saying, "For Heaven's sake, let girls be better educated; let them have some better objects of thought, some more solid occupations." But after a few hours' conversation with an oracular literary woman, or a few hours' reading of her books, they are likely enough to say, "After all, when a woman gets some knowledge, see what use she makes of it!

Her knowledge remains acquisition, instead of passing into culture; instead of being subdued into modesty and simplicity by a larger acquaintance with thought and fact, she has a feverish consciousness of her attainments; she keeps a sort of mental pocket-mirror, and is continually looking in it at her own 'intellectuality;' she spoils the taste of one's muffin by questions of metaphysics; 'puts down' men at a dinner-table with her superior information; and seizes the opportunity of a *soirée* to catechise us on the vital question of the relation between mind and matter. And then, look at her writings! She mistakes vagueness for depth, bombast for eloquence, and affectation for originality; she struts on one page, rolls her eyes on another, grimaces in a third, and is hysterical in a fourth. She may have read many writings of great men, and a few writings of great women; but she is as unable to discern the difference between her own style and theirs as a Yorkshireman is to discern the difference between his own English and a Londoner's: rhodomontade is the native accent of her intellect. No — the average nature of woman is too shallow and feeble a soil to bear much tillage; it is only fit for the very lightest crops."

It is true that the men who come to such a decision on such very superficial and imperfect observation may not be among the wisest in the world; but we have not now to contest their opinion — we are only pointing out how it is unconsciously encouraged by many women who have volunteered themselves as representatives of the feminine intellect. We do not believe that a man was ever strengthened in such an opinion by associating with a woman of true culture, whose mind had absorbed her knowledge instead of being absorbed by it. A really cultured woman, like a really cultured man, is all the simpler and the less obtrusive for her knowledge; it has made her see herself and her opinions in something like just proportions; she does not make it a pedestal from which she flatters herself that she commands a complete view of men and things, but makes it a point of observation from which to form a right estimate of herself. She neither spouts poetry nor quotes Cicero on slight provocation; not because she thinks that a sacrifice must be made to the prejudices of men, but because that mode of exhibiting her memory and Latinity does not present itself to her as edifying or graceful. She does not write books to confound philosophers, perhaps because she is able to write books that delight them. In conversation she is the least formidable of women, because she understands you, without wanting to make you aware that you *can't* understand her. She does not give you information, which is the raw material of culture, — she gives you sympathy, which is its subtlest essence.

A more numerous class of silly novels than the oracular (which are generally inspired by some form of High Church or transcendental Christianity) is what we may call the *white neckcloth* species, which represent the tone of thought and feeling in the Evangelical party. This species is a kind of genteel tract on a large scale, intended as a sort of medicinal sweetmeat for Low Church young ladies; an Evangelical substitute for the fashionable novel, as the May Meetings are a substitute for the Opera. Even Quaker children, one would think, can hardly have been denied the indulgence of a doll; but it must be a doll dressed in a drab gown and a coal-scuttle bonnet, — not a worldly doll, in gauze and spangles. And there are no young ladies, we imagine, — unless they belong to the Church of the United Brethren, in which people are married without any love-making, — who can dispense with love stories. Thus, for Evangelical young ladies there are Evangelical love stories, in which the vicissitudes of the tender passion are sanctified by saving views of Regeneration and the Atonement. These novels differ from the oracular ones, as a Low Churchwoman often differs from a High Churchwoman: they are a little less supercilious and a great deal more ignorant, a little less correct in their syntax and a great deal more vulgar.

The Orlando of Evangelical literature is the young curate, looked at from the point of view of the middle class, where cambric bands are understood to have as thrilling an effect on the hearts of young ladies as epaulettes have in the classes above and below it. In the ordinary type of these novels, the hero is almost sure to be a young curate, frowned upon, perhaps, by worldly mammas, but carrying captive the hearts of their daughters, who can "never forget *that* sermon;" tender glances are seized from the pulpit stairs instead of the opera-box; *tête-à-têtes* are seasoned with quotations from Scripture, instead of quotations from the poets; and questions as to the state of the heroine's affections are mingled with anxieties as to the state of her soul. The young curate always has a background of well-dressed and wealthy, if not fashionable society; for Evangelical silliness is as snobbish as any other kind of silliness, and the Evangelical lady novelist, while she explains to you the type of the scapegoat on one page, is ambitious on another to represent the manners and conversation of aristocratic people. Her pictures of fashionable society are often curious studies, considered as efforts of the Evangelical imagination; but in one particular the novels of the White Neckcloth School are meritoriously realistic, — their favorite hero, the Evangelical young curate, is always rather an insipid personage.

The most recent novel of this species that we happen to have before us, is "The Old Gray Church." It is utterly tame and feeble; there is no one set of objects on which the writer seems to have a stronger grasp than on any other; and we should be entirely at a loss to conjecture among what phases of life her experience has been gained, but for certain vulgarisms of style which sufficiently indicate that she has had the advantage, though she has been unable to use it, of mingling chiefly with men and women whose manners and characters have not had all their bosses and angles rubbed down by refined conventionalism. It is less excusable in an Evangelical novelist than in any other, gratuitously to seek her subjects among titles and carriages. The real drama of Evangelicalism — and it has abundance of fine drama for any one who has genius enough to discern and reproduce it — lies

among the middle and lower classes; and are not Evangelical opinions understood to give an especial interest in the
weak things of the earth, rather than in the mighty ? Why,
then, cannot our Evangelical lady novelists show us the operation of their religious views among people (there' really are
many such in the world) who keep no carriage, " not so much
as a brass-bound gig," who even manage to eat their dinner
without a silver fork, and in whose mouths the authoress's
questionable English would be strictly consistent? Why
can we not have pictures of religious life among the indus-
trial classes in England, as interesting as Mrs. Stowe's pictures of religious life among the negroes ? Instead of this,
pious ladies nauseate us with novels which remind us of what
we sometimes see in a worldly woman recently " converted; "
— she is as fond of a fine dinner-table as before, but she
invites clergymen instead of beaux; she thinks as much of
her dress as before, but she adopts a more sober choice of
colors and patterns; her conversation is as trivial as before,
but the triviality is flavored with gospel instead of gossip.
In " The Old Gray Church " we have the same sort of Evangelical travesty of the fashionable novel, and of course the
vicious, intriguing baronet is not wanting. It is worth while
to give a sample of the style of conversation attributed to
this high-born rake, — a style that, in its profuse italics and
palpable innuendoes, is worthy of Miss Squeers. In an evening visit to the ruins of the Colosseum, Eustace, the young
clergyman, has been withdrawing the heroine, Miss Lushington, from the rest of the party, for the sake of a *tête-à-tête*.
The baronet is jealous, and vents his pique in this way : —

" There they are, and Miss Lushington, no doubt, quite safe; for
she is under the holy guidance of Pope Eustace the First, who has, of
course, been delivering to her an edifying homily on the wickedness of
the heathens of yore, who, as tradition tells us, in this very place let
loose the wild *beastises* on poor St. Paul! — Oh, no! by-the-by, I
believe I am wrong, and betraying my want of clergy, and that it was
not at all St. Paul, nor was it here. But no matter, it would equally
serve as a text to preach from, and from which to diverge to the de-

12

generate *heathen* Christians of the present day, and all their naughty
practices, and so end with an exhortation to ' come out from among
them, and be separate ; ' — and I am sure, Miss Lushington, you have
most scrupulously conformed to that injunction this evening, for we
have seen nothing of you since our arrival. But every one seems
agreed it has been a *charming party of pleasure*, and I am sure we all
feel *much indebted* to Mr. Grey for having *suggested* it; and as he seems
so capital a cicerone, I hope he will think of something else equally
agreeable to *all*."

This drivelling kind of dialogue, and equally drivelling
narrative, which, like a bad drawing, represents nothing, and
barely indicates what is meant to be represented, runs
through the book ; and we have no doubt is considered by
the amiable authoress to constitute an improving novel,
which Christian mothers will do well to put into the hands
of their daughters. But everything is relative ; we have met
with American vegetarians whose normal diet was dry meal,
and who, when their appetite wanted stimulating, tickled it
with *wet* meal ; and so we can imagine that there are Evangelical circles in which "The Old Gray Church" is devoured
as a powerful and interesting fiction.

But, perhaps, the least readable of silly women's novels
are the *modern-antique* species, which unfold to us the domestic life of Jannes and Jambres, the private love affairs of
Sennacherib, or the mental struggles and ultimate conversion
of Demetrius the Silversmith. From most silly novels we
can at least extract a laugh ; but those of the modern-antique
school have a ponderous, a leaden kind of fatuity, under
which we groan. What can be more demonstrative of the
inability of literary women to measure their own powers, than
their frequent assumption of a task which can only be justified by the rarest concurrence of acquirement with genius ?
The finest effort to reanimate the past is of course only ap-
proximative, — is always more or less an infusion of the modern spirit into the ancient form, —

> " Was ihr den Geist der Zeiten heisst,
> Das ist im Grund der Herren eigner Geist,
> In dem die Zeiten sich bespiegeln."

Admitting that genius which has familiarized itself with all the relics of an ancient period can sometimes, by the force of its sympathetic divination, restore the missing notes in the "music of humanity," and reconstruct the fragments into a whole which will really bring the remote past nearer to us, and interpret it to our duller apprehension, — this form of imaginative power must always be among the very rarest, because it demands as much accurate and minute knowledge as creative vigor. Yet we find ladies constantly choosing to make their mental mediocrity more conspicuous, by clothing it in a masquerade of ancient names ; by putting their feeble sentimentality into the mouths of Roman vestals or Egyptian princesses, and attributing their rhetorical arguments to Jewish high-priests and Greek philosophers. A recent example of this heavy imbecility is, " Adonijah, a Tale of the Jewish Dispersion," which forms part of a series, "uniting," we are told, " taste, humor, and sound principles." " Adonijah," we presume, exemplifies the tale of " sound principles ; " the taste and humor are to be found in other members of the series. We are told on the cover, that the incidents of this tale are "fraught with unusual interest," and the preface winds up thus : " To those who feel interested in the dispersed of Israel and Judæa, these pages may afford, perhaps, information on an important subject, as well as amusement." Since the " important subject " on which this book is to afford information is not specified, it may possibly lie in some esoteric meaning to which we have no key ; but if it has relation to the dispersed of Israel and Judæa at any period of their history, we believe a tolerably well-informed school-girl already knows much more of it than she will find in this " Tale of the Jewish Dispersion." " Adonijah " is simply the feeblest kind of love story, supposed to be instructive, we presume, because the hero is a Jewish captive, and the heroine a Roman vestal ; because they and their friends are converted to Christianity after the shortest and easiest method approved by the " Society for Promoting the Conversion of the Jews ; " and because, instead of being written in plain language, it is adorned with that peculiar style of grandiloquence which is held by some lady novelists to give an antique coloring, and which we recognize at once in such phrases as these : "the splendid regnal talent, undoubtedly possessed by the Emperor Nero," — "the expiring scion of a lofty stem," — "the virtuous partner of his couch," — "ah, by Vesta!" — and "I tell thee, Roman." Among the quotations which serve at once for instruction and ornament on the cover of this volume, there is one from Miss Sinclair, which informs us that "works of imagination are *avowedly* read by men of science, wisdom, and piety;" from which we suppose the reader is to gather the cheering inference that Dr. Daubeny, Mr. Mill, or Mr. Maurice may openly indulge himself with the perusal of "Adonijah," without being obliged to secrete it among the sofa cushions, or read it by snatches under the dinner-table.

"Be not a baker if your head be made of butter," says a homely proverb, which, being interpreted, may mean, Let no woman rush into print who is not prepared for the consequences. We are aware that our remarks are in a very different tone from that of the reviewers who, with perennial recurrence of precisely similar emotions, only paralleled, we imagine, in the experience of monthly nurses, tell one lady novelist after another that they "hail" her productions "with delight." We are aware that the ladies at whom our criticism is pointed are accustomed to be told, in the choicest phraseology of puffery, that their pictures of life are brilliant, their characters well drawn, their style fascinating, and their sentiments lofty. But if they are inclined to resent our plainness of speech, we ask them to reflect for a moment on the chary praise, and often captious blame, which their panegyrists give to writers whose works are on the way to become classics. No sooner does a woman show that she has genius or effective talent, than she receives the tribute of being moderately praised and severely criticised. By a peculiar thermometric adjustment, when a woman's talent is at zero, journalistic approbation is at the boiling-pitch; when she attains mediocrity, it is already at no more than summer heat; and if ever she reaches excellence, critical enthusiasm drops to the freezing-point. Harriet Martineau, Currer Bell, and Mrs. Gaskell have been treated as cavalierly as if they had been men. And every critic who forms a high estimate of the share women may ultimately take in literature will, on principle, abstain from any exceptional indulgence towards the productions of literary women. For it must be plain to every one who looks impartially and extensively into feminine literature, that its greatest deficiencies are due hardly more to the want of intellectual power than to the want of those moral qualities that contribute to literary excellence, — patient diligence, a sense of the responsibility involved in publication, and an appreciation of the sacredness of the writer's art. In the majority of women's books you see that kind of facility which springs from the absence of any high standard; that fertility in imbecile combination or feeble imitation which a little self-criticism would check and reduce to barrenness; just as with a total want of musical ear people will sing out of tune, while a degree more melodic sensibility would suffice to render them silent. The foolish vanity of wishing to appear in print, instead of being counterbalanced by any consciousness of the intellectual or moral derogation implied in futile authorship, seems to be encouraged by the extremely false impression that to write *at all* is a proof of superiority in a woman. On this ground, we believe that the average intellect of women is unfairly represented by the mass of feminine literature, and that while the few women who write well are very far above the ordinary intellectual level of their sex, the many women who write ill are very far below it. So that, after all, the severer critics are fulfilling a chivalrous duty in depriving the mere fact of feminine authorship of any false prestige which may give it a delusive attraction, and in recommending women of mediocre faculties — as at least a negative service they can render their sex — to abstain from writing.

The standing apology for women who become writers without any special qualification is, that society shuts them out from other spheres of occupation. Society is a very culpable entity, and has to answer for the manufacture of many unwholesome commodities, from bad pickles to bad poetry. But society, like "matter," and her Majesty's Government, and other lofty abstractions, has its share of excessive blame as well as excessive praise. Where there is one woman who writes from necessity, we believe there are three women who write from vanity; and, besides, there is something so antiseptic in the mere healthy fact of working for one's bread, that the most trashy and rotten kind of feminine literature is not likely to have been produced under such circumstances. "In all labor there is profit;" but ladies' silly novels, we imagine, are less the result of labor than of busy idleness.

Happily, we are not dependent on argument to prove that Fiction is a department of literature in which women can, after their kind, fully equal men. A cluster of great names, both living and dead, rush to our memories in evidence that women can produce novels not only fine, but among the very finest; — novels, too, that have a precious specialty, lying quite apart from masculine aptitudes and experience. No educational restrictions can shut women out from the materials of fiction, and there is no species of art which is so free from rigid requirements. Like crystalline masses, it may take any form, and yet be beautiful; we have only to pour in the right elements, — genuine observation, humor, and passion. But it is precisely this absence of rigid requirement which constitutes the fatal seduction of novel-writing to incompetent women. Ladies are not wont to be very grossly deceived as to their power of playing on the piano; here certain positive difficulties of execution have to be conquered, and incompetence inevitably breaks down. Every art which has its absolute *technique* is, to a certain extent, guarded from the intrusions of mere left-handed imbecility. But in novel-writing there are no barriers for incapacity to stumble against, no external criteria to prevent a writer from mistaking foolish facility for mastery.   And so we have again and again the old story of La Fontaine's ass, who puts his nose to the flute, and, finding that he elicits some sound, exclaims, "Moi, aussi, je joue de la flute;"—a fable which we commend, at parting, to the consideration of any feminine reader who is in danger of adding to the number of "silly novels by lady novelists."

CARLYLE'S LIFE OF STERLING.

A S soon as the closing of the Great Exhibition afforded a reasonable hope that there would once more be a reading public, "The Life of Sterling" appeared. A new work by Carlyle must always be among the literary births eagerly chronicled by the journals and greeted by the public. In a book of such parentage we care less about the subject than about its treatment, just as we think the "Portrait of a Lord" worth studying if it come from the pencil of a Vandyck. The life of John Sterling, however, has intrinsic interest, even if it be viewed simply as the struggle of a restless aspiring soul, yearning to leave a distinct impress of itself on the spiritual development of humanity, with that fell disease which, with a refinement of torture, heightens the susceptibility and activity of the faculties, while it undermines their creative force. Sterling, moreover, was a man thoroughly in earnest, to whom poetry and philosophy were not merely another form of paper currency or a ladder to fame, but an end in themselves, — one of those finer spirits with whom, amidst the jar and hubbub of our daily life, ·

> " The melodies abide
> Of the everlasting chime."

But his intellect was active and rapid, rather than powerful, and in all his writings we feel the want of a stronger electric current to give that vigor of conception and felicity of expression, by which we distinguish the undefinable something

called genius; while his moral nature, though refined and
elevated, seems to have been subordinate to his intellectual
tendencies and social qualities, and to have had itself little
determining influence on his life. His career was less exceptional than his character : a youth marked by delicate health
and studious tastes, a short-lived and not very successful
share in the management of the *Athenæum*, a fever of sympathy with Spanish patriots, arrested before it reached a
dangerous crisis by an early love affair ending in marriage,
a fifteen months' residence in the West Indies, eight months
of curate's duty at Herstmonceux, relinquished on the ground
of failing health, and through his remaining years a succes-
sion of migrations to the South in search of a friendly climate, with the occasional publication of an " article," a tale,
or a poem in " Blackwood " or elsewhere, — this, on the pro-
saic background of an easy competence, was what made up
the outer tissue of Sterling's existence. The impression of
his intellectual power on his personal friends seems to have
been produced chiefly by the eloquence and brilliancy of his
conversation ; but the mere reader of his works and letters
would augur from them neither the wit, nor the *curiosa felici-
tas* of epithet and imagery, which would rank him with the
men whose sayings are thought worthy of perpetuation in
books of table-talk and " ana." The public, then, since it is
content to do without biographies of much more remarkable
men, cannot be supposed to have felt any pressing demand
even for a single life of Sterling; still less, it might be
thought, when so distinguished a writer as Archdeacon Hare
had furnished this, could there be any need for another. But,
in opposition to the majority of Mr. Carlyle's critics, we agree
with him that the first life is properly the justification of
the second. Even among the readers personally unacquainted
with Sterling, those who sympathized with his ultimate
alienation from the Church rather than with his transient
conformity, were likely to be dissatisfied with the entirely
apologetic tone of Hare's Life, which, indeed, is confessedly
an incomplete presentation of Sterling's mental course after

his opinions diverged from those of his clerical biographer;
while those attached friends (and Sterling possessed the
happy magic that secures many such) who knew him best
during this latter part of his career, would naturally be
pained to have it represented, though only by implication,
as a sort of deepening declension ending in a virtual retrac-
tion. Of such friends Carlyle was the most eminent, and
perhaps the most highly valued; and, as co-trustee with Archdeacon Hare of Sterling's literary character and writings, he
felt a kind of responsibility that no mistaken idea of his departed friend should remain before the world without correc-
tion. Evidently, however, his "Life of Sterling" was not
so much the conscientious discharge of a trust as a labor of
love, and to this is owing its strong charm. Carlyle here
shows us his "sunny side." We no longer see him breathing
out threatenings and slaughter, as in the Latter-Day Pam-
phlets, but moving among the charities and amenities of life,
loving and beloved, — a Teufelsdröckh still, but humanized
by a Blumine worthy of him. We have often wished that
genius would incline itself more frequently to the task of the
biographer, — that when some great or good personage dies,
instead of the dreary three or five volumed compilations of
letter and diary and detail, little to the purpose, which two
thirds of the reading public have not the chance, nor the
other third the inclination, to read, we could have a real
"Life," setting forth briefly and vividly the man's inward
and outward struggles, aims, and achievements, so as to make
clear the meaning which his experience has for his fellows.
A few such lives (chiefly, indeed, autobiographies) the world
possesses, and they have, perhaps, been more influential on
the formation of character than any other kind of reading.
But the conditions required for the perfection of life writing
— personal intimacy, a loving and poetic nature which sees
the beauty and the depth of familiar things, and the artistic
power which seizes characteristic points and renders them
with lifelike effect — are seldom found in combination.
"The Life of Sterling" is an instance of this rare conjunction.

Its comparatively tame scenes and incidents gather pictu-
resqueness and interest under the rich lights of Carlyle's mind.
We are told neither too little nor too much; the facts noted,
the letters selected, are all such as serve to give the liveliest
conception of what Sterling was and what he did; and though
the book speaks much of other persons, this collateral matter
is all a kind of scene-painting, and is accessory to the main
purpose.   The portrait of Coleridge, for example, is precisely
adapted to bring before us the intellectual region in which
Sterling lived for some time before entering the Church.
Almost every review has extracted this admirable description, in which genial veneration and compassion struggle with
irresistible satire; but the emphasis of quotation cannot be
too often given to the following pregnant paragraph : —

"The truth is, I now see Coleridge's talk and speculation was the
emblem of himself.   In it, as in him, a ray of heavenly inspiration
struggled, in a tragically ineffectual degree, with the weakness of flesh
and blood.   He says once, he ' had skirted the howling deserts of infidelity.'   This was evident enough ; but he had not had the courage,
in defiance of pain and terror, to press resolutely across said deserts to
the new, firm lands of faith beyond ; he preferred to create logical *fata-
morganas* for himself on this hither side, and laboriously solace himself with these."

The above-mentioned step of Sterling — his entering the
Church — is the point on which Carlyle is most decidedly at
issue with Archdeacon Hare.   The latter holds that had Sterling's health permitted him to remain in the Church, he would
have escaped those aberrations from orthodoxy which, in the
clerical view, are to be regarded as the failure and shipwreck
of his career, apparently thinking, like that friend of Arnold's
who recommended a curacy as the best means of clearing up
Trinitarian difficulties, that " orders " are a sort of spiritual
backboard, which, by dint of obliging a man to look as if he
were strait, end by making him so.   According to Carlyle, on
the contrary, the real " aberration " of Sterling was his choice
of the clerical profession, which was simply a mistake as to
his true vocation : —

" Sterling," he says, " was not intrinsically, nor had ever been in the highest or chief degree, a devotional mind. Of course all excellence in man, and worship as the supreme excellence, was part of the inheritance of this gifted man ; but if called to define him, I should say artist, not saint, was the real bent of his being."

Again : —

" No man of Sterling's veracity, had he clearly consulted his own heart, or had his own heart been capable of clearly responding, and not been bewildered by transient fantasies and theosophic moonshine, could have undertaken this function. His heart would have answered, ' No, thou canst not. What is incredible to thee, thou shalt not, at thy soul's peril, attempt to believe ! Else-whither for a refuge, or die here. Go to perdition if thou must, but not with a lie in thy mouth; by the eternal Maker, no ! "

From the period when Carlyle's own acquaintance with Sterling commenced, the Life has a double interest, from the glimpses it gives us of the writer as well as of his hero. We are made present at their first introduction to each other ; we get a lively idea of their colloquies and walks together, and in this easy way, without any heavy disquisition or narrative, we obtain a clear insight into Sterling's character and mental progress. Above all, we are gladdened with a perception of the affinity that exists between noble souls, in spite of diversity in ideas, — in what Carlyle calls "the logical outcome" of the faculties. This "Life of Sterling" is a touching monument of the capability human nature possesses of the highest love, the love of the good and beautiful in character, which is, after all, the essence of piety. The style of the work, too, is for the most part at once pure and rich ; there are passages of deep pathos which come upon the reader like a strain of solemn music, and others which show that aptness of epithet, that masterly power of close delineation, in which, perhaps, no writer has excelled Carlyle.

We have said that we think this second "Life of Sterling" justified by the first; but were it not so, the book would justify itself.

THE GRAMMAR OF ORNAMENT.

" THE inventor of movable types," says the venerable Teufelsdrockh, "was disbanding hired armies, cashiering most kings and senates, and creating a whole new democratic world." Has any one yet said what great things are being done by the men who are trying to banish ugliness from our streets and our homes, and to make both the outside and the inside of our dwellings worthy of a world where there are forests, and flower-tressed meadows, and the plumage of birds ; where the insects carry lessons of color on their wings, and even the surface of a stagnant pool will show us the wonders of iridescence and the most delicate forms of leafage ? They, too, are modifying opinions, for they are modifying men's moods and habits, which are the mothers of opinions, having quite as much to do with their formation as the responsible father, Reason. Think of certain manufacturing towns where the piety is chiefly a belief in copious perdition, and the pleasure is chiefly gin. The dingy surface of wall pierced by the ugliest windows, the staring shop-fronts, paper-hangings, carpets, brass and gilt mouldings, and advertising placards, have an effect akin to that of malaria ; it is easy to understand that with such surroundings there is more belief in cruelty than in beneficence, and that the best earthly bliss attainable is the dulling of the external senses. For it is a fatal mistake to suppose that ugliness which is taken for beauty will answer all the purposes of beauty ; the subtle relation between all kinds of truth and fitness in our life forbids that bad taste should ever be harmless to our moral sensibility or our intellectual discernment ; and, more than that, as it is probable that fine musical harmonies have a sanative influence over our bodily organization, it is also probable that just coloring and lovely combinations of lines may be necessary to the complete well-being of our systems apart from any conscious delight in them. A savage may indulge in discordant chuckles and shrieks and gutturals, and think that they please the gods, but it does not follow that his frame would not be favorably wrought upon by the vibrations of a grand church organ. One sees a person capable of choosing the worst style of wall-paper become suddenly afflicted by its ugliness under an attack of illness. And if an evil state of blood and lymph usually goes along with an evil state of mind, who shall say that the ugliness of our streets, the falsity of our ornamentation, the vulgarity of our upholstery, have not something to do with those bad tempers which breed false conclusions ?

On several grounds it is possible to make a more speedy and extensive application of artistic reform to our interior decoration than to our external architecture. One of these grounds is that most of our ugly buildings must stand; we cannot afford to pull them down. But every year we are decorating interiors afresh, and people of modest means may benefit by the introduction of beautiful designs into stucco ornaments, paper-hangings, draperies, and carpets. Fine taste in the decoration of interiors is a benefit that spreads from the palace to the clerk's house with one parlor.

All honor, then, to the architect who has zealously vindicated the claim of internal ornamentation to be a part of the architect's function, and has labored to rescue that form of art which is most closely connected with the sanctities and pleasures of our hearts from the hands of uncultured tradesmen. All the nation ought at present to know that this effort is peculiarly associated with the name of Mr. Owen Jones; and those who are most disposed to dispute with the architect about his coloring must at least recognize the high artistic principle which has directed his attention to colored ornamentation as a proper branch of architecture. One

monument of his effort in this way is his "Grammar of Ornament," of which a new and cheaper edition has just been issued. The one point in which it differs from the original
and more expensive edition, namely, the reduction in the size
of the pages (the amount of matter and number of plates are
unaltered), is really an advantage; it is now a very manage-
able folio, and when the reader is in a lounging mood may be
held easily on the knees. It is a magnificent book; and those
who know no more of it than the title should be told that they
will find in it a pictorial history of ornamental design, from
its rudimentary condition, as seen in the productions of savage
tribes, through all the other great types of art, — the Egyptian,
Assyrian, Ancient Persian, Greek, Roman, Byzantine, Ara-
bian, Moresque, Mohammedan-Persian, Indian, Celtic, Mediæval, Renaissance, Elizabethan, and Italian. The letter-press
consists, first, of an introductory statement of fundamental
principles of ornamentation, — principles, says the author,
which will be found to have been obeyed more or less in-
stinctively by all nations in proportion as their art has been
a genuine product of the national genius; and, secondly, of
brief historical essays, some of them contributed by other
eminent artists, presenting a commentary on each characteristic series of illustrations, with the useful appendage of bib-
liographical lists.

The title "Grammar of Ornament" is so far appropriate
that it indicates what Mr. Owen Jones is most anxious to be
understood concerning the object of his work, namely, that
it is intended to illustrate historically the application of principles, and not to present a collection of models for mere
copyists. The plates correspond to examples in syntax, not
to be repeated parrot-like, but to be studied as embodiments
of syntactical principles. There is a logic of form which
cannot be departed from in ornamental design without a
corresponding remoteness from perfection; unmeaning, ir-
relevant words or clauses, that tend no whither. And as a
suggestion towards the origination of fresh ornamental design, the work concludes with some beautiful drawings of

leaves and flowers from nature, that the student, tracing in
them the simple laws of form which underlie an immense
variety in beauty, may the better discern the method by
which the same laws were applied in the finest decorative
work of the past, and may have all the clearer prospect of
the unexhausted possibilities of freshness which lie before
him, if, refraining from mere imitation, he will seek only such
likeness to existing forms of ornamental art as arises from
following like principles of combination.

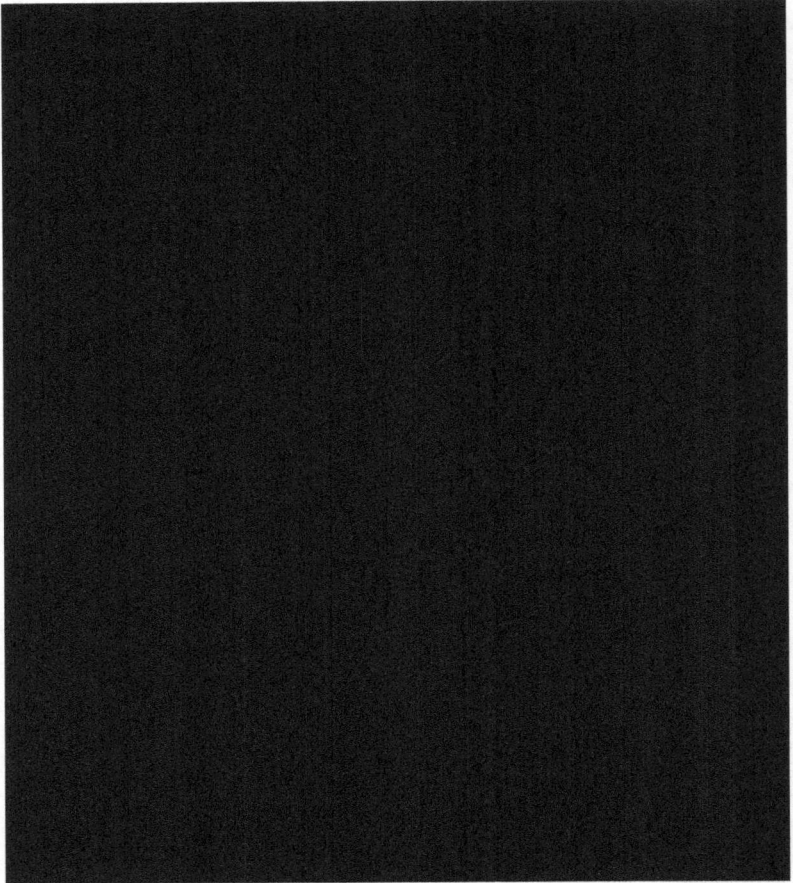

University Press: John Wilson & Son, Cambridge.

www.ingramcontent.com/pod-product-compliance
Lightning Source LLC
Chambersburg PA
CBHW030325270326
41926CB00010B/1507